In my industry, the low price provider is king—but thanks to the hard work of Dr. Steinmetz and Bill Brooks, I've never even had to consider cutting my company's prices. Instead, we've broken away from the pack as "the only choice" regardless of price. No matter what you sell or who you sell it to, you owe it to yourself to read this book!

—James A. Canale
CEO and President
Net2 Technology Group, Inc.

This book is the definitive work on full-margin selling for executives, sales managers, and salespeople alike. It is, undoubtedly, the ultimate source for selling at full price, fee, or margin.

—Jim Taylor
CEO
Thomas Group

Finally, a book that allows salespeople to understand the impact of "cutting prices" and how to increase sales margins! This is a must-read book for all sales personnel, especially those who want to "make it up in volume."

—Robin Wall
Vice President of Sales
Dearing Compressor & Pump Co.

A practical handbook for CEOs, general managers, and sales managers struggling with how to meet competition in the marketplace and at the same time preserve the profit margin required not only to stay in business, but prosper over the long term.

—Edward E. Newcomer
Chairman of the Board
E. E. Newcomer Enterprises, Inc.

We constantly preach the importance of margins as we have far greater potential to positively influence that outcome, than gross sales revenue itself. A few points on the top line translate to huge gains on the bottom line. Bill Brooks' insights to help us get there have made a huge difference.

—James MacDonald
President
R. F. MacDonald Co.

This book reminds us to consider customer relationships in the context of a marathon, not a sprint. It shares our company's philosophy that building partnerships with customers and offering great service is vital to success. It's not just about winning customers . . . but keeping them for the long haul.

—Chuck Burns
Area Vice President
First Citizens Bank

How to Sell at Margins Higher Than Your Competitors

Winning Every Sale at Full Price, Rate, or Fee

Lawrence L. Steinmetz, PhD and William T. Brooks

WILEY

John Wiley & Sons, Inc.

Published by John Wiley & Sons, Inc., Hoboken, New Jersey
Published simultaneously in Canada

For general information on our other products and services or for technical support, please contact our Customer Care Department within the United States at (800) 762-2974, outside the United States at (317) 572-3993 or fax (317) 572-4002.

Wiley also publishes its books in a variety of electronic formats. Some content that appears in print may not be available in electronic books. For more information about Wiley products, visit our web site at www.wiley.com.

Library of Congress Cataloging-in-Publication Data:

ISBN-13 978-0-471-74483-2 (pbk.)

ISBN-10 0-471-74483-2 (pbk.)

Printed in the United States of America.

10 9 8 7

PREFACE

This is the thirteenth book I've written. Every time I write a book, I wait until it's almost time for page proofs before I write the preface because I like to reflect on what the book really is about in order to say a few succinct statements about the book for the prospective reader.

For this particular book, I am especially mindful of something I wrote in the preface to my first book in 1992. I wrote:

> The perspective I got for this preface came from a vacation I took just a week ago. I happened to read a piece of advertising literature of a small (albeit international) manufacturing company in one of the better-known ski resort towns in Colorado. The first paragraph of that company's literature proudly boasts: 'We are not just running a business, but living a lifestyle.' I'm sure the people who are running that company are proud of that statement; genuinely believe that one need not be too serious about running their business—that if you produce a good product, the product will sell itself and one need not worry about the vulgar details of operating a business in a business-like fashion. Another interesting part of this manufacturer's literature is that the enclosure with this literature compared this company's prices with competitors' prices and—you guessed it—this company's prices were lower than their competitors'. That's right. They allegedly have a superior product and, furthermore, can sell it at a price lower than their competitors' and (surely?) make money doing that.

Once you've read this book, you will appreciate the sarcasm in the above paragraph. I revisited that Colorado resort town just last week to check out how the business was doing. At no surprise to me, it has vanished without a trace. I pointed out in the original book that one cannot run a business successfully via a series of propitious accidents or in a cavalier manner. We make that point again in this book: Business is a game of margins, not a game of volume. Whether one is running a manufacturing company, a wholesale operation, a distributorship, a retail store, a construction company, a financial institution, or a professional service organization, all too many people operate these enterprises with the idea that one can sell at prices (fees, rates) lower than their competitors and still be successful. Oh, if it were only true—and that easy. That is not to say that one cannot have fun running a business or professional organization. Or that there is no time for a good quality lifestyle. But the basics of running a good (successful) business are not founded on a "fun first, the business (practice) will take care of itself" attitude. Too much water has gone under the bridge throughout history proving the point that a serious, professional manner has to be established at the helm by those running the operation.

Fortunately, history gives us many lessons in the good and the bad practices that happen in running a business—admittedly, mostly bad, but there are also good examples. The common threads that underpin the good and successful examples are what we have chosen to present in this new version of my original book. We have expanded it in many ways. We have added chapters on things such as the cardinal sins of selling and how to tell when a customer is lying about having a sweeter deal "down the street." I also added a chapter on how the salesperson can "hang in there" under intense pressure to cut the customer some kind of deal on the price. These additional chapters particularly enhance the book because, based on my experience consulting with companies and conducting more than 2,000 seminars on this subject since writing the first book, I have found these issues to be the more vexing problems for most salespeople. Fortunately, given the time period since publishing the first book, I have developed material that provides solutions to many of these problems.

The original book and this book are about how you sell things at prices higher than your competitors—not how to give things away. The organization of this book is much like the original book and essentially runs as follows: We start with FACTS—and the facts are that most companies do go broke and business is a game of margins, not a game of volume.

The second dimension of this book has to do with UNDERSTANDING. Selling at prices higher than your competitors requires an attitude and an understanding on the part of the salesperson. Some of that understanding includes the following: People (customers) don't buy on price alone. Furthermore, there are five factors on which one can compete in selling a product or professional service, and price is only one of the five. Quality, service, sales capability, and ability to deliver the product or professional service to the customer, when they need it, where they want it, *and* on time are the other factors. Each of those remaining four is far more significant than price. Another bit of understanding is that buyers really need and like a lot of things—and low price isn't necessarily one of them. Sales reps who intend to sell at prices higher than their competitors need to get inside the customer's head and understand how their customers' needs and likes can fit with their ability to command a higher price than competitors.

The third section of this book concerns REALITIES. Many business and professional people, as well as many salespeople, simply do not understand the *economics* of pricing. Most think they do; very few do. For example, have you ever asked a business or professional person or a salesperson how much additional volume of any product they have to sell (or service they have to provide) to make up for a price cut? Usually you'll get some vague answer, or some wide range of answers like: "Twenty to forty percent more, I guess." And, once in a while, you even get an honest answer such as, "Gee. I don't know." Business and professional people are their own worst enemies, as are sales representatives. They tend to blindly believe that somehow, someway, if they get price competitive (i. e., cut the price) that they will "make it up in volume." This section of the book, devoted to the realities of the marketplace, is absolutely essential for the business or professional person to understand if he or she is to sell at prices higher than competitors.

It is difficult, if not impossible, to cut price and make it up in volume while, on the opposite end, it is often possible to raise price, lose volume, and make far more money. People who have attended the seminars that I do on "How to Make Your Prices Stick" and "How to Sell at Prices Higher than Your Competitors" have, over the years, related numerous testimonials concerning the fact that raising prices is not the end of the world. Doing so does not cause sales to plummet, and often simply means that the company or the professional organization just makes more money with less aggravation and heartache for those endeavoring to earn a living in that business.

The newer part of this book is the material I added on how the salesperson can avoid being victimized by the hard-charging, demanding price-buyer who puts the salesperson in as awkward a position as the buyer can in an effort to get the salesperson to cut the customer some kind of deal on the price (or other terms of the sale). Many salespeople don't understand either what to do with an extremely demanding customer or how to tell when a customer is lying, fabricating, or not being 100% truthful with the salesperson about having "a sweeter deal down the street." In my extensive experience in dealing with these problems as a seller of my own companies' products and professional services and/or presented to me as a problem that a trainee needed help with, I have had the luxury of time to develop answers to these types of questions and issues. I make the particular point that one does not, as a salesperson, want to call a customer a liar. But customers do lie, or fabricate stories that are not fully true, in an effort to get a salesperson to shoot him/herself in the foot and unnecessarily cut the price or squander away the possible profitable side of the deal. This all new section of the book is an especially valuable addition to the manuscript.

The final and major portion of this book has to do with WHAT TO DO ABOUT IT. Thus, the bulk of this book addresses such things as how to handle price pressure, price resistance, and price competition. We spend a lot of time talking about how to face up to and handle price cutting by your competitors, as well as how to determine if it really is price that is the problem in the mind of the customer. We devote attention to understanding the basics of this statement: Your customer will tell you when your prices are too high—as well as tell you when your prices are too low. By analyzing those indicators of overpricing and underpricing which we develop, the sales rep can determine very accurately whether or not he/she should be able to realize a higher selling price in the marketplace.

Yet another very fundamental system of coping with price pressure in the marketplace is the material that we develop in this section on tricks used by those serving in the role of procurement officers, purchasing agents, or buyers in attempting to get the sales representative to cut his/her own price. From the feedback I have received from my seminar attendees, identifying these tricks has given salespeople strong support in foiling the attempt of buyers to get salespeople to cut their prices.

In this section of the book, we also discuss closing sales in the face of price resistance, as well as sales techniques to use in facing down price resistance. Finally, we address the question of "Stoppers"—the methods and techniques that sales reps use to stop customers from beating on them for additional price reductions.

All in all, I'm very pleased with the end result. I've been doing seminars on this subject for so many years I hate to think about when I started. In this book we have assembled a hard-nosed, let's-face-life-with-reality look at how those companies and individuals who make a lot of money selling at high prices manage to do so. They don't do it by cutting prices, fees, or rates. They do it by knowing the realities of selling at prices higher than one's competitors. They face facts, they understand customer buying motives, they face the realities of the economics of selling products and services, and they know what to do about the customer who says, "Your prices (fees, rates) are too high." Furthermore, they do not become duped by the overly aggressive or out-and-out unscrupulous customer. They face reality, work professionally, and have a good time running their business (or practice) AND enjoying life to its fullest because of their success.

I hope the reader will find this book every bit as productive as those who have heard me speak these words in public and private seminars—and

I wonder what the people who worked for that manufacturer in the mountains in Colorado are doing now . . .

LAWRENCE L. STEINMETZ, PhD

Boulder, Colorado

In 1992, Larry Steinmetz graciously asked me to write the introduction to his original book on this topic. Not only was I thrilled to do so, but also I became hooked on his concepts and the breakthrough ideas that his book offered.

Now, more than 13 years later, I have had the privilege of co-authoring the newest, most up-to-date, cutting-edge version of those original ideas in this, its latest version.

This book is intended to deliver to you, the reader, ideas, strategies, tactics, and concepts not available anywhere else in the world. After selling for well over 35 years and speaking, training, and consulting with sales organizations for more than 27 of those years, I am fully convinced that the single biggest issue confronting most sales organizations and salespeople is how to defeat lower priced competitors. Period.

Whether you are a business owner, executive, sales executive, sales manager, or salesperson, this book has great value for you. Dr. Steinmetz and I approached this book with the premise that whether you sell tangible products, an intangible service, large or small ticket products, or anything in-between, there is great value for you within its covers.

Having said that, I invite you to prepare to learn things that can and will deliver great margins to your business. However, please be warned: The ideas you find here could revolutionize your business. They could also, however, cause you great concern as you examine some of your current pricing, selling, and business practices. However, if you face reality and take action, your entire career will be revolutionized. I guarantee it.

WILLIAM T. BROOKS, CSP, CPAE, CMC

Greensboro, North Carolina

CONTENTS

CHAPTER 1

EMPLOYERS CAN FAIL OR GO BROKE— AND YOURS CAN, TOO

Our basic problem has been our 14 quarters of losses. And that's because the price of the equipment we build has been less than the cost.

—Norman J. Ryker

It is, indeed, an unfortunate fact: *Most* businesses fail. They start off, expand a lot or a little, and then they die. Statistically, 16 out of 17 businesses that start in the United States will fail and/or go out-of-business—most of them in the first two years of their existence. The average life expectancy of all businesses in the United States is estimated at 7.5 years. In fact, one of the headlines used to promote a series of highly successful business management seminars has been, *If your business is not 8 years old, the odds are it never will be!* No less a business giant than Thomas J. Watson, the builder of IBM, in the very first paragraph of his book, *A Business and Its Beliefs,*[1] wrote:

> Of the top twenty-five industrial corporations in the United States in 1900, only two remain in that select company today. One retains its original identity; the other is a merger of seven corporations on that original list. Two of those twenty-five failed. Three others merged and dropped behind. The remaining twelve have continued in business, but each has fallen substantially in its standing.
>
> Figures like these help to remind us that corporations are expendable and that success, at best, is an impermanent achievement which can always slip out of hand.

Watson wrote that in the middle of the last century. As we enter a new century, the situation is potentially far worse.

1

It is a statistical reality that most businesses do sooner or later fail. For us to state that most businesses fail is just as true as it is for us to tell you that if you are not 80 years old, the odds are you never will be. The average life expectancy for people in our society is just short of 80 years: For women it's just at 80 years and for men it's 74 to 75. But on average, we will all be dead by the time we're 80. And, on the average, most businesses will be dead before they are 8 years old.

SO MOST BUSINESSES FAIL—WHAT'S THAT GOT TO DO WITH MAKING MY PRICES STICK?

Most businesses end up in bankruptcy court and are liquidated or sold off because they aren't making any money. But why should we talk about failure? This book is about success—about how to sell at a premium price and how to make a profit for yourself and your employer. Right? Not necessarily. However, we would argue strongly that one of the first things you need to recognize is that the fundamental problem in making your prices stick is that you're competing with many people and businesses who are actually going broke. And when businesses start losing money, *they cut their prices.* In a desperate attempt to try to stay alive, they slash their prices because they've always been told that they can make it up in volume. They think if they can just sell more, then surely they will come out on top. But that doesn't work. When was the last time you saw a business that had a going-out-of-business price *increase?*

Most people have no idea how many businesses actually do fail in the United States. It is estimated that there are 800,000 new businesses started in the United States each year, yet there are only about 11,000,000 businesses existing in the country at any given time. Let's relate that number to another relevant statistic. According to the U.S. Census Bureau, there are approximately 293,000,000 Americans. That means that there is roughly one business for every 27 people. Roughly, only about 40 percent of our population work outside of the home. That means that we have approximately one business for every 11 people employed outside the home. Therefore, if we have 800,000 new businesses starting each year, and we have only 11,000,000 businesses, the failure rate *has* to be rather extensive. If it were not, we would eventually have more businesses than we have people to run them.

Maybe we should say that *fortunately,* half of those 800,000 businesses that start fail the first year. And that *fortunately,* half of the remaining half fail the second year. This means that roughly three out of four businesses that start fail in the first two years of their existence. And you need to keep that in mind when you come home from a hard day of selling, with your nose bloodied, and your knuckles skinned up, and you say to yourself, "We are getting killed; we are getting hammered out there. How can those guys sell at that price? If they can sell at that price, we can, too."

Well, Mr. or Ms. Sales Professional, you have only part of that right. *They* can sell at that price—and go broke and *you can, too!* If you base your price on your competitor's price—and they are going broke—you will, too. Typically, someone among your competition is going broke and usually is cutting prices on the way out. Owen Young, who is credited with having built General Electric, once said, "It's not the crook we fear in modern business; rather it's the honest guy who doesn't know what he is doing."

It May Be Illegal to Be Crooked, But It Isn't Illegal to Be Stupid

Whom would you rather compete against, a crook or an idiot? If you think about it, you'll no doubt decide in favor of a crook. Have you ever seen a crook sell below cost? Have you ever heard anybody call the Mafia *poor business people*? You may not approve of the Mafia and their "business," but you have never heard anybody say they don't know how to make money. And lots of it!

Now, let's address the idiots. Have you ever seen an idiot sell below cost? Which idiot? And on what day do you want to talk about? You see, Owen Young was right. Fundamentally, it is not the crook we fear in business, but rather it is the honest idiot. The people (or organizations) who don't know what they are doing are the ones who foul up the works. And fundamentally, they are the ones giving away their products and services by cutting their prices.

Causes of Business Failure

Typically, when a business does go bust, especially if it gets into enough trouble to file bankruptcy, three things occur:

1. They experience a period of declining gross margin;
2. Wages, as a percentage of sales, begin to increase; and
3. Sales volume begins to increase.

In this book—because we are dealing with the subject of how to make your prices stick—we are going to deal in depth with only two of those three things: declining gross margin and increasing sales volume. Wages are a whole different issue, deserving its own book.

Declining Gross Margin

A declining gross margin indicates that there is a pricing problem. The way to calculate gross margin (GM) is by subtracting the cost of goods sold (COGS) from sales:

$$\begin{aligned}
\text{Gross margin} &= \text{Sales - Cost of goods sold} \\
\$35 &= \$100 - \$65 \\
35\% &= 100\% - 65\%
\end{aligned}$$

The only way that gross margin (as a percentage of sales) can go down is if a business cuts its prices or fails to raise its prices when its costs rise. That's it. Even though that can occur three different ways, the bottom line is the same: The sales price is too low relative to the cost of goods sold. These three ways are shown in the box titled, "The Three Ways Gross Margin Can Decline."

Declining gross margin should inevitably send a signal to an organization that it is experiencing a pricing problem that will ultimately result in trouble. It clearly signals either an inability or an unwillingness to sell its products or services at a high enough price in comparison to the costs. Most organizations that file for bankruptcy due to operational reasons have had a clear history of declining gross margin for a significant time before they ever filed. They often will blame it on "cost increases," but the real culprit is a declining gross margin: Their selling price was too low relative to their cost.

In fact, one of your authors recently had a conversation with the CEO of a firm that had to sell out before bankruptcy. And sell out he did. What did the former owner say? Here it is: "If I had increased price and cut capacity to half, we'd be in business today." His error, which he now sees, was that he did the exact opposite.

Wages, as a Percentage of Sales, Begin to Increase

A second condition that normally prevails when any entity fails financially is that wages, as a percentage of sales, begin to increase. This normally occurs because the organization just has too many people on the payroll or too many people making too much money. There often are too many people sitting around on their hands, watching other people who are also sit-

The Three Ways Gross Margin Can Decline

A. If you *cut* price $5 to sell something, situation A transpires:

Situation A

	Dollars	Percent	Dollars	Percent
Sales	$100	100%	$ 95	100%
COGS	65	65%	65	68%
GM	$ 35	35%	$ 30	32%

B. If you don't cut price to get a sale, but *fail* to raise price when your costs go up $5, situation B transpires:

Situation B

	Dollars	Percent	Dollars	Percent
Sales	$100	100%	$100	100%
COGS	65	65%	70	70%
GM	$ 35	35%	$ 30	30%

C. If you find your costs are going up $5 and raise your price only by the amount of your cost increase, situation C transpires:

Situation C

	Dollars	Percent	Dollars	Percent
Sales	$100	100%	$105	100%
COGS	65	65%	70	67%
GM	$ 35	35%	$ 35	33%★

★*Note:* Your dollar gross margin stays at $35, but your gross margin as a percentage of your sales goes down from 35% to 33%. In short, raising your price the same dollar amount as your cost increase is a de facto price cut. You must raise your selling price the same percent as your percent increase in costs if you are to maintain your gross margin percent in the face of rising costs.

ting around on their hands. However, as we've suggested, that's a subject that falls into another area of business management and not what we want to talk about here. However, for the decision-making executive, that is certainly an area that should be monitored constantly. Why is that? Because it often proves difficult to downsize a work force even if people don't have anything to do. Executives must never allow wages as a percentage of sales to increase above a point where they have good profitability, or their organizations will likely go broke—even if they don't have a problem in making prices stick.

Sales Volume Increases

Surprisingly, most entities that go broke do it during a period of an increase in sales volume. This statement shocks most people (especially those involved with sales) because most everyone mistakenly believes that a business fails as a result of a lack of sales volume. The facts are, however, that business is *not* a game of volume. *Business is always a game of margin*. If a business doesn't maintain gross margin at an adequate level, it is going to go bust, *regardless* of its sales volume. Cheap seats, cheap products or services, and giveaway prices really do have a way of attracting more and more customers. Have you ever seen a yard sale go wanting for customers? We don't think so. Lots and lots of items for sale and all at very low prices.

Business Is a Game of Margin, Not Volume.   Many large company leaders seem to sincerely believe, albeit blindly, that volume and market share are the secrets to business success. If that is the case, then why are multiple billion-dollar corporations filing bankruptcy every year in the United States? In the years between 2000 and 2004, 23 of the 40 biggest bankruptcies of all time occurred.

The year 2001 was a record year for big dollar bankruptcies—there were 257 major organizations that filed in the United States in that year alone. Since then, we've seen even more high-profile bankruptcy filings such as Enron, Kmart, and WorldCom—the record holder with assets worth more than $103 billion on the day before its default and credited with a bankruptcy worth $11 billion.

Westpoint Stevens, once one of the largest home fashion manufacturers in the United States, filed for Chapter 11 protection before agreeing to be bought by an investor group, WL Ross & Co., which had already purchased failed textile companies Cone Mills and Burlington Industries. The Fleming Companies, which not only was a supplier to Kmart, but owned IGA and Piggly Wiggly grocery stores, filed for bankruptcy in 2003 with revenues of $15.6 billion.

Delta Air Lines filed a report with the Securities and Exchange Commission that it would likely incur a net loss for 2005, and as we go to press in October, the airline has filed for bankruptcy. (Like many airlines, Delta narrowly avoided bankruptcy once in 2004 when its pilots agreed to concessions.) The same day, Northwest Airlines also filed for bankruptcy protection, negatively affected by union troubles, an out-of-date "hub-and-spoke" model, and increasing fuel costs.

"As goes General Motors, so goes the nation," was a famous expression of the 1960s. But as we write this, there is speculation in some very prestigious business journals that General Motors itself may be bankrupt by the year 2020 or before.

Even these few examples should provide a fairly graphic picture that business is, indeed, not just a game of volume and market share. A business must maintain an adequately high price against its costs (a high gross margin), or it is going to follow these well-known predecessors down the well-traveled path to bankruptcy court.

But We Can Make It Up in Volume.   When businesses get into financial difficulty, it's inevitably because some genius gets the bright idea that one can cut price and make it up in volume—to at least be "competitive." Most people get that idea when they take a course in economics. In fact, if you have anything to do with selling or pricing, one of the *worst* things that may have ever happened to you was taking Econ 101 when you went to college.

Just to emphasize the point that the bulk of our population thinks that the only way to do business is to cut price and make it up in volume, consider what happened as a result of airline deregulation. Way back in 1978, then-President Jimmy Carter deregulated the airline industry. This meant that the airlines were free to charge any price they wanted. How many raised prices? Answer: None. How many kept the same prices? Answer: Virtually none. They all, in varying degrees, began to *cut* their prices. How many airlines have filed for bankruptcy since deregulation? Answer: Hundreds. And some predict that the twenty-first century will see a further culling of the airline industry so that just a few airlines survive.

It could be argued that the first airline to really figure this out was Southwest. Here was an airline that intelligently attacked key issues head-on and won. However, it took them a long time after deregulation to enter the scene and become competitive. Perhaps they learned from the losers. Some of the traditional airlines have (and are) going broke, because they are cloned knockoffs of the model. Southwest keeps labor costs down by hiring younger, non-union employees and sustains margin with a series of maneuvers that cut costs. For example, flying a limited number of aircraft models eliminates training redundancy, a huge parts inventory, specialized tools, and other costs. In addition, they eliminated the wasteful hub concept and, instead, fly from point to point. The result? They *can* sell cheaper seats, but keep labor costs in line, control other expenses, and still sell more seats. However, they are a minority player, and it took many years for someone to discover the formula. We cannot help but wonder what the future holds for them as costs, labor demands, and all the rest potentially escalate. There are other airlines merging and following suit as well—making the terrain even more competitive.

Some airlines that have filed for bankruptcy since deregulation include:

Air Florida Systems	Metro Airlines
America West Airlines	Midway Airlines, Inc.
Braniff International (twice)	Northwest Airlines
Capitol Air, Inc.	Pan Am Corp.
Conquest Industries, Inc.	People Express
Continental Airlines (twice)	Provincetown Boston Airlines
Crescent Airways Corp.	StatesWest Airlines, Inc
Delta Airlines	Tower Air, Inc
Eastern Air Lines, Inc.	Trans World Airlines (three times)
Fine Air Services Corp.	UAL Corp. (United Airlines)
Frontier Holdings (twice)	US Airways, Inc.
HAL, Inc.	Vanguard Airlines
Hawaiian Airlines, Inc. (twice)	Western Pacific Airlines
Kitty Hawk, Inc.	

The ability to fail creatively is widely documented. The depths have not as yet been plumbed as to the new, novel ways somebody is going to figure out how to mess up a business. *But they all go back to one common pattern: They cut the price (to make it up in volume).* If you think you can match (or sell below) your competitor's prices, you need to understand that you will have an on-going, lifetime battle for survival that, sooner or later, you are going to lose.

WHY COMPANIES CUT PRICE WHEN THEY GET INTO TROUBLE

Perhaps you've heard the story of the industrious entrepreneurs who set out to make their fortune by buying watermelons for a buck each and selling them for $10 a dozen. And, like any good joke, it is readily adaptable to anything. Just change the subject—watermelons, exit signs, carpeting, hammers—and make the local meathead the butt of the joke. The way we originally heard it ran as follows:

> There were these two guys from Texas who had a little money and an old pick-up truck. They heard they could buy these watermelons in Mexico for $1 each and they decided that they could sell them for $10 per dozen.

So, they went to Mexico, loaded the truck with watermelons and headed toward Dallas, selling off these watermelons for that $10/dozen. They did a great business and sold out of watermelons before they even got halfway to Dallas. But, while sitting on the side of the road, counting their money, they noticed they were a little short of the amount they had started with. They wondered what the problem was since they had done a brisk business and it finally dawned on them—what they needed was a bigger truck.

Although you may have thought this was a new story, there is clear evidence that it has been around for over a century. Paul Nathan,[2] who wrote *How to Make Money in the Printing Business,* published the following in 1900:

If there is any one thing in the business management of a printing office that particularly commands the utter disapproval of successful printers as being worse than other evils that beset the trade, it is the cutting of prices. The method of getting work by lowering the price has absolutely nothing to recommend it, and it is contrary to common sense. The practice is absolutely wrong in principle, and the reasoning advanced in its support, stripped of its verbiage, is the equivalent of that of the old apple-woman who bought apples at a cent each and was selling them at ten cents a dozen, and when asked how she could make any money at that replied: "By doing a very large business."

When a business gets into trouble, it has a cash-flow problem and a margin problem—not a profitability problem. For example, let's consider the following:

Question: Do the vendors to your company care whether: (A) you're profitable or (B) pay your bills?

Answer: (B) pay your bills.

Question: Do an organization's employees care whether: (A) their employer is profitable or (B) meets its payroll?

Answer: (B) meets its payroll.

An organization gets into trouble when it can't pay bills and/or can't meet payroll. It has a cash-flow problem (or more correctly, a cash-trickle problem). This creates an intolerable situation for the organization. If the bills aren't paid, it will be cut off from needed services and supplies; if payroll isn't met, there will be no one to do the work. So, the first thing executives start worrying about is, "How can we get some cash? . . . How can we get that cash in the fastest way?" You guessed it. It has got to *sell* something! How to sell that something? Use the old standby: *Cut the price.* Unfortunately, cutting the price immediately creates the three danger signs that signal the organization may soon become a bankruptcy statistic: (1) gross margin goes down, (2) wages as a percentage of sales go up, and (3) sales volume begins to increase.

Gross margin must go down when prices are cut. But do most organizations cut wages when they cut prices? No. So then, wages as a percentage of sales go up—and sales go up because of the lower prices. Again, remember that those are the three conditions that *virtually always prevail* when an organization really gets itself in trouble and ends up filing bankruptcy or having to sell off or merge because it isn't making any money.

Many salespeople have the feeling that when they're out in the marketplace, the only way to sell and compete is to cut price when the competition starts cutting its price. They think, "Hey, we're getting killed. We're getting hammered. Our competitors are selling at a lower price than we are. They keep cutting price. We can't compete on an unlevel playing field. And, if those guys can sell at that price, we can too." So they go back to the boss, and say, "Hey, boss, we're getting smashed out there. Those guys are selling at a lower price. And we need to do the same thing or we won't ever be competitive." Well, the bottom line is—*If those guys can sell at that price and go broke—you can, too.* Just because your competition is selling at a price or offering products or services at a price lower than you are, it doesn't mean you can—or should even try to—meet their price, because most of that competition is going broke.

Maybe you *still* don't believe that most businesses go broke. Perhaps you think it's only the little start-up companies that lose it—not the big boys that "really know what they're doing." Do you think that big businesses don't go broke? Let us give you another example. *Inc.* magazine, way back in May of 1988, reported that, "We should not expect that our large corporations somehow possess a corporate fountain of youth. We should not mourn the fact that, in the 11 years between 1970 and 1981, 29 percent of the 1970 *Fortune 500* companies vanished as companies . . ."[3] The article went on to say that the " 'vanishing rate' of a *Fortune 500* company is only two-and-a-half times less than the vanishing rate of a garage start-up today." Did that continue? Let's take a look.

Other notable bankruptcies ($100,000,000 or more in assets) in the early 2000s have included: Mirant Corporation; Spiegel, Inc.; Penn Traffic Company; NRG Energy, Inc.; Solutia, Inc.; Amerco; Alterra Healthcare Corporation; Pillowtex Corporation; Conseco, Inc.; Global Crossing, Ltd.;

NTL, Inc.; Adelphia Communications Corporation; Genuity, Inc.; Exide Technologies, Inc.; Viasystems Group, Inc.; Consolidated Freightways Corp.; Roadhouse Grill, Inc.; President Casinos, Inc.; Archibald Candy Corporation; Florsheim Group, Inc.; TransTexas Gas Corp.; Jacobsons Stores, Inc.; Kasper A.S.L, Ltd.; Geneva Steel Holdings Group; Guilford Mills, Inc.; Formica Corporation; Oakwood Homes Corporation; Consolidated Freightways Corporation; Globalstar, LP; Highlands Insurance Group Inc.; Farmland Industries; National Steel Corporation; Budget Group Inc.; XO Communications; Today's Man; Piccadilly Cafeterias; FAO, Inc.; iPCS Inc.; Neenah Foundry Company; Magellan Health Services; Congoleum Corporation; Eagle Food Centers Inc.; Cone Mills Corporation; Wherehouse Entertainment Inc.; . . . and the list goes on.

Notice that what we are talking about doesn't just involve an isolated segment of the business world. Failure occurs in all avenues—big and small, established and start-up. But there is a commonality that exists—most failing companies believe they can cut their prices and make it up in volume, but they fail to consider what happens to their gross margin when they try to compete that way. As the quote at the start of this chapter says, "The cause of our losses is that the *price* of the equipment we build *has been less than the cost.*"

CHAPTER 2

BUT COMPETITION KEEPS CUTTING MY PRICE

No business opportunity is ever lost. If you fumble it, your *competitor will find it.*

—Business Quotes

Just because your competition cuts its price doesn't mean that you can or should even expect to survive if you do the same thing. Why is that? Because if your competitor has more money to lose than you do, you will go broke first. The important thing to remember is that *your competition does not cut your price; **you** cut your price.* Your competitor may offer its product or service at a price lower than you offer yours; but you cut your own price. Pogo the Possum said it all years ago: "We have found the enemy and he is us." If anything occurs that causes your price to go down, it's a *self-inflicted* wound.

CUSTOMERS ONLY BUY ON PRICE— OR DO THEY?

Unfortunately, many businesses and salespeople operate under the false notion that people (and businesses) buy on price—and price alone. Nothing could be farther from the truth. Our research clearly shows that price is almost never the primary reason why anybody buys anything. In fact, if price were the only reason anybody bought anything, then only one seller—the one with the lowest price—would sell all there is to sell of that product. But that has never happened in the real world. So there must be some other reasons why customers buy from different sources.

There is also another bit of evidence corroborating that prospects and customers don't buy primarily on price. If price were the only reason anybody bought anything, we wouldn't need salespeople. In fact, we wouldn't even need people to answer the phone or give a quote. A computer could

12

handle sales presentations and the Internet could accept the orders. Of what earthly use would a salesperson be if customers bought only on price and aggressively searched for the best price? They would just call 800 numbers, cruise the Internet to get the lowest quotes, and then place their orders by clicking the appropriate button on the websites of their choice.

Are You Wearing the Cheapest Shirt or Blouse You Could Buy?

To further examine the flawed logic about people buying (or not buying) strictly on price, let's try a simple test. Right now, are you wearing the cheapest shirt (blouse, dress, etc.) you could buy? You may seriously believe that you are, but even so, let's explore this further. Would you have bought it if it didn't fit? What about the color and style? What if you needed it right away, and it was on backorder? Well, then, what was more important? Price or fit, color, style, or availability? No doubt, you did consider the price, but what was *the* real deciding factor? Even if you still believe it was the price— at least you can see that price *alone* did not determine your decision. What about your shoes? Would you buy the cheapest pair if they pinched your toes? And again, what about style and color? Would you have bought them if they were chartreuse? And had spots?

You might be thinking, "Yeah, but . . . !" Yeah, but you are talking about consumer goods. I sell in the business-to-business environment. I deal with the trained bad actors that my prospects and customers send to school to learn to buy on price. If you think businesses buy on price, next time you are around a group of senior management types, ask for a show of hands of all those in the group whose companies buy and use the cheapest machinery and equipment on the market. It would be surprising if even one of them raised a hand. People don't buy on price, and neither do businesses—at least not very many of them. Many *say* they do; and many even *think* they do. And most of your customers will tell you they do because *they are trying to get you to cut your price.*

Do You Buy Because of Price?

Many people think they buy because of price, and maybe you still think you do. So let's conduct another brief test: Consider the previous two paragraphs about price; price-buying the shirt, blouse, or dress you are wearing and the shoes you are wearing. Then take a moment to answer this question: Are you really a price-buyer?

Yes _____   No _____

WE'D CAN ANY SALESPERSON WHO WORKED FOR US WHO WAS A PRICE-BUYER! CAN HIM OR FIX HIM

You may have a little trouble reading the above heading because it is printed on the page backward. That is because we wanted you to honestly answer the question of whether or not you are a serious price-buyer. If you hold that heading up to a mirror, it will quit looking like gibberish and will read as follows: WE'D CAN ANY SALESPERSON WHO WORKED FOR US WHO WAS A PRICE-BUYER! CAN HIM OR FIX HIM.

There are two reasons for this statement, and they both hinge on the same principle: *Price is virtually always more important in the mind of the seller than in the mind of the buyer.* One experiment we conducted on customer buying motives involved 100 experienced purchasing managers and 100 inexperienced ones. They were asked how much of several products they would buy from various vendors. Almost every one of the inexperienced buying group picked the *same* vendor, who was mathematically the lowest priced. But *none* of the experienced buyers picked the lowest priced vendor. Interestingly, their vote was split between two other vendors at the rate of about 5 to 1. We asked those who picked the vendor most widely selected by the experienced buyers why they picked that vendor, and they said, "history of delivery." We asked those experienced buyers who picked the other vendor and they said, "quality standards of the vendor."

In another bit of research we conducted with the same type of experienced, trained buyers, we further proved that they didn't buy solely on price. The price they were after was one that was "justifiable." What did we discover? They wanted something else ("history of delivery") with a price that would make it easy for them to justify *not* buying from the cheapest vendor. What does this tell you?

THE HOT STOVE PRINCIPLE

This principle, loosely stated, says that if you have ever seen a cat jump on a hot stove, you'll probably never see that same cat jump on the stove again, even if it is cold. In fact, the cat will likely never jump on ANY stove again, ever! Once burned, you, too, have probably learned your lesson. Prospects and customers learn lessons just like cats, and just about as quickly.

What makes a business buyer awaken at 3:15 A.M. in a cold sweat thinking, "I'm going to get fired!"? It isn't that they paid too much for a product or service. What will get them canned is *if the cupboard is bare!* "We

---

The Typical Salesperson's Idea of What Is Taught in Purchasing and Buying Seminars

How to Buy on Price—A One-Day Seminar

A. Why you want to buy on price.

B. Why you don't want to pay too much.

C. Knowing your numbers—a practical exercise on accurately identifying the lowest bid price.

D. How not to be confused about quality—that stuff is all the same anyhow.

E. Service—service—everybody says theirs is the best.

   • Why service is unimportant.

   • Even if their service is better, there are eight good reasons not to pay extra to get it.

F. All salespeople are liars—therefore, you must only buy on price.

G. Ascertaining the lowest number-basic math secrets you can use to be sure you're committing to the lowest price.

H. So what if they can deliver it yesterday when you absolutely have to have it—there are lots of good reasons to buy from the cheap guy anyway.

I. How to beat them up on price.

---

don't have parts." "We don't have material." "We are out of supplies." "Where's that software I was supposed to get?" Those are the statements and questions that haunt purchasers of business services or products, procurement officers, and anyone else whose career depends on intelligently buying goods or services. Not answering the question: "How much did you pay?" The same person who tells you that "parts are parts" knows very well that parts aren't parts when they *don't have any parts!* Terror is the only emotion in the buyer's mind when his or her superior says, "Where are those . . . (parts) (supplies) (tools) (fuel) (materials) (updates) (trainers) (manuals) (etc.)? Now I have to shut this place down. . . . Send a crew of people home. . . . Can't fill this order. . . . Can't complete this job." And then says, "It's all your fault. You're done!"

If there is any doubt that price is not as important as delivery, quality, and even service, here is a simple experiment that can be conducted in your own organization. First thing tomorrow, go to the person who pays invoices in your organization and ask for a 100 percent accurate list of vendors that your company *paid* during the past two years. Having done that, you now have a list of all the vendors who actually made a sale to your organization. That is, you ordered, they shipped, and you paid. Nothing less constitutes a sale. (A sale is not ever final until the customer's check has cleared the bank.) Now, with that 100 percent accurate list of your vendors, go to the people in your organization who purchased things from them, and ask them to review the list. Find out which vendors they bought from a year ago— but didn't use last year—and find out which vendors your organization used last year to supply the same products or services that your organization had bought from *other vendors* a year before. Ask your organization's buyers *why* they quit using the vendors they did, and what was most important in their minds when they picked the new vendors they used to replace the ones they dropped.

In a study of 64 firms, we discovered that *price* was the reason for dropping a particular vendor only 8.1 percent of the time. But in an astounding 70.2 percent of the cases, a *delivery* problem was the trigger event that caused one vendor to be replaced by another.[1] This makes the following four points:

1. A delivery problem is virtually always the trigger event that causes loss of a sale to an existing customer.
2. Your customer does not care *why* you screwed up the delivery. He only knows two things: (1) it isn't there, and (2) it is *your* fault. And please remember, delivery is not just with hard, tangible goods. Think about this for a minute. How about service, promised documents, electronic codes, Internet design, and so on. Delivery relates to *all* products or services. What you sell isn't the issue. Delivery is.
3. Your customer does not care *how good* your reason was for screwing up the delivery. He doesn't even care if *your reason is true!* Even if you have pictures of the fire, flood, hurricane, tornado, volcanic eruption, earthquake, or other catastrophe that caused the delay, he still only knows two things: (1) It isn't there, and (2) it's your fault.
4. You screw up delivery *one time,* and your customer will find another supplier—*because he has to.* He wouldn't have ordered your product or service if he didn't want and/or need it—and need it on time.

MOST SALESPEOPLE THINK PRICE IS MORE IMPORTANT THAN IT IS

It is not unusual to find salespeople who think price is more important than other factors when it comes to a customer's decision to purchase. The research we described indicates clearly that price is more important in the mind of the seller than it is in the mind of the buyer. That takes us back to the two reasons that make a price-buyer a poor prospect as a salesperson (and why we say we'd can any salesperson who worked for us who was a price-buyer). The reasons are:

1. *Price-buying salespeople project their feelings onto their customers.* *Projection* is the word psychologists use to communicate the idea that people transfer (or impute) their ideas, feelings, and emotions onto others. The same concept applies to the salesperson who says, "I'm just like anybody else, I put my pants on just like anybody else." He or she also says, "I'm just like anybody else. I buy on price. Therefore, my customer buys on price." But that is faulty logic. Just because you buy on price doesn't mean that your customer buys on price, any more than just because you are a good driver means your customer is a good driver or that just because you put your pants on, left leg first, while sitting down, means that your customers do the same thing. Maybe they put their pants on right leg first, standing up. Just as we easily can think of four different ways people put their pants on, we can think of at least four different motives that people have for buying something . . . and price is only one of them.

Projection means, in essence, it takes one to call one. It takes a price-buyer to call a price-buyer, and studies show clearly that price-buyers "see" (at least they think they "see") a lot of price-buyers. But that is because all buyers look like price-buyers to a price-buying salesperson!

2. *Price-buying salespeople tell the customer they think their own prices are too high—inviting their customers to beat them up on price.* It is literally true that salespeople who think their prices are too high and "know" in their heart, gut, and brain that the customer can "get it cheaper down the street" will indicate that belief to their customers. They do this as much by things they don't say and do as by things they do. And the number one thing they don't do that invites the customer to beat them up on price is that they don't talk price.

What Happens When You Don't Talk Price?

In one study conducted a few years ago, up to 94 percent of salespeople, when making a sales call, would not talk price *until* the customer asked about the price. Further, 44 percent of the salespeople, when asked the price, would change the subject; and about one-third would never even say the price out loud, preferring to write it down or point at it.

Do you have any idea what not discussing price says to your customer? It says you are scared. After all, if your price was such a good deal, you'd be willing to talk about it, wouldn't you? And if you are one of those who writes it down, or points at it—"Here, you can see our price is . . . ," are you afraid of your voice cracking or that you'll sound nervous if you *actually* verbalize your price? Salespeople who are nervous about their price almost always signal to the prospect that they are nervous (and think their price is too high) by the way they (don't) handle price. Coughing, choking, stuttering, stammering, pointing at the price, changing the subject, clumsily and unprofessionally avoiding the issue—all clearly signal to the prospect that you are not comfortable with your price. Until you can credibly, comfortably, and confidently tell your prospect, "This is the price. I sell a lot of it at this price, and I fully expect your order at this price," we can guarantee your prospect will beat you up on price.

There is an acid test you can use to determine if you can credibly handle price. You must be able to handle price like you handle the time of day:

Question: "What time is it?"

Answer: "It is 3:15."

Question: "What is your price on this?"

Answer: "The price is $200."

How would you do? Better yet, how do you actually feel about this? Can you verbalize your price as comfortably as you can tell someone what time it is? Try it—out loud. Now.

However, avoiding the statement of the price, or showing a lack of credibility in handling the price, aren't the only things that signal to the prospect that you will negotiate. One of the other ways you invite your prospect to beat you up on price is to use adverbs and adjectives when you present or discuss it. Therefore:

Never use adverbs or adjectives when you present or discuss price.

Adverbs and adjectives are a flag to the prospect that your price is negotiable. Consider, for example, the implication of the statement, "Our *usual* price is $200," versus the statement, "Our price is $200." Adverbs and adjectives limit, modify, or specify things about the noun, pronoun, verb, adjective, or adverb with which they are used. Therefore, they clearly imply that *there is more than one kind* of noun, pronoun, verb, adverb, or adjective. When you say, "Our usual price is . . . ," you make the customer think that you have more than one price; that you will negotiate. Try substituting any of the following adverbs or adjectives for the word "usual" in

the previous sentence, and see what you get—or use your own special adverb or adjective:

Suggested	Usual
Regular	Lowest
Normal	Best
List	Reduced
Book	Basic
Asking	Quoted

Adverbial and adjectival phrases are also used like adverbs and adjectives,
but they are used to "cushion the blow" of giving the price to the prospect.
These always signal to the prospect that the salesperson's price is negotiable
or that the salesperson feels his or her own price is too high. These cush-
ioning techniques take on a variety of forms:

- Those that clearly show that you are afraid that your price is too high:
  —"You'd better sit down before I give you my price."
  —"Buckle your seatbelt before I lay this price on you."
  —"Isn't it a crime, the price they charge for this stuff these days?"
  —"Are you ready for this?"
  —"The best I can do is . . ."
- Those that flatly state that your price is negotiable:
  —"You know I want to work with you on this."
  —"You know we've valued having you as a customer over these
  many years."
  —"I've been selling to you for a long time, Mr. Customer, and I sure
  don't want to lose your account."
  —"We really want to start doing more business in your industry."
  —"I can let you have it for only $200, if . . ."
  —"Since you are one of our larger customers, maybe we can work
  with you a little on this price."
- Those that invite or challenge the customer to look around or do com-
  parison pricing. These include jewels such as:
  —"Our price is lower than anybody's."
  —"Comparatively speaking, I think you'll find that we have the best
  price in town."
  —"By buying from us, you can use these for as little as 23¢ each time
  you use it in a normal year."
  —"Our new, reduced price is . . ."
  —"Why, in the overall picture, using our product will hardly cost
  you anything."

- Those that clearly state: *beat me up*. Examples include:
  —"Tell me where I need to be."
  —"What do I have to do to get your business?"
  —"Am I in the ballpark?"
  —"How's 27¢ sound to you?"
  —"Would you be willing to pay $40 for this?"
  —"Could you pay $40 for this?"
  —"Of course, I can give you an even better price, if . . ."
  —"You do intend to buy a lot from us this year, don't you? If you think you might order more than X amount this year, I might be able to work a better price for you."
  —"Of course, you know these cost more if you only buy two at a time. But if you bought three, I could maybe knock off another 50 percent."
  —"Well, we look at each order separately."
  —"Is $15 okay?"
  —"You know, we're giving you one heck of a deal here."

Eye movement also alerts the customer that you can be bludgeoned on price. Your eyes inevitably reveal your sincerity—unless, perhaps, you are an Oscar-winning performer. When you say a price you don't really believe, you'll almost always break off eye contact and look down. There is a lot of research about this topic that we can't cover here. You may want to spend time learning more about it on your own.

Other factors that signal to prospects that your price is negotiable include:

- Appearing to be overly eager to write the order
- Volunteering quantity discounts
- Stressing nonprice issues and avoiding talking about price
- Saying, "wow," or otherwise indicating that this is an exceptionally large order
- Making a clearly standard price quote
- Initiating options that would lower the overall price

The way you handle your price will largely determine the probability that you will get your price. Until the salesperson can handle his or her price credibly, confidently, and comfortably, he or she will have a very difficult time selling at prices that are higher than his or her competitor. More will be said about how to do this in later chapters.

CHAPTER 3

DETERMINING YOUR COMPETITIVE ADVANTAGE

You must determine your competitive advantage and use it to differentiate your product, or you will be seen as selling a commodity.

You must sell your product or service on the basis of some competitive advantage. That advantage will boil down to one or a combination of five fundamental things: (1) price, (2) quality, (3) service, (4) advertising/promotion/salesmanship, and/or (5) delivery. We'll deal with price, quality, and advertising/promotion/salesmanship in this chapter. We'll discuss salesmanship and service in Chapter 4, and nonsalesmanship (why, when, and whom not to sell to) and delivery in Chapter 5.

PRICE

One facet of your competitive advantage could actually be your price. It is true that a few people and businesses really do buy products and services based solely on price. And we know that many salespeople (maybe you) face customers who *say* the only important thing is price. But, as we've indicated, our research clearly shows that price is virtually *never the primary reason* a person buys anything. It is seldom even the secondary reason. Usually, it's a third consideration at best. Many salespeople might say, "If you don't think people buy on price, why don't you follow me around on some sales calls. Why, just yesterday I had a prospect say to me that there are only three important things when he buys: The first one is price, the second one is price, and the third one is price."

We know your prospects will tell you that—because they are trying to get *you* to cut *your* price. But customer-buying behavior belies their words.

21

In fact, many people get nervous even thinking about buying something that is low priced. Indeed, an analysis would likely show that there are more people who actually buy products or services on the basis of the price being *high* than there are who will make a purchase on the basis of the price being low. You've probably even heard people who contemplate making a purchase saying, "The only thing that really worries me about this deal is that the price seems so low."

If you don't think people buy based on *high* price, let's consider another example. Would you go to the low-price bidder for your own, personal brain surgery? Probably not. Because fundamentally, deep down, you really feel that you "get what you pay for," and the thought of going to the low-price bidder for your brain surgery messes with your mind. Most of us have a gut feeling that price intrinsically has something to do with the *quality* and the *value* of the product or the service that we are buying. In fact, most of us feel that price makes a statement about not only the quality of the product or service, but even to some degree, about the advisability of doing business with the low-price seller.

Price Makes a Statement about Credibility

If we told you we had a brand new Rolls-Royce parked out front that we'd let you have for $87,000, the first thing you'd ask us is, "What's wrong with it?" And the second thing is, "Do you have title to it?" because you probably couldn't believe that we would offer to sell you a new Rolls-Royce for $87,000 unless something was wrong with it or it was stolen property. Price does make a statement. A statement not only about the quality of what you are selling, but also about the very advisability of making the purchase. If your price is too low, the prospect thinks there may be something wrong with the item.

Now, let's look at the flip side. If we told you we had a new Rolls-Royce we'd sell you for $600,000, what would you say? You'd probably say something like, "Really? What makes that car worth $600,000? I want to see that car right now." *Translation:* "Tell me, show me, sell me on why I, or anyone, would pay you $600,000 for that (or any) car."

Again, price does make a statement—a very strong statement. Just as people will believe you when you tell them your products/services are cheaper (and they will believe that in every sense of the word—in price, quality, and value), they will also believe you when you say your products/services are higher priced (again in every way—price, quality, and value). Salespeople who sell at premium prices know that they can use a high price to make a credibility statement about their product or service being better; that is, if it costs more, it probably is worth more. And they know that by acknowledging that their price is higher than their competitors' prices, they trigger a "the hell you say" response in their customers that creates the most *receptive, responsive* atmosphere in which to sell their product.

QUALITY

Low price is only one way for you to compete. And it's also the dumbest thing to try to compete on for customers. If you want to earn a serious income as a salesperson, you'd better learn two things: The first is to compete on something other than low price. And, second, the only aspect of virtually any product or service that is extremely important to every prospect is quality. How important and viable, as a competitive advantage, is the quality of your product or service? It's probably very important. In some cases, it can be the most important reason your prospect buys (Figure 3.1).

Selling Quality

Selling quality is easy. But only *if you have quality and you know what it is.* The truth is that virtually everybody does have quality. Unfortunately,

Figure 3.1
Bicycle Helmets

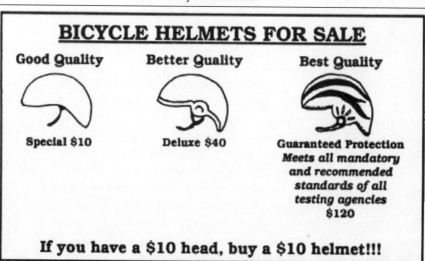

not everyone knows what quality means—and consequently they have a tough time selling it.

Most salespeople will tell you that quality means "best." *Quality does not mean best.* Quality means conformance to standards and expectations—to your *prospect's* standards and expectations. Quality means the *right* stuff; not the best stuff. Quality is the *correct* stuff for your prospect's requirements and needs, not the best stuff made.

The word *quality* and the word *best* are not synonymous. For example, what is a quality tire for your car? The only way to answer that question is to ask another question: What are you going to use the car for? Are you talking about an Indy 500 tire? Are you talking about a racing slick? Perhaps you are talking about a snow tire. Go out and buy the best racing slicks you can get, put them on your power-traction wheels, and see how fast you can accelerate in six inches of snow. Or put racing slicks on your front wheels and see how fast you can stop on wet pavement, going downhill. You might say that you bought the "best tires money could buy," but you'll be disappointed in their performance under those conditions.

Quality does not mean best. If quality means best, then why do we always have to define quality? Why does the mail-order catalog say "good quality" baseball glove, "better quality" baseball glove, and "best quality" baseball glove? The catalog could just as easily describe its "good quality" glove, its "lesser quality glove," and its "worst quality glove ever stitched together." But they are all *quality* gloves. Each one meets a specific set of customer standards and expectations.

Quality Can Be the Wrong Stuff

Many salespeople can't make their prices stick, because they try to sell either too high a quality or too inferior a quality for the needs of the customers. If you want to sell quality, you better have "the right stuff." If you don't have the right stuff for your customer, you have a problem. A salesperson is a fool if he or she tries to jam the wrong stuff down the prospect's throat. Selling certainly includes telling your prospects that your stuff is the correct stuff (and why it is the correct stuff) for them. But if your stuff is *not* the right stuff—if you are selling high-quality walnut wood and your customer only needs cheap plywood—the only way you'll get your customer to buy the wrong stuff is to cut your price. If they're building fine furniture, they might buy your walnut. But if they're putting in subflooring, they won't: They don't need it, don't want it, and can't afford it. The only way you'll sell them high-quality walnut for subflooring is to cut your price.

But I Sell a Commodity—And You Have to Sell Any Commodity Solely on Price

Let us make another strong statement about salespeople. Not only would we fire any salespeople who worked for us who are, themselves, price-buyers; but we'd also fire any salespeople who worked for us who viewed our product as a commodity. Let us explain why we say that.

Many salespeople feel that they are in a commodity business, and they believe because of that, they absolutely must sell on price. Nothing is further from the truth. Selling a commodity doesn't mean that you automatically must sell it on price. A *commodity,* by definition, is any item for which there is extreme competition; one that has no discernible distinguishing difference that separates it from the others. For example, suppose we have two water glasses for sale that are identical. If we tell you one sells for two pennies and the other sells for one penny (and you are buying water glasses), which one are you going to buy? You are going to buy the one-penny glass. Other things being equal, people buy on price. Right?

Many people believe that—other things being equal—all customers buy on price. But even that is not true. First off, other things are seldom, if ever, equal. Second, and more important, *it is the salesperson's job* to make sure the customer knows (1) that other things are *not* equal, and (2) that the customer knows why he or she should buy the salesperson's (higher priced) commodity item. A salesperson must differentiate his or her company's product and services from the competitor's some how, some way. That is what selling is all about. Otherwise, a computer could answer the phone, direct the customer to a price quote on the web, and all orders could be filled digitally as well.

Furthermore, there is ample evidence that even when the product is equal to another identical product, people don't always buy on price. For example, if we were to offer to sell you a gallon of gasoline for $3.00 or an identical gallon—and we mean *identical* gallon—for $3.10, would you pay us the $3.10 or the $3.00? You will probably say that you'd only pay the $3.00. But the truth is many, many people will pay the $3.10—as is evidenced by the *billions* of gallons of gasoline sold in the United States to people who *use their credit cards instead of cash.* At many service stations in the United States, when you punch "credit" instead of "cash," you have voluntarily elected to pay a premium for the *identical* gasoline—not just *almost* identical—*the identical*—gasoline. And consider what you pay for the same gasoline if the attendant pumps the gas for you.

Consider what you voluntarily pay for gasoline when you turn in a rental car and haven't topped off the tank—50 to 80 percent more. But that's different, isn't it? After all, your company is paying for it, and we all know that companies, if not individuals, *always* buy on price, don't they? Even if it is advertised that the price of gasoline is the same for cash or credit card—how about the APR (18 percent per annum or more) paid on any unpaid credit card balances?

The facts are, other things are never equal—and even if the product is identical to another, prospects don't necessarily buy on price. Remember: They *say* they do because they are trying to get *you* to cut your price. But their behavior belies their words! The point is, even if one is selling a commodity—a genuine commodity—people still don't buy on price. Household consumers don't and businesses don't, either.

While we are on the subject of commodities, incidentally, you should understand that most "commodities" are not commodities. For example, coal isn't coal, oil isn't oil, grain isn't grain, peanuts aren't peanuts, and cement isn't cement. If you believe cement is cement, why don't you go to Skokie, Illinois, to the Portland Cement Association, and make a statement such as "cement is cement." We guarantee it won't be long before they are going to ask you, "What kind of cement are you talking about?" There are different kinds of cement, even though most people who buy cement will tell the cement salesperson that "cement is cement." And even when you are talking about the *same kind* of cement, any given manufacturer of cement can differentiate its product from a competitor's by simply putting its brand name on its product. In essence, this tells the company's customers that "this is cement like the other guy's, but we made it, and by buying *ours,* you are getting *our* quality control, *our* service, *our* delivery, *our* company's policies and procedures, *our* way of doing things, *our* billing procedures, *our* order turnaround, *our* friendly service, *our* care and attention, *our* ease of doing business, plus all the other differentiating factors we offer."

Yes, But You Are Buying It from Us

Wholesalers and distributors and other resellers are, of necessity, often selling the same stuff. Let's say you are a soft-drink vending business and you carry Coca-Cola, 7 UP, and Pepsi products. Your competitor, another vending company, also carries Coca-Cola, 7 UP, and Pepsi products. Now, Coke's Coke. And 7 UP's 7 UP. Right? All Coca-Colas are made to the same formula, and all 7 UPs are made using the same 7 UP formula. Therefore, if you are going to sell Classic Coke against your competition, who also sells Classic Coke, then you've got to sell on price, don't you?

No! You don't have to sell on price. Let's say you sell your Coca-Cola through vending machines at a hotel. Why don't you check the price of

Coca-Cola in a vending machine at that hotel and compare it to the price of Coca-Cola in the hotel's restaurant, on the room service menu, and at that same hotel's gift shop? Likely you will find three, if not four, different prices for the same stuff, being sold at the same place and time. Put simply, you can sell on several things other than price. This includes not only being easier, better, and more convenient to do business with, but also advertising/promotion and professional selling acumen, as well as location.

How important are advertising, promotion, and acumen in selling? Well, if the customer doesn't know about your product or service, you're not going to do very well at selling it. Years ago, an exceptionally successful woman who started an incredibly profitable business gave us this little rhyme:

> He who has a thing to sell
> and goes and whispers in a well
> is not so apt to get the dollars
> as he who climbs a tree and hollers.

DO YOU APPROVE OF SELLING?

How significant are your capability and your willingness to sell? Our experience tells us that they often make all the difference in getting a sale. *The truth is that many salespeople really don't like selling.* In fact, a lot of salespeople think selling is just a notch above ambulance chasing. The truth is lots and lots of the salespeople we've assessed *fundamentally don't approve of selling as a profession*—and our educated guess is that about 90 percent of the general population doesn't approve of selling at all.

Salespeople *sell* things to people. In contrast to what? A mechanic. A mechanic is the word that we use to describe the salesperson who believes the product ought to be so good *it will sell itself.* The mechanic is the salesperson who still believes in the flawed "better mousetrap" theory. This person believes that people show up and buy things . . . without being asked to (more on this in Chapter 4).

How do you feel about the person who calls you at 6:30 in the evening when you're having your dinner and tries to sell you light bulbs? There ought to be a law against that, right? Well, there are laws against it. For evidence as to how strongly people have thought for a long time that there should have been a law against telemarketing, see *USA Today,* Tuesday, June 11, 1991, p. 18. In 1991, there were already laws in existence in 28 states against it. In subsequent years, very strong efforts have been made to further legally control telemarketing throughout the United States, such as the "National No Call Lists." That same article also pointed out that 28 percent of the telephone numbers even way back then were already *unlisted,* primarily because the telephone subscriber did not want to receive sales calls—and was willing to pay a premium for an unlisted number to avoid such calls.

However, if you think telemarketing is just interrupting someone's dinner to try to peddle light bulbs, you may not be salesperson material. Some of the greatest marketing success stories we can tell you are about people who have gone into telemarketing to tell prospects about products that the prospects wanted or needed but did not know were available. Telemarketing has the potential to be a real service to customers. Think about this: While many people may consider the dinner-time phone call intolerably inconsiderate of their privacy, there are many home-bound individuals who have limited access to shopping and welcome this type of service.

Most people have a certain degree of antipathy towards selling, especially when it's done aggressively—and salespeople do, too. A lot of salespeople think the old "shucks, golly, gee whiz, I don't imagine you'd want to buy this" approach to selling is too strong—let alone telling a customer that he needs, wants, and can afford your product or service and ought to buy it.

Most people have heard of H. Ross Perot by now. He's the guy who built Electronic Data Systems (EDS) long before he became even better known for running for president of the United States. Years ago, it was reported that he was worth about $2.4 billion—and that he had made all that money in about 30 years. Do you know how much money that is? If he had invested that money at 5 percent interest, his interest income would have been about $325,000 per day! We're not saying everybody can sell like H. Ross Perot. But we do think salespeople can learn a lot from someone like him. There was a classic article about Perot in *Business Week,*[1] which talked about his selling skills:

> Perot's initial challenge was to rise above his own success. He joined IBM in Dallas in 1956 after graduating from Annapolis and finishing his tour of duty. Though he was ignorant of computers—he thought the company just made typewriters—Perot quickly became a problem. He was so good at selling computers that his superiors didn't know what to do with him. He was already making so much money as a salesman that a promotion would have meant a pay cut. Perot, wanting action, said he wouldn't mind taking a pay cut to be promoted or even a smaller sales fee if IBM would turn him loose. IBM obliged, slashing his commission by 80% and raising his quota. Perot filled his 1962 sales quota on January 19th.

Nineteen days to fill his new, higher quota—and one of those was New Year's Day, and another four of those days were weekend days. In reality, he only had 14 working days to fill his new, higher quota.

Forget about Perot the politician or business icon. Think about Perot the salesperson. Not everybody can be as great at sales as H. Ross Perot, but most can do a lot better than they do. The first way to improve is to learn that there is a lot more to selling than price. Even if you're selling a commodity, and even if your competitor's quality is identical to yours, you still don't need to sell on price. Maybe your competitive advantage is advertising, positioning, promotion, or, as was in Perot's case, sales skills, acumen, and ability. Or maybe it is something known as *service*.

CHAPTER 4

SERVICE AS YOUR COMPETITIVE ADVANTAGE

Anyone who thinks the customer isn't important should try doing without him for a period of 90 days.

—Business Quotes

How important is service in selling your product? It can be *the one, single thing* that makes or breaks your sale. Service is incredibly important. And the good news is that it is *easy* to compete on service, because very few businesses really (we mean, really) *want to compete on service. Most businesses are run by the people who work in a business, and most people run businesses for themselves.* As a consequence, they often treat the customer as an unnecessary inconvenience.

WE ARE YOUR FULL-SERVICE BANK— WE ARE OPEN FROM 9:00 TO 5:00

Businesses often give minimal service to their customers, but they tell themselves that they give a lot. Your friendly, full-service bank is probably a good case in point. If your bank is so full of desire to give you good service, why are so many only open to actually lend you money from 9:00 to 5:00—except every holiday known to mankind and weekends when they are either open for a few hours or closed altogether—and will only lend you money if you don't need it? Why aren't they open from 8:00 to 5:00 . . . or even 6:00, and all day Saturday? We'll tell you why: Because the bank's management and employees don't want to be open then. Many a banker's basic idea is: You can't be playing golf or be home by 5:15 P.M. unless you close by 5:00 P.M.—and it is hard to get in a good duck hunt and still get to work

30

wearing a business suit by 8:00 in the morning. And that has nothing to do with you having to work until 5:00 and be at your office by 8:00 A.M. while needing to get to see a live banker (not an ATM) before 8:00 A.M. and after 5:00 P.M.!

And how about this old line (if you believe people whose job is to give you service really do want to actually serve you): "I'm from the government, and I am here to *help* you." And they say that with a straight face. Much like the professor who says, "The university is really a nice place when the students are gone," or the flight attendant who says, "Take any seat, we have a very light load" (notice you're not a person or passenger—you're part of the "load"). And then there's the customer service representative who takes the phone off the hook so he can "get his job done," or the desk clerk who says, "If that phone would only quit ringing, I could make some headway." The list could go on and on—but you get the idea. You seldom hear anyone say, "This was a great day at the office. I was so busy I didn't have time for lunch."

SELLING SERVICE INSTEAD OF PRICE—OR EVEN QUALITY

One of the all-time great success stories in business and selling was that of Tom Monaghan—the guy who originally built Domino's Pizza. Monaghan's worth was once estimated to be at least $450 million before he gave a lot of it away; he sold the company in 1998 for $1 billion. How did he achieve that wealth? His success came from selling service—*charging for pizza,* but *selling* service. The key to his sales success was his now famous sales slogan: "Domino's (Pizza) Delivers in 30 minutes or less." Was it the best pizza in town? Very few will argue that it is or was the best. Was it the lowest priced pizza in town? Hardly. Not even close. In fact, it is still more apt to be among the highest priced. Was he the most effective salesperson in town? Very few would argue that he wasn't, because he was able to get the word out that he would do what he said he would do. And he did it. Was it because he had no competition? Nope—he had a competitor on every corner. Then what was his secret to success? He delivered pizza on time—like he said he would. Period.

How many pizza shops are willing to guarantee pizza delivery in comparison to how many rely on the premise that they cook "the best pizza in town" in order to sell their product? By our own count in a few selected cities, less than 28 percent of the pizza shops in the United States actually deliver pizza. Most think that if they *cook* good pizza, customers will beat a path to their door. Their mentality is: "If you want good pizza, *come to me* and I'll cook it for you. But don't expect me to deliver it. We aren't starting that nonsense. If we do that, the next thing you know, you'll actually want it *hot* when we get it there!"

At a recent seminar, an attendee who was in the refrigerator and freezer supply business for hotels and restaurants in the Miami area told us that in the metropolitan Miami area about 1,100 new restaurants open each season. But he also said that the total number of restaurants in Miami had not changed significantly in the past 10 years. This means that about 1,100 restaurants *fail* in Miami each year.

It is no secret that in the United States the restaurant business has an incredibly high failure rate. The reason for that is that most people who operate restaurants are merchants who run their business *for themselves* and treat the customer like a necessary evil. If you ever talk to people who have failed in the restaurant business, you will find that their thinking before they opened their restaurant often went something like this:

> I'm going to open a restaurant, cook good food, serve generous portions, and charge fair prices. No, I'm not going to do any advertising. No, I'm only going to do word-of-mouth advertising. I know if I cook good food, serve generous portions, and charge fair prices, the world will beat a path to my door.

Wrong. You can't go into the restaurant business and succeed because you want to cook good food. You have to want to *sell* the food that has been cooked, whether it is good or not. Not all successful restaurants have the best food around, but most that are successful know how to *sell* it. If you don't know how to sell your product, we don't care how *good* your product is, you likely will find your business another statistic in the failed business column. It's that simple, straightforward, and fundamental.

THE BADLY FLAWED BETTER MOUSETRAP THEORY

> If a man can write a better book, preach a better sermon, or make a better mousetrap than his neighbor, though he builds his house in the woods, the world will make a beaten path to his door.
>
>   —Ralph Waldo Emerson

You can have an unbelievably good product, but if you don't know how to sell it, you won't make any money. If you believe in the theory that he who has a better mousetrap will find the world will beat a path to his door, you have no business in business. Ralph Waldo Emerson is credited with making that statement. And that makes it doubly interesting, because he was not a successful businessperson at all. In fact, Ralph Waldo Emerson apparently had a fair degree of contempt for businesspeople and sales types in particular. However, somehow his maxim about the better mousetrap has lived on to become an often quoted misconception in business literature.

Let's make one thing very clear: If the world is beating a path to your door, *your prices are too low.* Would you like to know how to stave off the thundering herd? You don't need to call out the military. Just raise your prices. Anyone can cut prices and sell a lot, but still go broke. *Selling* occurs when you have the world buying your products and services *even though* (or because) your prices are higher than your competitors'. It's easy to get people to line up outside your door when the word on the street is that you are giving your stuff away.

Do You Really Like to Provide Your Customer Great Service?

Many salespeople (and businesses) really don't like to provide their customers service at all. Let alone *great* customer service. In fact, it could be argued that *most companies* don't like to give their customers service. They reason that the only way that you "sell" anything is to be "competitive," that is, have a low price. And they certainly don't seem to accept—let alone practice—the idea that service is the responsibility of *all employees* to the customer.

We have a friend who sells carpeting. He is a very good salesperson and manager. A few years ago, his company was having trouble with its northwest division, so he was asked to go out to Seattle to shape things up. When he got there, to his amazement, he discovered that the company's customer service telephone number was an *unlisted phone number.*

We've been telling that story about the unlisted customer service telephone number for years, and you would never believe the number of "I've got a better one" stories that we've heard. One of the "better ones" involves the owner of a company who was upset when he discovered that many of his firm's happy customers were using the company's 800 number to call in free to get information about the use and application of his company's products. Feeling that it was a waste of company resources to fund these free telephone calls, this genius-of-selling-skills decided that the only way to cut down on this "abuse" was to eliminate the 800 number. That is real world-class thinking, isn't it? However, we should point out that one of the quicker thinkers in the seminar had a suggestion for this guy's boss. He suggested that the company install a 900 phone number. That way the company could actually *make* money when the customers called in their queries! And, just recently, we had a distributor of chiropractic examination tables tell us that one of his suppliers had just canceled his 800 telephone number because, "the only people who ever called us were our customers." So, whom do you want calling you?

SALESPEOPLE SHOULD PERSONIFY CUSTOMER SERVICE

Many salespeople don't seem to understand that they must personify customer service. In most business organizations, the only person the customer ever talks to, perhaps the only person the customer ever sees, is the salesperson. Often, when something goes wrong, the only person that the customer can go to is their salesperson. Unfortunately, most companies have all sorts of barricades preventing the customer from talking to anyone other than that salesperson (unless, of course, they have an exceptionally good customer service department).

We have made it our personal avocation to study sales professionals who make big dollars. One thing all of them seem to have in common is that *they take care of their customers.* They understand that their job is not simply to throw the order on someone's desk or to enter it into an order-entry database, but to be sure that once the order is entered, everything occurs as it should. That doesn't mean that they're telling the truck drivers what to do; the warehouse people which orders to pick and ship; the manufacturing people which job to run on which day; or the people in credit, collection, or customer service what to do and when to do it. It does mean that they are the watchdogs who ascertain that those things that were *promised* to their customer are actually going to *transpire.* That product is going to be shipped on time; that special information, parts, and services are going to be given; and that marketing and sales help is going to be provided.

Salespeople who are successful at selling at premium prices know that nobody pays big bucks for excuses—nobody! No prospect or customer wants to put up with a bunch of half-baked excuses as to why things that were promised did not occur, and they certainly won't tolerate being aggravated and inconvenienced by slipshod performance on the part of their vendor. A smart salesperson assumes total responsibility for (and takes personal accountability for) bird-dogging or otherwise pestering those in their organization to ensure the promises made to prospects and customers are fulfilled.

CHAPTER 5

WHY YOU REALLY SHOULDN'T MESS WITH PRICE-BUYERS

When our vendors were in the lobby, it looked like they were waiting for root canals.

—Michael Bozic

Certainly some of the most essential factors in selling any kind of a product or service revolve around the selling organization's proficiency in advertising, promoting, and selling its offerings. And most people would readily agree that branding, advertising, and promotion can significantly help-or badly hinder-the sales of any product or service. As the old adage goes, 50 percent of advertising works; but the unfortunate thing is that we don't know which 50 percent.

Presumably, those branding, advertising, and promotion efforts are in the hands of experts in your organization, and those people know which 50 percent to use and which 50 percent not to use—if that's even possible. For our purposes, however, we'll assume that this is an area over which you have no control. As a salesperson, you either benefit from productive promotion or have to overcome the unproductive. But we do think we can add something about the selling dimension relative to this competitive factor, and that is: Salespeople who are the most successful *don't mess with price-buyers*. That's right—they know when *not* to sell and to *whom* not to sell.

There's probably not an experienced salesperson anywhere in the world who hasn't had the unhappy experience of accepting an order from a prospect and, after the fact, wishing that he or she had never even met the new customer. One of the most difficult things for salespeople to understand is that the pure price-buyer is devoted to one fundamental, single-minded proposition: "You are not going to make any money on me.

35

Period." Therefore, it is incredibly foolhardy for any salesperson to waste time trying to sell to someone with that mind-set. The pure price-buyer is going to squeeze every drop of blood out of you and your organization before they place the order. There's nothing more professionally disgusting than seeing a salesperson trying to cajole an order out of someone who simply has no intention of allowing anyone but himself to "make a buck."

There are nine key reasons you shouldn't mess with these people. Here they are:

1. *Pure price-buyers take all your sales time.* If you're an experienced salesperson, reflect back over the past six months of your selling experience and ask yourself this question: Where have I spent most of my sales time? Inevitably, if you haven't been able to eliminate them, it has been with price-buyers.

The price-buyer has no qualms whatsoever about wasting your time. Invariably, their attitude is, "I've got to get a good deal no matter how long it takes." They will beat and pound on you, asking you to "squeeze a little extra out of here" or "cut them a deal on this or that." Then they'll tell you that they "need some time to think it over" and will ask you to "come back in a couple of weeks," at which time they'll beat and pound on you again. The pure price-buyer has one mentality: We can waste *your* time or *my* money. Guess which one they prefer to waste?

2. *They do all the complaining.* Pure price-buyers do this for the following reasons:

- *They believe that complaining builds character in salespeople.* They learned long ago that complaining will almost always get them some sort of price concession or special deal. The basis of that logic is that most people do not believe that someone complains unless there really is something to complain about. Therefore, most people who hear complaints from their customers believe that there must be something seriously wrong or they wouldn't complain in the first place. Because of this, the salesperson is inclined to say to his or her boss, "This customer's really unhappy. We'd better do something about it, or we're going to lose this account. Maybe we should cut them some kind of a deal to make them happy."

    People who study negotiation skills learn quickly that complaining *does* get concessions from salespeople. Therefore, those who teach negotiation seminars to purchasing professionals, for example, teach them to complain. It almost always gets some kind of concession from the selling organization in the form of a discount, rebate, throw-in, or some other "extra."

- *They want full measure.* These prospects or customers want 100 percent satisfaction. But you really need to recognize one thing: Their notion of 100 percent satisfaction will almost always exceed your idea of 100 percent satisfaction. In fact, you might interpret any pure price-buyer's notion of 100 percent satisfaction as more like 125 percent satisfaction.

3. *They forget to pay you.* One of the most interesting things about pure price-buyers is that once they've told you that they are "paying good money for this stuff" and "you had better make it right"—and you attempt to "make it right"—they then forget to pay for what they bought.

Most price-buyers are also slower payers. Anybody to whom money is so important tends not to settle accounts quickly. Anybody who is willing to beat the daylights out of you for an extra one quarter of 1 percent is more than willing to take that extra discount in the form of the time-value of your money by slow pay of your account. By the way, they also fail to pay other suppliers. So, at least you're not alone.

We'll even bet we can give you a list of your price-buyers, with 80 percent accuracy, just by looking at your receivables. Why is that, you ask? Because price-buyers are notoriously slow payers, and they can almost always be identified through their lousy, slow, or delinquent payment records.

4. *They tell your other prospects or customers how little they paid you.* People who are proud of their buying skills are sure to brag about how little they paid for something. But bragging is an interesting thing. Bragging does not count unless you are bragging to somebody who appreciates what you are bragging about.

Consider this scenario. A man just cut a great deal on a load of drywall he bought. Who's he going to brag to about that? His 13-year-old son after school? "Sit down, son, I'd like to tell you about knocking the soup out of this sales guy on this drywall today." Will the son say, "Gee, Dad, that's a terrific story. Tell you what. I'm going to get my buddies in here because they'll want to hear about this, too."

The reality that people brag about what they do is not necessarily bad. But it does create difficulty for you if you are trying to sell your product or service at a high price. The reason is that the price-buyer who cuts a particularly good deal will run down the street telling all your other prospects and customers how little he or she paid you for something, thereby conditioning them to expect the same low price.

In fact, bragging about what they've bought from you and how little they paid for it is, perhaps, the most debilitating thing that price-buyers can do to you. Not only have they beaten you up on price, but they encourage other prospects to do the same. Therefore, those other prospects will come at you with the same kinds of expectations the pure price-buyer did, thinking that they can get the same terms.

5. *They drive off your good customers.* With all their nagging, complaining, distractions, and unwillingness to pay their bill as agreed, they also wear you down to the point that you have little time and energy left to provide superior service to your good customers.

Have you ever had a good day turn sour? Have you ever had a day when you couldn't wait to get home and get your feet up, and you realized that it was about 9:15 in the morning when you began to feel that way? Almost always, it is dealing with a pure price-buyer that makes you feel like that. They love to tell you how insensitive or incompetent you are and how "they're not going to pay that bill until you do this, that, and the other thing," and that "you've got to make this right," and why "there's a problem with that," and that "you're going to have to fix it before I do anything."

Invariably, it is the price-buyer who gets you so psychologically beaten up that you get to the point where you don't feel like dealing with even your very good customers. What do you say to yourself then? "Why should I sell more to anybody? I get grief from the bad ones and don't have the time to deal with the good ones."

6. *They're not going to buy from you again, anyway.* Pure price-buyers appear to be loyal to only one vendor. The lowest priced one. The only way they're going to give you another order is if your price is even lower next time, and they'll only continue to order from you as long as your prices stay low. They will continue this until your organization goes broke, at which time they're going to say, "I knew they were going broke. Their prices were too low. I could have told them that."

It is unfortunately true, however, that price-buyers, deep down, have no real loyalty to *any* provider, vendor, source, or so-called "partner." If you do anything for them, under any conditions, you can still bet that the minute someone else comes along with a lower price, they're going to jump ship. The pure price-buyer is devoted to the sole proposition that, "You're not going to make any money on me," and appreciates, respects, and remembers nothing good that you've ever done for him or her in the past 4,000 years.

7. *They require you to "invest up" to supply their needs—and they blackmail you for yet a lower price.* One of the other things that a pure price-buyer is apt to do to you is require you to "invest up" in software, inventory, land, building, machinery, equipment, technology, trucks, warehouse space, and even people to supply their needs. Once they get you fully invested, they will then beat on you for yet a lower price. They will do that by declaring that they'll have to receive a lower price or they'll give their business to somebody else.

Many larger retailing companies are notorious for having done this over the years. They go to small manufacturers and give them big orders, watch them increase their inventories, put additions on their plants, upgrade systems, buy new machinery and equipment, hire and train people, and generally "invest up" to supply that big customer's needs. Then, when the big customer has a pretty good idea that the little vendor has a need for their volume just to survive, they'll blackmail them to receive even a lower price with the threat of "yanking all of the business" unless some very drastic price concession is made.

Large companies have no particular reason to worry about whether you fail (other than the short-term inconvenience of changing suppliers). They figure there are more fish in the sea, and they can always get what they need from someone else. Some of the most tragic small business failures have occurred because the small guy gets mesmerized by being associated with the big guy and then finds out that the big guy simply squeezes out all the blood. It's kind of like the big guy saying, "Which way do you prefer to die? Fast or slow? A bullet between the eyes now or starve to death over the next few months?"

It should be noted that it's not really a function of whether or not your customer is big in terms of being a gigantic organization. It's only a question of whether the big customer is big *to you*. If a customer is worth $100,000 in sales, it may not seem like a very big customer unless you are doing only a million in total sales. Then that customer is buying 10 percent of your total volume, and that's a lot. Here's our basic precept: If you ever have a customer whose purchases are more than 10 percent of your volume, you are probably vulnerable to this kind of blackmail. That's Russian Roulette at its most dangerous.

8. *They destroy the credibility of your price and your product or service in the eyes of the end users.* Another major problem of selling to price-buyers at the low price they demand occurs if and when you sell to someone who, in turn, resells your product or service. This is particularly problematic if you are a manufacturer.

If your reseller is a price-buyer who is able to extract a low price from you, you can bet that he or she will turn around and resell your product or service to the end user at a low price as well. Part of the reason for this is that resellers feel that their customers buy on price largely because *they* buy on price. And they believe that if they can get a low price deal themselves, they can turn around and resell at a low price and presumably still maintain their margins.

The problem with reselling at a low price is that the reseller destroys the credibility of your product or service—and the price of it—in the eyes of the end user. The retailer or distributor who buys at a low price and then resells at a low price is, in essence, telling the end user that this product is not worth the big price that others are paying for it. After all, if it were worth more, it would cost more. Any number of the "discounters," "clubs," "wholesale outlets," and other nationally known discount retail operations have completely destroyed manufacturers of products by doing this.

9. *They steal any ideas, designs, drawings, intellectual property, information, and knowledge they can get their hands on.* Pure price-buyers often have little or no scruples when it comes to stealing anything they can get their hands on. They will ask you to "show them what you can do," or "prove you have the capacity," or "give us your ideas and then we'll think about it." And when they say, "give," they literally mean, GIVE.

You are foolish or at least naive if you fall for those ideas about developing a relationship with a customer by proving yourself to them unless the customer is ready, willing, and able to pay for your insight. That is why we have patent and copyright laws. Elsewhere in this book you will find two ways to protect yourself from this theft. And never forget this admonition—if your ideas are worth anything, they must be paid for.

Delivery—The Ultimate Competitive Advantage

One thing that you can compete on successfully, consistently, and long term is delivery: Your ability to put your product or service offering in your customer's hot little hand, when and where he needs it. Delivery is absolutely the one thing you *must* be competitive on if you want to sell at a higher price than your competitor. In many industries, a company's ability (or inability) to deliver a product or service in a timely, agreed-on manner can literally make or break it.

Have you ever wondered why your customers go to all the trouble of explaining to you that they can get the very same thing that you sell at a lower price somewhere else? If they can really get it cheaper somewhere else, why don't they just go there and get it? Why do they waste all that time telling you, "I can get it cheaper from the other guy"?

There are really two reasons. One is because they really *can't*—and they are misrepresenting the price or your competitor's ability to deliver the product or service offering on time, and/or it really isn't the same stuff. What they are really saying is that they want everything *you* can give them,

---

**Reasons Customers Don't Get It Down the Street
for a Cheaper Price**

Reason 1: They can't get it:

- They misrepresent your competitor's pricing.
- The same stuff isn't available now.
- It isn't the same stuff.

Reason 2: They can, but:

- They don't really want to.
- They'd better not buy it there.
- For some reason, they can't (even though it is available) because your competitor won't sell it to them.

---

but at a lower price. But they also want *your* ability to deliver, *your* investment in inventory, *your* way of doing business, *your* service, *your* quality, *your* people, and *your* investment in machinery and equipment.

The second reason price-buyers tell you they can get it cheaper from the other guy is because they *can* get it, but *they don't want to, better not,* or *can't* because your competitor won't sell it to them. Let's analyze what that really means.

When prospects tell you they can "get the same stuff from someone else, for less money," you always want to silently ask yourself this essential question: Then why are they even talking to me? Because if they really can get *the same stuff* down the street, *right now,* for less money, why are they bothering to talk to you?

REASON 1: THEY CAN'T GET IT

They Misrepresent Your Competitor's Pricing

We hope this dose of real-world reality doesn't burst your bubble, but it's a fact that prospects stretch the truth, especially when it is to their advantage. One falsehood that many will tell you is that the other guy's price is "lower" when it really isn't. They will claim that the other guy's price is lower because of "other things" that the other guy will do. Then claim that your competitor will pay the freight, give better terms, offer a longer warranty, and so on. Or your prospects will do the reverse—insist that the other guy's price ($98) is lower than your price ($100) when they know that the *real* cost is not lower. For example, let's say your price is $100, but you pay the freight, give credit for 30 days, and will ship to all four of your customer's job sites at no extra charge. You also sell in less than case lots. Your competitor, whose price is $98, is cheaper—says your customer—completely but conveniently overlooking the fact that your competitor's $98 price is COD, and that your competitor will not sell in less than case lots, will not pay freight, and does no shipping to job sites. So, whose long-term cost is really cheaper?

Another form of fabrication that super-desperate, price-driven prospects or customers may engage in is actually to counterfeit or forge your competitor's quotations, thereby "substantiating" your competitor's lower prices. Today's high-tech copy machines make this form of fraud child's play. We once talked to a purchasing manager who actually bragged to us about not only how simple such fraud was to do, but how effectively it worked for him. Unbelievable, you say? Not really. Distressing? Yes. But out of the realm of possibility? No!

The Same Stuff Isn't Available at This Time

Marvin Schutt, the late executive director of the National Sporting Goods Association, used to tell this story years ago to make this point. We'll refer to it now and again later, because it's that good. It seems that this guy wanders into a sporting goods store and wants to buy a can of tennis balls. "How much are your tennis balls?" he asks.

The merchant says, "That six-can pack is $17.99."

The customer says, "$17.99! Why I can get the exact same six-can pack of tennis balls down the street at your competitor's store for half that much."

"Well, I'm sorry, sir, I can't let you have it at that price," says the merchant. "I guess you'll have to go down there and get them."

"Well, I would, but I can't," replies the customer.

"Why can't you?" asks the merchant.

"He's out of tennis balls right now," says the customer.

"Oh, well, you can come back when I'm out. Mine are only a buck for a six-can pack when I don't have any. I always give everybody a great deal when I'm out, too," retorted the merchant.

Unfortunately, many salespeople just don't seem to fathom how important delivery really is. They don't seem to understand that, usually, when customers are saying that they can get it cheaper, they're really trying to get *your* quality, *your* service, and *your* delivery *at the other guy's price*. Because if they can really get a better deal, they would be down the street *getting it* and wouldn't be wasting their time trying to con you into cutting your price.

You can't find a retail salesperson anywhere with any degree of experience who hasn't seen this scenario played out. You learn quickly, if you are a good judge of actions instead of words, that if your prospects could really get a better deal (quality, service, and on-time delivery) that they would be down the street buying it—not wasting time telling you how much better a deal they "can" get from your competitor.

It's the Same Stuff . . . But It Really Isn't the Same Stuff

Another fabrication that price-conscious prospects will attempt to tell you is that they can get "the same stuff" somewhere else for less money. But it simply is not *really* the same stuff. It is easy to say that "the same stuff" is the same stuff even when the quantity, size, quality, color, weight, performance characteristics, volume, shape, taste, feel, smell, range, power, texture, and on and on, aren't even close. It's your job to know (or verify) what the competition really is offering and not to fall for such a gross misrepresentation of the truth.

One of your authors regularly encounters this with a complex, sophisticated assessment system that he offers for salesperson screening and selection. Prospect after prospect tells him that he or she can purchase an assessment product that measures the same capacities for much less money. However, when he proceeds to ask whether the other assessment measures values, cognitive process, talents, and skills—and also compares all of these to the job's standards—his prospects quickly backpedal to admit that the other product is primarily a behavioral assessment only and does not compare a candidate to a unique sales position's benchmark.

REASON 2: THEY CAN GET IT, BUT . . .

The second reason your prospect will spend a lot of time telling you he can get the same stuff cheaper, is that he can, *but*. But what? Here we go . . .

They Don't Really Want To

It is easy to say, "I can get the same stuff down the street for less money," especially when you really can. But, often, what the prospect knows is that, although he can get the *same stuff* for less money *right now,* he doesn't really want to do so. Why not? Because you (and/or your employer) are better and easier to do business with; you are more reliable and easier to work with; you have better service, better hours, better trained people; you have quicker order turnaround time, offer a better warranty or guarantee, honor your commitments, have simpler and easier to understand invoicing, record keeping, and so on. In short, many prospects will tell you, truthfully, that they can get it cheaper—but they really do know that you and your organization offer the best buy. They just want you to cut your price—even though they are going to buy from you anyway.

They'd Better Not Buy It There

What do we mean that he or she had "better not" buy it there? They'd better not—because their boss said so. Many prospects can tell you, truthfully, that they can get the same stuff from your competitor for less money. The part they won't tell you, of course, is that they'd better not buy it there, because someone very powerful in their organization *told them* that they'd better not get it there, for whatever reason. And, usually, the people who flex that kind of muscle: (1) have a good reason for doing so, (2) accept no other sources, and (3) know that savings of a few dollars "over there" is just plain stupid.

They Can't Get It There, Even Though It's Available

The third reason that prospects will tell you that they can get your stuff somewhere else cheaper is that they can't, even though they can. This is *not* double talk. The real truth is, even when it is widely known that your competitor is offering the same stuff at less money and can deliver it, your prospect actually can't buy it from your competitor *because your competitor won't sell it to them*. Why not? There are lots of reasons, including:

- Your prospect is a jerk—lies, steals, takes advantage, is a difficult person to deal with, and/or sets up too many obstacles for ease of doing business.
- Your prospect hasn't paid for the last stuff they bought—a point that will only surprise the most naïve reader. Here's a little philosophical thought—if you aren't going to be paid for it, you may as well charge more for it . . . and you can even write off a bigger loss!

- Your competitor won't sell it to your prospect as a matter of policy. For example, some buyers for governmental agencies face this problem—potential vendors won't even give them a quote, let alone write up the order for them, due to the difficulty of the process, paperwork, slow pay, and so on.

Your prospect certainly will try to get you to cut your price and will tell you they can get the same stuff somewhere else for less money. But if that were true, why would they spend so much time telling you about their better deal? The point is, you should always learn to waste some of this type of prospect's time (professionally, of course) and see how diligently they will really work at telling you how they can get the same stuff, cheaper. If they can—you are history. The reason that prospects will spend time telling you they can, but don't run you off, is because they can't or, if they can, they don't want to or better not do so.

As we have continually emphasized, delivery is usually the, single trigger event that can cause loss of up to 70 percent of your business with existing customers. Conversely, the ability to deliver the right stuff at the right place at the right time with good service will actually make you sales and help you retain customers. Of all the things that any enterprise can compete on, the most significant, most important is delivery. If your employer has delivery problems, you will have difficulty selling *at any price,* let alone a *premium* price. If your organization has a spotty track record on delivery (or quality or service), you will start losing sales. Anybody can cut price, get an increase in sales volume, foul up delivery, have quality problems develop, find service falling to pieces, and go broke.

Products and services are sold—and prices stick—because a business gives its customers quality, service, and on-time delivery. And these companies that know how to create a brand and promote and sell those three things—quality, service, and on-time delivery—will have prospects wanting to do business with them. But all those things cost money. If you are going to give your customers what they *need* and *want,* you've got to charge a premium price. The good news is: Those organizations that have historically charged premium prices have: (1) survived the longest, (2) made the most money, and (3) been able to pay the highest wages, salaries, and commissions to the people who work for them.

CHAPTER 6

WHAT BUYERS AND CUSTOMERS REALLY NEED— HINT: IT ISN'T LOW PRICE

If your customer truly needs a low price, you can't afford to sell to him.

—Cletus Peichl

Most organizations go broke be-
cause they legitimately believe they can sell low and make it up in volume. We have consistently shown that those who are successful are the
ones that charge premium prices—and know *how to sell* their product or
service. However, the ability to sell isn't just a function of salesmanship.
And it really isn't a function of having the highest quality (although, admittedly, it is very difficult to peddle genuine junk for very long and survive). What do prospects really need? What do they really buy? Someone
who is a legitimately qualified prospect must have certain characteristics.
What are they?

Many salespeople succumb to buyer pressures to cut prices because they
have never really analyzed what the customer needs versus what he or she
says he or she needs (or wants). Buyers do not need a low price. They will
tell you they do, they may even think they do, and they certainly are pressured to try to get a low price. But they don't really *need* a low price. In
fact, if they truly *need* a low price, you'd better not take their order because
they may not be able (or willing) to pay you. Let's examine some of the
things that buyers really do need.

THEY NEED TWO OR MORE VENDORS

Sole-sourcing is very perilous. In a world where there are thousands of potential vendors, sole-sourcing is just plain dumb. A fire, flood, tornado,

hurricane, software crash, earthquake, volcanic eruption, labor exodus, or a labor strike can cause any single vendor not to be able to ship or provide a product or a service on time.

Sole-sourcing is short-sighted, and most buyers can't afford it. For example, many people argue that the federal government is a price-buyer, but even the government has tight rules and standards that regulate sole-sourcing contracts. Even if there are many, many vendors, sole-sourcing is dangerous, because if you do sole-source and something happens to that source, you must quickly—and we mean overnight—come up with another source. This is not always easy to do, especially if you're dealing with a large volume or a highly customized product; some sort of extensive, sophisticated service; or intricate demand. If you don't have a track record, if you don't have a history of good payment, if you don't have an ongoing relationship, other vendors may not even sell to you. They don't know you, don't need you, have managed to get along without you as a customer up to now, so why should they help you? And if they've ever tried to deal with you in the past, they may not trust you. Would you want to be in that position?

Street-smart prospects learn early that sole-sourcing is dangerous. So most won't do it. That means, by definition, that one vendor *can* charge a higher price than the lowest price bidder and get the business. Also, virtually all customers who buy in bid situations reserve the right to reject any and all bids. That is generally stipulated because they know that if they accept the lowest bid, they are vulnerable to any idiot who writes down a very small number on a piece of paper and gets the bid, but then fails to perform.

CUSTOMERS NEED ON-TIME DELIVERY

More than anything else, customers need on-time delivery. And this is true whether you sell a hard-goods product, a high-quality service, data, or information. If you can deliver on time, you don't have to sell at the lowest price. If you can't deliver on time, forget about commanding a higher price—and with the possible exception of the very short term, forget about selling at any price. There will be more to come on this later, but keep this concept in mind. Many businesses eventually have delivery problems because they have gotten too much business due to their prices being too low.

THEY LIKE THE IDEA THAT THEY'RE CUTTING A DEAL

If you are ever in a negotiated versus sealed-bid situation, you must remember that many buyers in that environment think they must "cut a deal." In other words, they don't want to be merely "order placers." In those situations, trial pricing is the only solution. This generally works because of the way most people are paid (or ultimately rewarded) not on how little they *spend,* but on how much they *save.* Thus, if you ask a significantly higher price than your competition, but tell your prospect you can "knock more off" than your competition, you can still have a higher selling price, but it's one that gives your customer a bigger "savings" by buying from you rather than your competitor. The following example illustrates how this can work.

Let's say you're selling Fords and your competitor is selling Chevrolets; you're asking $20,000 for your car and your competitor is asking $18,400. But let's say you're willing to take (in a negotiated bid) $18,000 for your Ford—and your competitor is willing to take $17,600 for his Chevrolet. You have an excellent shot at getting the sale at the $18,000 price over your competitor's $17,600. Why? Because if you're selling your Ford, asking $20,000, but willing to take $18,000, you can give your customer a savings of $2,000 per unit. If your competitor is asking $18,400, but will go to $17,600, he can only show his customer an $800 per unit savings.

You probably feel that we don't really "get it." Isn't the real savings $400? The difference between the $18,000 and $17,600? Yes, but you can't prove that savings to your boss if you are a buyer. After all, a Ford isn't a Chevrolet. You can't say, "I saved $400 because I bought a Chevrolet" *because you can't prove that.* While a Ford may be very similar to a Chevrolet, it isn't a Chevrolet. Even if they have all of the same features and options, the cars aren't identical. *You can prove* you saved $2,000 per unit by buying the Ford, but you can only prove that you saved a mere $800 per unit if you bought the Chevrolet.

Whenever you are in a negotiated bid environment and you have a differentiable item, trial pricing works. We personally don't like to do it because it smacks of purposely questionable selling, but it does work. If you ask a high price, or at least a higher price than your competitors, and are willing to negotiate a wider spread, the buyer is hard put to refuse it. If the buyer buys from you, he or she can report to the boss, "Hey, when I bought those four new Fords I saved $8,000. Had I bought those four new Chevrolets, I would only have saved $3,200."

Incidentally, the reciprocal of this tactic (that you might successfully use trial pricing because of how many people are paid) is a very important principle. Here it is: As a salesperson, never tell any prospect exactly how *you* are paid. This is particularly critical if you are paid by commission. Unfortunately, if some prospects know you are paid by commission, they believe you are motivated to sell at any price. Why? Because a little bit of something certainly beats a lot of nothing, doesn't it? Let's say you are paid a 7 percent commission rate. If you sell $1,000 worth of product, your commission is $70. If you sell it at only $900, your commission is only $63. Granted, you're going to make more money if you sell at the full $1,000, but you may not get the sale at all at $1,000 and 7 percent of nothing is nothing. Most anybody would rather get $63 in commission than get nothing. And that is why, if some prospects know you are paid a commission on your sales dollars, they believe you will be motivated to sell at a low price . . . or at *any* price.

So *never* tell prospects you're paid on any sort of commission. If they ask you how you're paid, or try to wheedle it out of you, do the right thing and avoid the discussion. Jokingly tell them you've got a 50-year contract that is noncancellable. It's none of their business how you're paid anyway, is it?

Another thing you should never tell a prospect is that there is a contest underway (and that you are going to get a free cruise if you sell another $40,000 worth of whatever you sell this month). Once prospects know you *really* want (need) a sale, they'll know you are willing to give away the store at any price, just to run up your sales volume and qualify for that free trip.

They Need Respect

Sure, we all need respect. Give them a little, and they might think about buying from you.

They Need Help and Guidance on Complex Purchases

Here is your real chance to sell. People who make multiple, varied, or complex purchases often are not as knowledgeable as you might think about what they are buying. If you, as a salesperson, see your role as being an educator or teacher to a harried prospect, you can get an advantage on your competition. A lot of salespeople still mistakenly believe that selling is telling jokes, being friendly, and finding out the other guy's price so they can slide in under it. They don't work at educating their customers, and they fail to give that extra dimension of valuable knowledge and service that earns the prospect's respect and loyalty. Don't ever expect a prospect or existing customer to buy strictly from loyalty. But, instead, recognize that if you are a knowledgeable, helpful representative of your products or services, you will always have access to the ears of your customers. This gives you the opportunity to present the reasons why they should pay you a premium price: You have not only helped educate them about what to buy, but you have communicated your ability to deliver the kind of quality product or service they need, on time, and you can back up their confidence in you with impeccable, ongoing support.

THEY NEED TO BUY WHAT THEY ARE TOLD TO BUY

Many people in buying and purchasing jobs don't really decide on their own what to buy—no matter what they tell you. Why is that? Because often, those who own the problem your product or service solves, don't own the buying role. Studies show that 85 percent of the time the person who is in the buying role has little or no real say in what they buy. In fact, in 32 percent of the cases, they really have *no* say whatsoever in the purchase decision. Don't forget that, because that little-known gem substantiates the very need for you to do backdoor selling. Professional buyers, of course, hate backdoor selling because it works. You, too, may react negatively to this suggestion, thinking, "Hey, guys, don't talk to me about backdoor selling—you try that and you'll get thrown out the front door."

In fact, an old, but still reliable *study*[1] on this issue reported that:

> Purchasing managers indicated they do not like a salesperson who practices backdoor selling; that is, by-passes the purchasing manager to talk directly with the end user of the product. Thirty-six percent of them complained about that.

And that's exactly why you want to do it. It works!

It's like playing any sport or other activity where there is an adversarial game or direct challenge. If they don't want you to go there, that's exactly where you should go. If they don't care whether you go there, there's no point in going. The subtle touch to this approach is that you've got to learn how to do backdoor selling tactfully and diplomatically. Realize most prospects will resent it, but they'll resent it because it is so incredibly successful. And, remember, even if you don't do it, your competition probably will do it.

The real secret to this strategy is never to be in a position to have to use it in the first place. You need to position yourself with those that have the most power, influence, and real decision-making authority before you ever get too far immersed in any sale. Remember this, it is far easier to be handed down than it is to try to work your way up once you've engaged at a lower level. If you can't enter accounts at a high enough level, you should seek the help of the person with whom you are dealing to get to the more powerful person. Remember, they don't sell your product or service. You do. Show them that it is to their advantage to help you influence the right people. However, as a last measure, this backdoor selling strategy might be your last, best option.

Later we're going to talk about prospect avoidance strategies. One of them is that prospects will try to stiff-arm you; that is, they say, "We can't pay any more than $18." That, my friend, is the one open invitation to do backdoor selling. Just ask "Why?" They'll inevitably say, "Because my boss (or whomever) said so." When they tell you because "so and so" said so, they are clearly identifying the individual to whom you should have been selling in the first place. They are naming the individual who really is the decision maker. Learn to use that knowledge. This is the point at which you say, "Gee, I can't believe they said that." Or, "I'm sure they want to get the right stuff. Maybe we should talk to them together?" The real truth, though, is that if you're a real pro you should have learned this much earlier in the sale, anyway, shouldn't you?

Backdoor selling is incredibly persuasive, but if you do it poorly, please remember that you are going to get thrown out in the snow, rain, or mud. So you have to learn how to do it diplomatically. Not just because in 32 percent of the situations a corporate buyer has no say in what they buy and you must sell to decision makers, but because while it's in only 32 percent of the situations in which they have no say, those situations *cover 68 percent of the dollars spent.* In other words, the bigger the ticket, the stronger the probability that the buyer has no say in what they buy, so you must get to the decision maker for bigger ticket sales (and the sooner the better). Also remember that big tickets come in two ways: It is a very expensive item, or it is a cheap item that they need a lot of.

Backdoor selling is highly risky, but works because people other than mid-level staff people often have a significant say, or at least some say, in what is bought. The people in engineering, information technology, and the plant manager—the people who are going to use the product in an application—all have a lot to do with the purchase decision, maybe everything. But maybe they don't. You've got to learn where the power is. A good example of this (and where it is virtually an art form) is the way commercials for the Saturday morning children's shows are designed. Why do you think they advertise cereal on those shows? Is it because little kids have a concern about the nutritional value of what they're eating? No. It's because the advertisers are trying to persuade the *decision maker* (the kid) to tell the *buyer* (the parent) to go out and get the right cereal. That's all there is to it.

Many salespeople forget this Iron Law of backdoor selling: Forgiveness is far easier to secure than is permission. Don't ask for permission to do backdoor selling, just do it. You can seldom get permission, but you can almost always get forgiveness. But remember to be careful, gentle, and astute. Don't be reckless.

THEY NEED TO GET WHAT THEY BUY— QUANTITY, QUALITY, TIMELINESS

They need to get what they've ordered. They need to have it on hand, in place, so that they don't have to shut down. We want to emphasize, one more time, the critical importance of your ability to deliver your product or provide excellent service to your customer, on time and in top condition, as you promised.

THEY NEED TO MINIMIZE INVENTORY CARRYING COSTS WITHOUT JEOPARDIZING THEIR ENTERPRISE'S NEEDS

Your prospect may need "just-in-time inventory"—nothing late, while not having too much on hand. This is a tough requirement, and if they can be convinced that you can deliver on time you have a strong selling advantage. Any astute operation needs to try to minimize inventory carrying costs. But understand one thing: All this time-worn business about statistical quality control and the continuing trend to have just-in-time delivery emphasizes the importance of just one thing: *delivery,* not price. They'll tell you they want low price, but they will *cut you off* as a vendor if you foul up delivery.

THEY NEED TO BUY FROM A TECHNICALLY CURRENT AND FINANCIALLY SOUND VENDOR

Have you bought a ticket on People Express Airlines lately? They sure were cheap. But they're out of business and have been gone for years and years and years. Have you ever tried to buy from *any* company that eventually went out of business? It's very hard to do, but the price is (was) right, isn't (wasn't) it? Most low-price competitors go broke and usually do so quickly. Years ago, People Express Airlines went from nothing in sales to more than $1 billion in sales and back to nothing in five short years. One day they were out there selling, and the next day the doors were locked, the phones shut off, and all the rest that goes with failure. Most astute prospects learn early in the game that you've got to buy from whoever is going to deliver quality product, on time. If they don't, they're going to be in a job-threatening situation when they or their employer doesn't have the needed products or services. Any smart business-to-business buyer is far more concerned about the probability of your being able to deliver on time, than your low price. Oh . . . they're also concerned about whether you're going to be around at all. Or, at least they should be. Shouldn't they?

THEY NEED MORE CERTAINTY ON A ITEMS (COMPARED TO B OR C ITEMS)

A items are what we call the items a prospect must *never* be without. B items are important, and there should never be any problem with their availability. C items are so ubiquitous that we don't need to worry about them. Customers need A items; items that are really critical to their business. For example, an airline needs fuel (A item) more than they need ice (B item). If you're a drinker, you might not agree with that, but most drinkers will agree that they would rather run out of ice than out of fuel, particularly at 30,000 feet. However, if they run out of cocktail stirrers (C item) probably no one will get too upset. Thus, lack of B and C items will not put the airline out of business, but lack of item A spells major disaster for the company. That is the real difference between a demand and nondemand item, and you need to know where your product or service fits into this hierarchy.

THEY NEED PRODUCTION/PERFORMANCE CAPABLE VENDORS

Here, one more time, is the old delivery factor. If you simply do not have the capability (capacity, know-how, or experience) to get what you sell to your customer, on time, in good shape, and totally functional, you aren't going to get the order (or at least subsequent ones) no matter how good your price. As we've already mentioned, you can see this clearly in bid situations when the low bidder doesn't get the job because the people vetting the bid are afraid that bidder can't perform to specifications.

THEY NEED COURTESY, SPEED, AND TIMELY ACTION ON THE PART OF SALESPEOPLE IN ACCEPTING ORDERS, ANSWERING QUESTIONS, AND RESPONDING TO ORDER PROBLEMS OR DELAYS

The number of salespeople who really don't want to talk to their customers is amazing. It is not unusual to hear salespeople check their voice mail and, on hearing that they have none, respond with, "Great!" If they do have any, they may say or think, "Well, did she want me to call her today?" or, "I'll call them later," or, "I'll tell him I couldn't return the call, but I'll make sure that I'll call him later."

THEY NEED SPEED AND ACCURACY IN INVOICING AND ACCURATE COST INFORMATION

We have a friend in the public seminar business who gave us an example of how important such a "minor" thing as fast and accurate invoicing can be. He said, "I cut off one of my suppliers, a printer. You want to know why? Because he wouldn't itemize what various cuts and folds were costing, and I couldn't make a decision as to whether or not I wanted to continue with a specific brochure that I was using. I think this guy thought I was trying to figure out where he was getting ahead of me on price, but that wasn't my motive. My problem was, I wanted to know if the special fold was worth doing. He wasn't trying to beat me on the price, I don't think, although it was a negotiated sale. But he couldn't (or wouldn't) tell me the breakout on the cost so that I could make an intelligent business decision. I just decided I couldn't afford to do business with him. And then he called me and wanted to know if his price was too high. I told him, 'Your service is no good. And I don't want to do business with you.'"

THEY NEED ORDER AND SALES SERVICE DEPARTMENT HELP

We once talked to a contractor who developed shopping centers, and he told us that one of his biggest problems was getting sales service and information from salespeople, especially when he was getting into something about which he had little knowledge or experience. The example he used was that he was trying to get information on automatic doors (at entry ways for supermarkets, hotels, and airports) that he needed to install. His concern was over safety, product liability, and the maintenance of the doors. Apparently the salespeople he talked to didn't think that those questions were important. The fact that they could offer him the lowest prices was what they believed should be the major topic of conversation. He said he didn't buy from the lower price guys, but rather bought from the one company that gave him the answers (and assurances) about his concerns.

They Need Quality Transportation Carriers Used by Vendors

If you ship a tangible product and it shows up broken or unusable, you either have a transportation carrier problem or a packaging problem. If it leaves your place in good shape, but it gets torn up in transit, it's because whoever is shipping it tore it up (this is most commonly the case), or because you didn't package it correctly for the type of transportation carrier you used. In either event, you still have a delivery or a quality problem. Please understand that failure to get a tangible product in the hands of your customer both intact and on time is almost a sure-fire way to lose a customer—not because of your price, but because the product can't be used or is unacceptable when it gets there (or it is too much trouble to use), and your customer will start looking for another vendor.

Delivery—You Can't Sell at a High Price without It

Delivery is an incredibly significant component of your ability to sell at a high price. The good news is, *if you raise your price,* you probably can eliminate your delivery problems, improve your gross margin, profitability, and earn bigger commissions and bonuses—even though your competitors have a lower price than you do. The reason low price vendors have delivery problems is that in order to sell at a low price, they have to cut back on everything. The volume that may be created by the low price usually results in an inability to produce enough product on time. The first thing that happens is they get late on shipments. Then, of course, because of rushing, quality gets bad. With poor quality, customer complaints start rolling in, and then service goes down the tubes. Planned sales volume of quality goods, with on-time delivery, means that you can sell at a higher price than your competitors.

CHAPTER 7

THINGS BUYERS WOULD LIKE BESIDES A LOW PRICE

The bitterness of poor quality remains long after the sweetness of low price is forgotten.

—Anonymous

We have already clearly established that prospects will tell you they need a lower price, but what they say isn't always true. What your prospect really needs are the things we outlined in Chapter 6. And if that prospect truly and absolutely needs only a low price, you likely can't afford to sell to him or her. Period.

Of course your prospects would like a low price. But they're probably realistic enough to understand that they are, in the final analysis, going to get what they pay for and that if they buy from your lower priced competitor, they will probably set themselves up for problems—some of which ultimately will be intolerable. So, *never* compete on low price. Instead, concentrate your efforts on providing the customer with what he needs, and of course, charge an appropriate (premium or high) price for that performance on your part.

Prospects and customers like a lot of other things besides low price, and some of these other things can be just as persuasive as a low price in getting your prospect to buy. Let's take a look at some of the things that you can provide to your prospects to get them to buy from you at a price higher than your competitor's.

AN EASY, "NO BRAINER" RELATIONSHIP

When it's easy to do business with someone, it makes your life easier. If you can provide your prospects and customers with an easy relationship in which they get what they want, when they need it, on time and in good shape, you'll probably find it easier to make that sale at a higher price.

Reliability and Dependability

People like to know that they can rely on you. This knowledge almost always is built over the history of your relationship. It is a foolish (and rare) customer who will drop a known provider to save a few pennies to buy from an unknown source. When prospects or customers tell you they can "get it cheaper down the street," you might remind them that they know they can rely on you and that there may be a serious question mark down the street.

Predictability

Customers not only like reliability, they like predictability. Your predictability is based on your past relationship and reputation. Most people who study behavior know one thing: What someone has done in the past will likely indicate what he or she will do in the future. Again, if you've got good marks in your past relationship, you've probably got an edge over your competition for future relationships.

Reaction to Their Needs

Most people like to think of themselves as being a little bit "different." "You don't understand, our business is different from those other guys'," is a very common refrain we hear from prospects. And, to some degree, they are right. Therefore, a good way to ingratiate yourself with your prospects is to be flexible and responsive to their specialized needs. Such flexibility virtually always warrants a purchase order, even at a higher price.

Short Delivery Times

Even those prospects and customers who do not say they need or do not aggressively pursue the concept of "just-in-time" delivery still like short delivery times, and that is true no matter what the product or service is. Everybody wants it yesterday. If you want to sell at premium prices, you will certainly want to cater to your prospects and try to provide quick turnaround times between the placing of the order and the delivery of your offering.

HELP AT REDUCING COSTS BY REALIZING SAVINGS

Most prospects would like you to help them accomplish their goal of minimizing their costs and realizing economies in their operations in order to enhance their organization's bottom line. Anything you can do to help them realize genuine savings will be of great value to them. But don't think that by cutting your price you're going to help them achieve genuine savings—particularly if your organization goes broke and fails to deliver as promised, wreaking all kinds of havoc for them because you've caused cash problems by selling too cheaply. Recognize that giving genuine help has to do with providing advice and assistance relative to uses and applications of your products and services in the hands of your customer, not just giving a low price.

BREADTH AND DEPTH OF QUALITY

Prospects and customers like to know that historically you have had both breadth and depth in quality, and they want you to be able to react to their changing needs. That means that they want you to not only have breadth, but also depth in your ability to react to the things they're trying to accomplish by buying your product or service. That has a great deal to do with seeing to it that they are getting the right quality and maximum utilization of the product or service they're buying from you.

TOTAL PRODUCT OFFERINGS

It is inconvenient to deal with six or eight vendors for different products when one or two will do. A complete line or a full offering simply makes it easier for the prospect to accomplish an important goal—getting the right product, advice, expertise, service, or information at the right place at the right time. Having a full product line will often help you to get orders simply because you offer prospects the ease, efficiency, and the convenience of buying from one company rather than from multiple sources. And this is true whether you're selling software, insurance, financial services, heavy equipment, or any other product or service, whether tangible or intangible.

KNOWLEDGE, COMPETENCE, AND FOLLOW-UP

We all like to know that "we're in good hands." Salespeople who are serious about following up on orders, making sure that everything's right, and who are quite thorough in processing and expediting requests and are available after the sale is made find that this activity gives them an opportunity to sell at a preferential price.

WILLINGNESS TO "GO TO BAT" FOR THE CUSTOMER WHEN PROBLEMS ARISE

All customers like to have somebody in their corner. Your customers will appreciate—and likely pay a premium price for—genuine help if and when any kind of problem arises. You can win customers for life when you are willing and able to help them in those crisis situations.

COMPLETE KNOWLEDGE OF YOUR PRODUCT OR SERVICE OFFERINGS

Your customers expect you to know a lot about what you're selling. That means that you can assist them in making the best choice in buying what they want or expect to buy from you. If you don't know the full breadth of your own product line or service offerings, you're not going to be very convincing to a customer as to why he or she should buy from you—particularly at a premium price.

KNOWLEDGE OF YOUR PROSPECTS' AND CUSTOMERS' PRODUCTS AND SERVICES

Not only do your prospects and customers expect you to know your own product and services, they expect you to know *their* products or business. How can you help them if you don't know what it is they're trying to do? How can you expect to convince them to buy your products or services from you when you don't know what uses and applications they have for them if they do buy it from you?

PREPAREDNESS FOR SALES CALLS

There are too many salespeople who simply "wing it." And if you're a real talker, a genuine word merchant, you will eventually have serious problems as a salesperson because you may mistakenly believe you can talk your way into or out of anything. If you don't adequately plan for your sales call (i.e., understand your customer's products and services or how they expect to use

---

The Lowest Bidder

It's unwise to pay too much, but it is worse to pay too little. When you pay too much, you lose a little money—that's all. When you pay too little, you sometimes lose everything, because the thing you bought was incapable of doing the thing it was bought to do. The common law of business balance prohibits paying a little and getting a lot—it can't be done. If you deal with the lowest bidder, it is well to add something for the risk you run. And if you do that, you will have enough to pay for something better.

—John Ruskin (1819–1900)

---

your product or service), you've got big problems if you expect someone to pay you a premium price.

REGULAR, PREDICTABLE SALES CALLS

People like predictability. People who are responsible for buying decisions like to know that the salesperson will come around on a regular, predictable basis. The salesperson who shows up on a hit-or-miss basis is not perceived as being reliable and is generally viewed as a questionable source. Nobody pays a premium price to a questionable vendor.

TECHNICAL EDUCATION ABOUT WHAT THEY ARE BUYING, IF RELEVANT

Not all products or services that are sold are super-technical ones. But some prospects must buy things that are technical. The salesperson who can and will provide a prospective customer with adequate technical education may very well get preferential treatment when it comes to winning the order at a premium price over their competitor's lower prices.

INFREQUENT SHORT SHIPMENTS

Most people who buy things are realists. Sometimes, problems do come up. Nobody likes nondelivery, but very few people expect 100 percent delivery 100 percent of the time. Normally, when a business can't ship a complete quantity, it will send out short shipments and backorder the rest. This is likely to be at least acceptable to most customers, assuming that the short shipment is enough to allow them to get through until the full order is re-ceived. But nobody likes worrying about whether or not the *rest* of the shipment is going to get there on time. And nobody likes to put up with too many short shipments, even if ultimately everything has worked out in the past. There is still the worry factor, and nobody pays big bucks to have to worry about a vendor delivering on time.

EASE OF INTERPRETATION OF VENDOR PRICE LISTS AND QUOTES

Being able to interpret the price that the salesperson is charging is impor-tant to a customer. If you, as a salesperson, can clearly point out to your prospect exactly what the price is in simple, understandable terms, you're more apt to get the order. It's this simple: A confused prospect buys noth-ing. If prospects have to figure out 87 different things to ascertain the real price, they're apt to give their business to your competitor, who gives them simple, quick, clean, and easy-to-understand quotations. Confusion erodes trust, and people or suppliers who are not trusted aren't paid premium prices. In the final analysis, they usually get no price because they don't make the sale.

EARLY NOTICE OF SHIPMENT OR PRODUCT PROBLEMS

If you ever do have shipping or product problems, let your customer know about them well beforehand. That, at least, will give them the opportunity to cover themselves by a substitute or some other source for the product or materials. It is hard to maintain customers when you force them to look for other sources, but it's nearly impossible to retain them when you give them too many nasty surprises. If you want to retain a customer, and you're going to have a shipment or product problem, at least let them know up front how you are going to help them get through the difficulty.

ADVANCE WARNING OF DISCONTINUANCE OF ITEMS

Again, people don't like surprises. If you are going to discontinue a prod-uct or service that your customer has been using, they'd like to know in ample time to cover their own self-interests relative to the unavailability of that product or service. Can they phase it out of their inventory? Can they avoid building an expensive marketing campaign around a product that isn't going to be available for them to resell? Can they avoid the expense of designing your software into their offering and then discovering that it's no longer available for them to use in making their system work? How about a financial product that is factored into a businesses benefit package and it is suddenly taken off the market? When your customer knows that you'll be alert and keep them on top of developments, you'll find that getting orders at a premium price is a lot easier.

UNDERSTANDABLE AND LEGIBLE SHIPPING DOCUMENTS

Not only do people like to get clear quotes and easy-to-understand invoices, they also like to receive understandable and legible shipping documents. Many people who buy things also have to receive or at least review those same things. Experience tells them (because of the unreliability of many sellers) that they had better compare what was received with what they were supposed to have received and what they are going to be eventually billed for having received. The more you or your organization can do to keep that task simple, the greater the probability that you will get preferential treatment . . . and your prospects will continue buying your product or service.

CHAPTER 8

YOUR COMPETITORS' DELIVERY PROBLEMS WILL GET YOU PROFITABLE SALES

Without a guarantee, customers won't complain—or come back.
—Christopher W. L. Hart

When your competitors encounter delivery, quality, or service problems, you can bet that their customers will start looking for alternative sources. And when a customer cuts off one vendor because of delivery, quality, and/or service and replaces that supplier with a new one, how do they go about picking the new source? On the basis of price? Of course not. When they are qualifying a new supplier, what is going to be the single, most important question on their mind? Price? No.

It will be something like this, "Am I going to get what I need when I want it? Am I going to have to go through all of these problems again?" When previously burned business-to-business prospects start asking questions about a potential supplier's ability to deliver quality product on time and back it up with great service, that potential vendor needs to be able to *prove* to the prospects that they can perform. They need to assure them that they can get what they need, where they want it, when they need it, without any excuses. The prospects need to know that the problems they've just wrestled with at your competitor's won't happen if they work with you.

THE ECONOMICS OF PRICING

Let's take a quick lesson in the economics of pricing. Most businesspeople (let alone most salespeople) don't seem to understand how selling at a high price ties in with a customer's decision to buy at a higher price. That is because sales types (and even business executives) often have no idea how much volume of product sales is required to make up for a price cut, or how much a loss of sales can be tolerated in the event of a price increase.

In Econ 101, or in some other equally theoretical course, you were told, "you could cut price and make it up in volume." One of your authors even had an instructor tell him that he could cut his price 10 percent and would only need to increase his sales volume by 10 percent to make up for the price cut. Well, that might be true if there was a 92 percent gross margin. But there just aren't many businesses anywhere with a 92 percent gross margin.

In the real world, if you cut your price 10 percent, your company will probably have to at least *double* what it's currently selling, and might even have to triple it or more. Unbelievable? Let us prove it to you. First, pick a product or service that you sell. Now ask yourself this: If I cut my price 10 percent, how much more volume do I have to sell of that product to make up for the 10 percent price cut?

If you don't have an exact, precise answer to that question, you have no business negotiating prices with your customer, or even commenting on the appropriateness of your product or service's price, *because you don't know what you're doing!* We want to show you how to answer that question for yourself. You've got to understand what happens in your sales environment if you start fooling around cutting price rather than learning to sell on some basis other than low price.

VOLUME SWINGS ASSOCIATED WITH PRICE CUTTING: DETERMINING HOW MUCH MORE YOU MUST SELL TO MAKE UP FOR A PRICE CUT—AND HOW MUCH LESS YOU NEED TO SELL IF YOU RAISE PRICES

This could revolutionize the way you sell if you *really* understand it. Many salespeople have no idea of how to figure out how the volume a company must sell is affected if it cuts its price. They just seem to think that somehow they can "make it up in volume." Well, the joke is on them. And it's an old, old joke! It is very difficult, if not impossible, to "make it up in volume" when you cut prices. One of the first things that you must understand is that the amount of volume you need to "make up" for any given price cut is *solely* a function of the margin you enjoy on what you sell.

Gross Margins—Who Gets What?

A typical manufacturer's gross margin will run somewhere between 30 percent and 35 percent, a retailer will usually run 35 percent up to 40 percent, and a typical wholesaler's will run 25 percent to 35 percent. Some service businesses' could even be higher. Therefore, many businesses realize gross margins on the products or services that they sell of about 25 percent to 40 percent. Some products or services may run higher, and some products may run lower, but that range will put a bracket around the products of about 95 percent of the product-oriented businesses in the United States.[1] Therefore, for our purposes here, we're going to use a 35 percent gross margin as a fair average for most businesses.

If you're curious about why some businesses' gross margins are higher than others', the answer is fairly simple: Generally, *the easier it is to sell anything, the lower the gross margin.* And that is simply because the people who enter those businesses usually don't know or care that much about selling. They just reason that, "I can sell that stuff."

As we've said earlier, the trouble is that most people don't like to sell. Consequently, more people enter these businesses, and because they tend to use low price as their sales tool, they bid down each other's prices to a "hard-to-survive" level. For example: more restaurants fail than jewelry stores. Everybody "knows," of course, that food is easier to sell than diamonds. Perhaps it's easier to sell food, but it is much harder to *profit* from selling food. Selling skills always bring higher rewards to the people who can sell. Giving things away seldom rewards the giver, at least financially, which may account for the low pay of social workers or others in various other helping roles or professions. It may be unfortunate, apparently unfair and cruel . . . but it's true.

No Pain, No Gain

Just because you are in a low-margin business, it doesn't mean you can't make money. There have been large fortunes made in low-margin businesses. But one truth does prevail: The lower the gross margin, the greater the pain and the greater the gain relative to cutting and/or raising prices in that business. For example, when a company cuts price 10 percent in a business that has products in the 35 percent gross margin range, they probably only will have to double the amount of product they sell at that price to "make it up in volume." But for a business with a 25 percent margin, the same 10 percent price cut will require that they sell more than three times as much volume to "make it up."

Conversely, when price is raised, the gain is greater in the lower margin business. For example, in a 35 percent gross margin business, when price is raised 10 percent, sales can fall about 34 percent and the company still will make the same amount of money it was making before the price increase. And if a company with a 25 percent gross margin raises prices 10 percent, it can probably lose 41 percent or so of its business, and still make the same amount of money! (We'll explain this in more detail in Chapter 9.)

If You Cut Price, You Must Sell *How Much* More?

Many will say "hogwash" to the concept that cutting prices 10 percent on a 35 percent margin will require you to sell nearly twice as much. And that if you raise prices 10 percent, you can lose 34 percent or so of your sales (and the corresponding quantities on 25 percent margins). Well, amazingly, it's true. Let's look at why. Consider this Profit and Loss Statement on a product we are selling:

Formula 1

Sales	1,000,000	1.00%
COGS	650,000	.65
Gross margin	350,000	.35
GS&A/Fixed	200,000	
Variable	150,000	.15
	0	

.20 profit potential on each one we sell
(Gross margin of .35 − Variable of .15 = .20)

Let's analyze our company's figures. The Profit and Loss Statement shows that we are selling $1,000,000 worth of product and our cost of goods sold (COGS) is $650,000. That gives us a gross margin (GM) of $350,000.

What does gross margin really mean? It means that when we sell something for a dollar, and it costs us 65¢ to have it to sell,[2] we've got a 35¢ gross profit (or a 35 percent gross margin) on our sales dollar. What that gross margin actually means is that our gross profit potential on any given dollar of sales is only 35¢, because we've got to pay for what it is that we've sold before we can make any money from it.

We must then subtract what are known as general, selling and administrative expenses (GS&A) from the gross margin. Some accountants call them SG&A (selling, general, administrative), while others call them operating expenses, but it all means the same thing. GS&A expenses are the costs of administering the sales and administrative operations of the business, the cost of the office, the cost of computers, telephone service, desks and chairs, the cost of customer service.

Of our GS&A expenses, some are fixed and some are variable. For example, in many businesses, office salaries are fixed. They don't have much to do with sales volume. Likewise, many other office costs are fixed: cost of occupying the offices, the heat, lights, utilities, insurance, and other such expenses. Those kinds of things are essentially the same from month to month, summer to winter, spring to fall. Other fixed costs are often budgeted costs and include such things as advertising and marketing costs. In our example, those costs are $200,000.

The other GS&A expenses are variable—those things that almost always vary with your sales volume. For example, when you sell something, you've got to invoice for it. If you didn't sell it, you wouldn't have to go to that expense. When someone pays the invoice by sending you a check, you've got to process the check, and so on. If you don't sell anything, you don't have these expenses: When you sell something, you do. In addition, there are many other kinds of GS&A expenses that vary with your sales volume. One example might be that you have to reorder things to replace what you've sold, or you won't have anything to sell in the future. Other variable GS&A expenses are credit and collection costs (the more you sell, the more credit and collection activity you must engage in) and customer service costs. In addition, commissions on sales are a variable expense. The point is, your variable expenses are expenses that essentially occur *because you sold something,* and the more you sell, the more of these costs you incur. Let's say our variable GS&A expenses are running $150,000. In our example, that means we're breaking even on the sale of this product.

As we've emphasized over and over, business is really a game of margin, not volume. Here's why: After you have paid the costs that are directly incurred each and every time you sell something, you only have a few pennies (percent, margin points) left from the sales dollar and this is your potential profit. This is because each time you sell another item, the direct costs are again incurred for the sale of that additional product, the same as those costs were incurred by each and every sale of each preceding item. Therefore, looking at Formula 1, we can see that the profit potential on the sale of any given product is 20¢ (obtained by subtracting the percentage of each sales dollar that goes for the cost of the product we sold and the cost of GS&A expenses directly attributable to that sale). This profit potential is most easily calculated by subtracting our variable GS&A expenses from our gross margin. For example, if our variable expenses are $150,000, they are 15 percent of our sales price. So really, when we sell something for $1, and we've got 65¢ cost of goods sold (which leaves us a 35 percent gross margin), we must still subtract our variable expense percent (15 percent) from that gross margin percent to determine what our true profit potential is on any given dollar of sale. But 20¢ is still only a *profit potential,* as we still have not deducted our fixed costs.

In short, when we sell something for a dollar, and we've paid all the costs of having it to sell and the direct costs associated with selling it, we've really only got a 20¢ profit potential on any given dollar of sales. And that 20¢ has to cover our fixed costs. On $1 million in sales, 20¢ on the dollar is $200,000, and our fixed costs are $200,000, so we break even at a million in sales. Up to the point of $1 million in sales, all of our 20¢ potential profit on each sale must be used to cover our fixed costs. At $1 million in sales, our fixed costs are covered; on any sales above $1 million those 20¢ pieces of profit potential remain as profit for the company.

The Break-Even Formula

From the previous analysis, you should be in a position to understand a formula that can be used to calculate your product or service's break-even volume. That is:

$$\text{Break-even volume} = \frac{\text{Fixed GS\&A costs (dollars)}}{\text{Gross margin (percent)} - \text{Variable expense}}$$

Your break-even volume is equal to your dollars of fixed GS&A costs, divided by your gross margin percent, minus your variable expense percent.

Let's see how the formula works. As we look at our Profit and Loss Statement (Formula 1), we see that fixed costs are $200,000, which is to be divided by our gross margin of 35 percent (.35 written as a decimal) minus our variable expense percent of 15 percent (.15 written as a decimal). That equals $200,000 divided by .20 (which is the profit potential that we have left when we subtract our variable expense percent from our gross margin). You can tell by looking at it (or by working out the formula yourself) that the answer then becomes $1 million. Formula 2 shows the calculations:

Formula 2

$$\text{Break-even volume} = \frac{\$200,000}{.35 - .15}$$

$$= \frac{\$200,000}{.20}$$

$$= \$1,000.000$$

What Happens When You Cut Price 10 Percent?

Now, let's take a hard look at what we do to ourselves when we cut the price of our product. If we cut our price 10 percent (let's assume that we sell the exact same amount of product—no more, no less—that way we can see exactly what happens to our margin as a consequence of that price cut) our revenues then would only be $900,000 (rather than $1,000,000), because we are getting only 90¢ for each item sold rather than $1 each. Our cost of goods sold, however, will still be the same $650,000, because we sold the exact same amount of product. Our gross margin, therefore, becomes $250,000.

The rest of the statement stays the same, except for the alarming reality that our company has lost $100,000. (But that, of course, makes sense. Because if we were doing $1 million in sales and were breaking even, but we cut our price 10 percent and sold the same amount, we are going to lose $100,000.) Formula 3 shows the results:

Formula 3

Sales	$900,000	100%
COGS	650,000	72.2%
GM	250,000	27.8%
GS&A/Fixed	200,000	
Variable	150,000	16.7%
	(100,000)	11.1% PP

Our cost of goods sold is .722 percent of our selling price, so our gross margin is .278. Notice, by cutting our price 10 percent, our gross margin fell from .35 to .278, which is more than a 20 percent drop in the gross margin. It is a .072 drop (from .35 to .278) as a percentage of *sales,* but a better than 20 percent drop as a percentage of the original gross margin of 35 percent. When we cut our price by 10 percent on a 35 percent gross margin, we actually cut our gross margin in excess of 20 percent:

$$35 - .278 = .072$$

$$\frac{.072}{.35} = .2057 \text{ or } 20.57\%$$

That's what happened to our gross margin—but there's more bad news. We have to look at our GS&A expenses to see the total impact of our price cut. Our fixed expenses are still going to stay the same at $200,000, and our variable expenses are going to stay the same at $150,000. But our variable expense percent has now become .167 of our selling price. And our profit potential (the spread that we realized by subtracting our variable expense percent from our gross margin) is now $.111, when before it was 20¢. Translation: If you cut your price 10 percent on a product with a 35 percent gross margin, you will cut your profit potential on each dollar of sales nearly in half, (from 20¢ on each one you sell to 11.1¢).

Remember the formula? There are three numbers we will need to calculate our new break-even volume. Formula 4 shows the results. Our $200,000 of fixed costs have stayed the same, but our gross margin has fallen from .35 to .278. Our variable expense percent has increased from .15 to .167, and the spread that we call profit potential, which was 20¢, is now only 11.1¢. Therefore, our new break-even volume can then be calculated. It is $1,801,801.80.

Formula 4

$$\text{Break-even volume} = \frac{\$200,000}{.278 - .167}$$

$$= \frac{\$200,000}{.111}$$

$$= \$1,801,801.80$$

That tells us that by cutting our price 10 percent on a product with a 35 percent gross margin, we're going to have to increase our sales volume from $1,000,000 of that product to $1,801,801.80 just to make the same amount of money we were making (i.e., to get back to our break-even volume).

By looking at Formula 5, we can see that with sales of $1,801,801.80, our cost of goods sold is $1,300,900.80 (.722 percent of the selling price). Our gross margin, in dollars, is $500,901.00 (.278 percent of sales). Of our GS&A expenses, our fixed expenses are $200,000 and our variable expenses are $300,900.76 (.167 of our sales). That leaves us with a 24¢ profit (because of rounding errors), but we think most readers would agree a 24¢ profit on $1,801,801.80 in sales is roughly break-even.

Formula 5

Sales	$1,801,801.80	100%
COGS	1,300,900.80	72.2%
GM	500,901.00	27.8%
GS&A/Fixed	200,000.00	
Variable	300,900.76	16.7%
	.24	

What all of this means is if you cut your price 10 percent on a 35 percent gross margin item, your sales volume has to increase from $1,000,000 to $1,801,801.80. That's an 80 percent increase in *dollar* sales, but a *doubling in the quantity* of product that you must sell. In fact, it is a little more than double. Why double and not 80 percent? Because you must sell $1,801,801.80 in sales dollars, but you are only getting 90¢ for each unit you sell. $1,800,000, at 90¢ each is twice as many units of product sold as $1,000,000 at $1 each. (It is also evident that you must double your sales when we look at our cost of goods sold, which has had to increase from $650,000 to $1,300,900.80; that is more than a 100 percent increase in the number of units of product that must be sold at cost.) Translation: On a typical business gross margin of about 35 percent on a product, if you cut your price 10 percent, you have to sell about twice as much. And that still isn't all the bad news. The lower your margin, the worse it gets. If the gross margin on your product is down around 25 percent, you will have to sell more than three times as much product to make up for the same 10 percent price cut.

IMPLICATIONS FOR THE REAL WORLD

Let's consider a couple of real-world implications of all of this:

Question 1: If you cut your price 10 percent, do you think you'd really sell twice as much volume in units?

Answer: Probably not, especially if your competition follows by cutting their price, too. The real truth is, you probably wouldn't sell a lot more and nowhere near twice as much.

Question 2: If you cut your price 10 percent and you get the orders for twice as much product or service levels, can you ship or service it? On time? With great quality?

Answer: Probably not. If you've got to ship twice as much product or provide twice as much service in the same amount of time, then you better be running at *less than half of your total capacity,* or otherwise you're going to be in the ignominious situation of having cut price and taken orders for product that you can't ship or services you can't provide on a timely basis. And remember, your business must be running at less than 50 percent of your capacity across the board, in every dimension of the business—plant, office, warehouse, number of employees available, ability to carry twice the inventory, accounts receivable, storage capacity, distribution, filing, data processing, telephone calls, customer service, and so on. If your business isn't at less than 50 percent of capacity in *all affected dimensions,* it will simply be physically impossible to ship to or service your customer on time, whether you get the orders or not.

For example, if you sell a product that is manufactured, before you ever consider cutting price, you need to think long and hard about this question: Can my organization *make* it and *ship* it on time, even if we get the orders? And if you sell as a wholesaler, distributor, or retailer, don't just think, "We'll just order more." You'd better give serious thought to this question: Can your manufacturers and suppliers ship to you—on time? And *will* they ship to you? Will they be willing to double your credit line? Do they have the capacity to ship to you? Maybe they do, but we'll bet that you have had the experience of hearing: "We'll have to put you on backorder. We might be able to ship that to you in four months." It's tough to cut price—and make it up in volume—especially if you really do *get* the orders.

Question 3: If you do cut price 10 percent, and you get the necessary quantity of orders to "make it up in volume," and you can ship it on time, who are you going to get as your new customers?

Answer: Price-buyers. Chiselers. Slow-payers.

Question 4: If you do drop prices, and are willing to put up with an increased number of price-buyers among your customers, are you really willing to do all that extra work, *but* not earn any more money for your organization?

Answer: You pull off all the above and you are only back to where you were breaking even on the sale of this product. It doesn't seem like a very intelligent decision to choose to work harder for the same amount or less money, does it?

CHAPTER 9

YEAH, BUT I'LL MAKE MORE MONEY IF I CUT MY PRICE—AND I DON'T CARE IF MY EMPLOYER DOES GO BROKE

I was looking for a job when I got this one.

—Anonymous

Many salespeople may have read Chapter 8 and thought, "Okay, so my company won't make any money if I cut my price. I will. And (honestly) I don't care if they go broke. After all, I was looking for a job when I got this one. I'll just go sell for someone else." Well, let's take a closer look at that idea.

WHAT HAPPENS IF YOU RAISE YOUR PRICE?

You can lose a lot of volume—maybe even as much as a third of it (on a 35 percent gross margin and 10 percent price increase) or more (41 percent of your volume on a 25 percent gross margin for the same price increase) and still make as much money. Let's see how these numbers work out because this powerful knowledge can give you more confidence, knowledge, and understanding of the serious implications that can occur if you do drop your price. We have continued numbering the formulas from Chapter 8:

Formula 6

Sales	$1,100,000	100%
COGS	650,000	59%
GM	450,000	41%
GS&A/Fixed	200,000	
Variable	150,000	13.6%
	$100,000	27.4% profit potential

In Formula 6, you can see that if we raise our price by 10 percent (we'll assume that we sell the same volume in order to determine the impact of our price increase on our margin), our total sales revenue will be $1,100,000. We're selling the same amount now, but we're selling it at $1.10. Our cost of goods sold (COGS), however, will remain the same at $650,000, because we sold the same amount, and it will, therefore, cost the same. Our gross margin (GM) will now be $450,000. With our higher selling price, our cost of goods sold is now a reduced 59 percent of our selling price. Therefore, our gross margin is 41 percent.

Notice, by raising our price 10 percent, our gross margin increases from .35 to .41 (about a 17 percent increase in our gross margin). Our fixed expenses are still going to be the same at $200,000, and our variable expenses will essentially stay at the same $150,000. But now we're going to realize a $100,000 *profit*.

However, that increased profit is not what we're concerned with at this point. What we're really trying to show here is what "miraculously" happens to our margins as a consequence of the price increase. Your variable expense percent is .136 of the selling price, and remember, our profit potential on a given dollar of sales is the spread we get when we subtract our variable expense percent from our gross margin. The profit potential on each unit sold was .20, but now it is $.274. By raising our price a mere 10 percent, we have increased our profit potential on every dollar of sales by 37 percent. Again, that's no magic act, that's just the way it is. And, again, by doing this we have the margin we need to use in our formula to determine how much actual volume we need to sell at these margins in order to break even. That will then tell us how much sales volume we can actually *lose* as a result of our higher price and still make as much money as we were making. Formula 7 shows those calculations:

Formula 7

$$\text{Break-even volume} = \frac{\text{Fixed GS\&A costs (dollars)}}{\text{Gross margin (percent)} - \text{Variable expense (percent)}}$$

$$= \frac{\$200,000}{.41 - .136}$$

$$= \frac{\$200,000}{.274}$$

$$= \$729,927.00$$

By using the formula, we have determined that the new sales volume required as a consequence of our higher price is only $729,927.

Formula 8 shows verification of this. We can see that if we multiply $729,927 by .59 (the percentage our cost of goods sold is of our new, higher sales price), you'll find that our cost of goods sold in dollars will be $430,656.93. Subtracting (or multiplying our sales by 41 percent, which is our gross margin) shows that our gross profit will be $299,270.07. The fixed GS&A costs are the same at $200,000. We can determine our variable expenses by multiplying sales by .136 (our variable expense percent). Our variable expenses are, therefore, $99,270.07. That comes to a perfect zero or break even (not even any rounding error problems).

Formula 8

Sales	$729,927.00	100%
COGS	439,656.93	59%
GM	299,270.07	41%
GS&A/Fixed	200,000.00	
Variable	99,270.07	13.6%
	0.00	

So, what's the real bottom line to all of this? By raising the price 10 percent on our product, our sales could fall from $1 million (where we started before we raised the price) to $729,927, a 27 percent decline in dollar sales. But remember, those are $1.10 dollars per unit because of our new, higher price. It's our cost of goods sold that will tell us how many *units* of sales we can actually lose in sales volume. That figure has dropped from $650,000 to $430,656.93: A figure that represents a 34 percent decline in the number of units that we actually need to sell at the higher price for us *to make the same amount of money we were previously making.* In short, if we raise our price just 10 percent on a 35 percent gross margin product, we can lose a little more than a third of all the sales we've been making and still make the same amount of money!

YEAH, BUT I'M NOT GOING TO MAKE AS MUCH

Let's deal with some reality here. Right now you may have (especially if you are paid on commission) some ambivalent feelings about all of this. It isn't the math that's bothering you. You understand that. Your ambivalence probably goes back to the "a little bit of something is better than a lot of nothing" philosophy. You're thinking: If I raise price and lose volume, *I'm* personally going to lose money because I'm paid a commission on sales, and that will hurt *my* checkbook. If I raise price and lose a third of my sales, my commission isn't going to go down by 33 percent, but it's going to go down.

Don't worry about that. Here's why: (1) It's doubtful that your sales will fall that much. Sure, they could; but most times they don't, and often they don't fall *at all*. They may even go up (premium pricing makes a statement—a positive, salutary statement). (2) Your ability to provide *better,* more *timely* delivery of *quality* product, backed by *superb* service to your customer will definitely improve when (or if) you do lose a little volume. This tends to ensure continued, profitable sales to your nonprice-buying customers. (3) Your employer almost assuredly will start making more money (unless total sales do fall by *more* than 33 percent), which means that you'll likely find bonus money in your paycheck and/or improving commission rates. This is especially true if your bonus is tied to organization-wide profits, and/or your commission *rate* goes up as your sales price goes up, and/or if your commission is somehow tied to your gross profit percentage. In short, you are worth far more as a salesperson, because the entire enterprise is making more. They won't want to lose you, and they are fools not to reward you. Good, profitable salespeople are hard to come by and are always well paid, in contrast to order-takers, who give away their product or service offerings.

WHY GO BROKE TIRED?

Two things salespeople who sell at premium prices learn early is that (1) if you continue to sell at a low price, your employer is eventually going to have to cut your commission rate (they have to when they start losing money), and (2) if you sell at a low price, you are going to inflict an *incredible* amount of work on *yourself* to try to maintain those (paltry) commissions. Here's why: Let's say you are selling $1 million worth of a product yourself ($650,000 at cost of goods sold). If you (and your employer) *raise* price 10 percent, you have to sell only $430,656.93 (in cost of goods sold) of this product. *Cost of goods sold* puts a definite dollar value on the number of units you must sell at your higher price to get back to the point where your employer is breaking even. Cost of goods sold is a way of putting a dollar value on how much work you (and your employer) must do—how many orders the employer has to get, produce, fill, ship, and deliver on time.

But the salesperson who cuts price by 10 percent has to sell, in terms of actual cost of goods sold, $1,300,900.83. That means that the salesperson who cuts price has to sell *three times* as much product on a unit-by-unit basis in order to enable his or her employer to make the same amount of money it would make if the salesperson were selling at the higher price. *If you're going to go broke, why go broke tired?* If you are going to have to find another job because your employer went broke, why do so much work to end up there?

If you (or your employer) are going to go broke because of a pricing error, you always want to go broke *overpricing.* Any fool can cut price, get volume, go broke, and grow tired. If you're going to make a mistake in pricing, you always want to make that mistake on the high side. It doesn't take nearly the work to go broke overpricing that it does to go broke underpricing.

NOBODY CAN MAKE ANY MONEY WORKING AT EL CHEAPOS

It's amazing, astounding, and perplexing that such a large number of people see volume and confuse it with prosperity and success—particularly when they see the volume being done at El Cheapos. Volume just creates a lot of hard work—not necessarily any profit.

When you work for El Cheapos, they probably aren't paying you very much money, let alone giving you any meaningful perks or benefits. Remember our earlier example of the defunct People Express Airlines? Many people thought that People Express Airlines was a very successful airline—when they looked purely at the volume the company did. But certainly the people who worked at People Express didn't make much money. In fact, they were actually pressured into buying stock in lieu of taking their earnings in wages. Then when the company went belly-up, who do you think the losers were? Who do you actually think paid for those cheap airline seats in which "everybody" was flying around? The People Express employees, of course.

Donald Burr, the founder and chief executive officer of People Express Airlines, put his finger on some of the absurdities of figuring that anybody working at a high-volume, low-price business is likely to have a highly rewarding financial career. For example, he was quoted in *Inc.* magazine as follows: "I knew I was in trouble when my mother was coming up to visit me and she said, 'I hope you don't mind, but I'm flying American. Just a few dollars more.' "[1]

One must certainly wonder why "Mommy" preferred to fly American Airlines—and pay a little more money. It seems likely that American Airlines was perceived as a better deal to her than People Express. And you must certainly wonder why "Mommy" had to pay for her own airline ticket, particularly when she was the mother of the president, founder, chairman of the board, and major shareholder of People Express Airlines. Would you have made your mother pay for her own airline ticket on your airline? And, unfortunately, this logic has continued with many, other similar business models since this first appeared almost four decades ago.

It's enlightening to look very closely at the welfare of employees who work for discounting operations. Ultimately, they, themselves never make any real money—because the company they work for never makes any real money.

WE WERE BUSY RIGHT UP TO THE LAST DAY

Just the other day one of your authors got off an airplane in Indianapolis, Indiana. The flight crew that flew the plane was riding on the courtesy bus with him to the hotel. A couple of the flight attendants were talking, apparently about a retail store. One of them said, "Hey, I hear that old Schwartzheimer's is going out of business."

The other one replied, "Oh, no. You're kidding. That's my favorite store. Why?"

The first one then said, "Gee, I don't know. Somebody said they weren't making any money."

The reply? "Oh, it can't be. Every time I've been in there, they have been jammed full of customers."

The coauthor felt like saying, "Let me get our Break-Even Formula out and explain it to you. I think I can explain why they were busy right up to the last day—but the employees didn't make any money, and the company went broke."

You've probably heard someone talking about having gone bust in a business. Almost always, if you ask him what happened, he will scratch his head and say, "Gee, I don't know. You know, we were busy right up to the last day." Remember what we said at the very beginning of this book? When businesses go broke, they virtually always do so during a period of a sales volume increase because they have cut their price. When they cut their price, their gross margin goes down, and their sales go up. But if sales don't go up enough, the company goes broke.

Have you ever worked for an unprofitable business? If you have, you probably learned that it's not much fun. Perhaps people who work at unprofitable businesses should consider putting signs in their offices that say, "It ain't fun if it ain't profitable." If you have worked for both profitable and unprofitable businesses, we think you would agree it's more fun when the enterprise is actually making money. We have never heard anybody complain about excessive frugality in successful businesses; but we sure have heard about "the need to tighten up" in an unprofitable one.

I STILL SAY I'D MAKE MORE MONEY SELLING AT THE LOWER PRICE

"Okay, okay," you say, "I understand that when organizations are operating on slim margins, everything has to be tight. But I could sell more at a lower price, and consequently, *I'd* make money even if (or until) my employer eventually does go broke." Even if your employer lets you cut your price, and you sell more product or services, it is unlikely that you'd actually make more money. Here's why: Imagine that you have been selling a million dollars worth of whatever it is you sell, and that your commission is 7 percent. That gives you a $70,000 commission income. Obviously, if your employer would let you cut the price by 10 percent *and you could double your sales,* your sales volume would go to $1,800,000 and you, of course, would receive 7 percent of the $1,800,000. So your commission income would rise from $70,000 a year to $126,000, and you'd certainly be better off, wouldn't you?

Maybe you would. But consider this. You'd be making $126,000, which would represent an 80 percent increase in your commission income. But *you'd have to be selling and servicing twice as much,* and in all likelihood, your competition would eventually counter with their own price cut, *which would put you back on a level playing field.*

Here's the point: Competition never fails to react. Discount your price by 10 percent, and you can bet your last penny that your competition will, too. However, that will put you back at the same relative price to your competitor. When that happens, what are the chances that you'll actually sell a significant *additional* volume, let alone twice as much? Once you're back on a level playing field, the only additional increase in sales volume that you will realize will come from prospects who have not been buying the product to begin with (the incremental customer for your product) or the existing customers who will buy a little more of your product (the one who thinks not only your product, but everybody else's that you compete with has been priced too high in the past). The probability of a significant increase in sales volume for your firm from these sources is very small because your competitors will get their share, too.

Once you're at the same price as your competition again, you're going to have to sell *twice* as much of what you sell. But even if you do that, you're only going to make *80 percent* more. That means that you're going to work twice as hard to make 80 percent more. So, let us ask you a straightforward question. If you're really willing to work twice as hard to make 80 percent more money, why don't you work twice as hard on the situation you already have so you can make *twice* as much right now?

The number of salespeople who just don't clearly understand that logic is amazing. It is even more amazing when you analyze the number of salespeople who fail to understand what is likely to happen if their employer does cut the price "so that they can sell more."

If you're paid by any form of commission, there's an incredibly high probability that when your employer cuts price, they're also going to cut your commission *rate*. Why will they do that? Because they cannot afford to pay you as high a commission rate when you are selling (giving away?) products or services at a lower price. As we have consistently emphasized: If we want someone to give away our product or service, we can go to the welfare department and hire social workers to do it.

Our own studies show that when the typical salesperson who's receiving a 7 percent commission rate cuts his or her price by 10 percent, he or she will probably experience about a 40 percent cut in commission rate. (Forty percent of 7 percent is .028 percent. If you subtract .028 percent from .07 percent you will be left with .042 percent.) Consider this. If you cut your price 10 percent and your sales volume increases from $1,000,000 to $1,800,000, but your commission is cut from .07 percent to .042 percent, that .042 percent of $1,800,000 is $75,600. If you go out and sell twice as much at your new lower price (in the face of your competitor's lowered price) your commission income will increase "dramatically" from $70,000 to $75,600—an 8 percent increase. Do you really want to sell and service twice as much to make 8 percent more—whether your employer goes broke or not?

The long and short of this whole discussion is that if you cut your price, you're probably not going to make significantly more money—you are just going to work harder, longer, and with greater frustration. And the reason you're not going to make significantly more money is that your long-term employer *can't afford to pay you any more money, because, frankly, you aren't worth more money, and they can't afford it anyway.*

Conversely, don't ever believe that if you raise your price, you aren't going to make as much money. We can guarantee you that if you sell at a premium price and keep your employer profitable, you're going to make a lot more money. Employers want to keep *profitable* salespeople on the payroll, and they pay them big bucks. But employers can't afford to pay big bucks to people who give things away. That is why an increasingly large number of smart businesses are compensating salespeople not just on the volume of sales they obtain, but against *gross margin* or *profitability* on those sales. They do this because they *have to* if they are going to remain in business. Some even pay escalating commissions or bonuses based on both margins *and* volume. Those are the ones we call "smart businesses."

CASE STUDY IN PRICING STRATEGIES

As the first part of this chapter describes, it is very difficult to cut price and make it up in volume. Yet, it seems that the woods are full of people (businesspeople—even highly educated businesspeople) who don't (or *won't*) understand bankruptcy. Again, airlines are the best example, and airline deregulation is a good case in point about the typical businessperson's propensity to cut price in the blind belief that "we can make it up in volume."

Remember, as we cited earlier, President Jimmy Carter deregulated the airlines in 1978. That meant that, overnight, the U.S. airlines were free to charge any price they wanted. We also asked earlier, "How many raised their price?" Our answer? None that we know of. And, as we pointed out in Chapter 1, the number of airlines filing for bankruptcy since airline deregulation has been staggering and still is growing as the twenty-first century unfolds.

The behavior of the businesspeople running U.S. airlines subsequent to deregulation proved that there is a latent bias on the part of most people in business to cut price. The moment they were free to charge any price they wanted, they all started cutting their prices.

Where does this bias come from? We'd like to share this thought that someone gave us a few years ago. Most of us learn that "you can cut your price and make it up in volume" in Econ 101, because that is where most of the preaching and mantras about cutting price and making it up in volume originate. Did it ever occur to you that the professor of economics who taught you Econ 101, who was working for a pittance, had a latent bias against high prices and high-income people? Did you ever think that perhaps this professor of economics had a latent desire to get you capitalist pigs to go out in the business world and *give away your products so his pittance would go a little farther?*

If you are ever going to make your prices stick, you must understand the real-world economics of pricing. Understanding what is required to "make up" for a price cut can instill a lot of courage in you as you battle against cutting your prices. Don't ever forget or lose sight of the Break-Even Formula. It can make you a pile of money, because it can destroy your notion that it is possible to cut price and make it up in volume. However, if you want to earn a solid living in sales, you need to remember that you are going to face a consistent challenge to hang on to a high price, because you will always find yourself competing with a fool who is going broke cutting prices. That's never going to go away. And, worse yet, when that somebody does go broke (which he or she eventually will) another someone else is going to come crawling out of the woodwork, declaring that, "these guys who are in the business are charging too much," and that, "we can cut the price, make it up in volume, and make more money."

Remember, there have been hundreds of airlines that have gone bust since deregulation, and there have been more than 200 new ones *started* since deregulation. We'll guarantee you that many of them have thought, "I'm smarter than those fools that are running those airlines. I can sell at a lower price and we'll make it up in volume because I took Econ 101." And this is not only true of airlines. Just look at the massive list of other bankruptcies we alluded to earlier and your competitors who are now gone— and even countless retail stores on every corner that couldn't make it, either. Face it, you're going to be hammered forever by price-cutting fools. Just accept that. But, ultimately if your price is to be cut, *you* will be the one who will cut it. And you'll do that because you don't know how to sell quality, service, and delivery (and you probably don't really understand the Break-Even Formula).

CHAPTER 10

HOW TO FACE A COMPETITOR'S PRICE CUTS

When you are in a price war, you learn to stay low.
—Billboard ad of a now-defunct automobile dealer in Michigan

Let's take a look at some of the more common situations that come up when you're faced with a cut in price by a competitor, and discuss what you might do about them.

Situation 1: You don't know for sure whether your competitor has cut his price or by how much.

Solution: Hold your price at the present level and watch your competitor, particularly in terms of volume of shipments and receipt of materials. If you just "hear through the grapevine" that your competition is offering their product at a lower price, try to determine if they are *really* offering that price. When your customer says, "I can get it cheaper down the street," you have to try to verify that. That's doing your homework. In the military, it's called intelligence. In sales, it's called pre-call planning.

We would never want to suggest that you do anything illegal, immoral, or unethical, but we will advocate that you learn to do a little legal and ethical spying. Is your competition *really* offering that lower price, or are they only offering that lower price when they can't ship it? Or is there some other catch—like, yes, the price is being offered, but only if you buy the purple ones with green and burnt-orange polka dots; or only if you buy version 1.0 when they're now on 3.0; or only if you buy a 92-year supply; or only if you agree *not* to buy from someone else for 46 years; or some other ridiculous, essentially unrealistic "requirement." Do some verification. And even if you determine they *are* offering that price, you still need to determine two more things: Are your customers *buying* at that price? And is the competitor who is offering that price both *shipping and receiving*? If customers are buying, and your competition is both shipping at that lower price and receiving, that says one thing. However, if they are shipping but not receiving, you can probably bet that they are dropping the line or they're going out-of-business.

Your first determination must be this: Are they charging that price, getting orders, and shipping and receiving at that price? If they aren't shipping, forget about it. No reason to cut your price. If they're charging that price and they're shipping but they're not receiving, still there's no reason to cut the price. They're soon going to run out of that product and aren't going to have any more to sell anyway.

You may be wondering: "How do I know if they're shipping and receiving?" It's disarmingly simple. Do a little homework. Call them and ask them. (You'll be surprised what motor-mouthed employees will tell anonymous telephone callers.) Or drive by their place and give it a "windshield appraisal." Often, you can tell how busy a place is by the inventory stored outside, the number of cars in the employee parking lot, or the number of cars in the customer lot. Or you can tell whether a business is busy just by driving around the block at quitting time, or by assessing how much smoke's coming out of the chimney, how many people are walking around, how many trucks are backed up at the loading docks. Walk through their store if you are a retailer. The creative things you can do to get information are only limited by your imagination.

Another thing you can do is check the local restaurants, coffee shops, and so on (where your competitor's employees go for breakfast, lunch, or after work). You'd be amazed what you can learn. Ask questions like, "How's business?" "Looking for programmers?" "You hiring anybody?" "How's that promotion going on X product?" and so on.

There are a multiplicity of other ways to get information about whether or not your competitor is (1) getting orders, (2) at the price claimed, and (3) shipping and receiving. So, Situation 1 is simple. If you don't know whether your competition has cut their price, find out. And even if they have cut the price, find out if they are both shipping and receiving. Don't do *anything* to your price until you are absolutely certain that all of the foregoing is happening.

Situation 2: Prices have been cut, but your volume is not being affected. Your sales are consistent, but they've cut their price.

Solution: Hold your price level until your competitor's price cut begins to significantly affect your volume. Maybe your competitor is at or near capacity and can't supply any more. If your competitor is selling at that price, and they're both shipping and receiving, but your volume's holding, your competitor is probably at or near capacity and can't ship any more.

For a good example of the consequences of not following this advice, you need only to look at what originally happened to the airline industry, again, starting with our oft-told saga of People Express and airline deregulation. Many airline companies said, "Hey, People Express is knocking the living daylights out of us. We have to do something; they're undercutting our prices." The smarter companies simply said, "Let them fill up their airplanes and we'll fly the others. They don't have many airplanes. They are all flying full, and it doesn't look like they can get many more planes. Nobody will sell (or lease) more airplanes to them, because they are having trouble paying their bills."

That worked for a while. But then the saga continued. Various other airlines started cutting prices because they "had to be competitive." But then they couldn't make any money. So they decided to pull the next trick—cutting costs. So they quit serving meals, cut down on the number of flights they offered, cut the flight crews, reduced the number of passenger attendants, laid off check-in personnel, and essentially started doing everything they could think of to reduce operating costs. Then passengers saw service as nearly nonexistent—checking bags became a nuisance, less baggage was allowed, tickets were nonrefundable and/or nonexchangeable, getting "bumped" on a flight that you had a reservation for was to be expected, missed connections were probably more common than making connections, arguments broke out between airline personnel and passengers who "wouldn't take it any more," and even more airline bankruptcies occurred.

And this occurred again years later with the success of the previously mentioned Southwest Airlines and the rise of other similarly structured low-priced airlines, a trend that promises to continue. However, this time the threat from discount airlines was real. These new airlines totally redefined the category of low cost. However, once again, conventional airlines failed to compete. They dropped fares, but couldn't contain costs. And the inevitable resulted.

And it continues. It started with the heinous terrorist attack on the United States on September 11, 2001, when airlines were grounded for a few days and then all kinds of new aggravations and inconveniences were (necessarily) put on the traveling public by the government. Security lines were seemingly interminable. Security personnel took away passenger's fingernail clippers and zealously started bomb-checking passenger luggage. Passengers having to show their IDs three times before boarding a plane became *de rigueur,* strip searching was not unheard of, and taking off one's shoes, belt, watch, jewelry, pen and pencil set, coins, money clips, and so on, was required of all passengers. Being wanded for contraband was considered a normal event.

The result of all this was that the business traveler, who really was the financial backbone of the airlines and for whom "time is money," found other ways to travel or alternatives to their need to travel altogether—web and teleconferencing, increased leasing of corporate jets, telephone bridge lines, and so on. As a result, more airlines filed for bankruptcy (after trying to fix everything by cutting prices), including such "biggies" as United Airlines, Delta, Northwest, and U.S. Airways. Bitter labor disputes followed because the bankrupt airlines tried to cut their workforce to lower operating costs, further exacerbating the service problem to their customers. Then United Airlines went to the old ploy of "fighting fire with fire" by starting its own discount airline. It is being reported that some of the airlines are planning to quit providing pillows and blankets for their passengers. What next—convert the toilets into extra seating capacity, or maybe just eliminate seats altogether and let people stand, strapping their arms to an overhead bar? (See Figure 10.1.)

Figure 10.1
Brother and Sister

Brother & Sister

The principle to be learned here is simple. Virtually all businesses are capacity limited. And discounters, no matter what they sell or service they provide, almost always end up with delivery problems that quickly convert into quality problems that rapidly become customer service problems that cause customers to look for other vendors. Using the airline example, in the end most business travelers would prefer to take a beating than have to fly on today's airplanes. And who is the backbone of airline revenue? Answer: business travelers.

Situation 3: Price has been cut, and your volume is being affected heavily. All right, now you're getting hurt on volume.

Solution: Hold your price, and consider whether you might be able to stem your volume loss with extra advertising, promotions, or customer acquisition strategies—or by way of better service or package dealing. Look at it like this: If you cut your price, you've got to get an incredible increase in volume (as the mathematics of pricing has explained). Second, if you cut price, you're probably going to hurt the image of your product. Third, it is mathematically true that, virtually always, if you will spend time and effort and money trying to make sure that you are giving your customer the quality, the service, and the delivery you've promised them, they won't go looking for other vendors. Spending money on correct quality, flawless service, and perfect delivery is virtually always less painful than if you cut your price. Just by way of example, if most businesses (assuming a 35 percent gross margin) tripled their budget for customer service, it would only take about a 5 percent increase in sales volume to make up for that effort. But if a business cuts price just 2 percent, it will have to do slightly better than 11 percent more in volume just to make up for that 2 percent price cut (see box pp. 88–89).

As we have mentioned previously, those entities that have survived the longest have charged the higher prices and made the most money. And, invariably, they have competed on delivery, quality, and service. They know that by cutting prices they would end up plugging up their business with unprofitable volume. And when they start having delivery, then quality, then service problems, they will drive off their most profitable customers.

The customer that any business gains because of low price is invariably the one that creates problems and destroys their ability to sell to a profitable (i.e., nonprice-buying) customer. You've got to be willing to say to a price-buyer (who is, again, solely devoted to the proposition that "you shan't make money on me"), "I don't really need your business. I can't even afford to do business with you."

Why It Is Almost Always More Sensible to Increase Your Activities in the Areas of Improving Quality and Customer Service, Spending More Time on Advertising and Promotion, and Ensuring That Your Delivery Is on Time, Rather Than Cutting Price

For most businesses (assuming a 35 percent gross margin on what they're selling), a tripling of their budget for customer service will only take about a 5 percent increase in sales volume to make up for that initiative in customer service.

Conversely, if they cut their price by just 2 percent, they will have to realize an increase in sales volume somewhere in the neighborhood of 11 percent just to make up for that 2 percent price cut.

If you are interested in the mathematics of this, read the next paragraph.

Let's say you are doing about $1 million in sales, and you are paying somewhere in the neighborhood of $5,000 for customer service activity. That would mean that you are spending approximately one-half of 1 percent of all sales dollars strictly for customer service.

Now, let's assume that you decide to triple the amount of money you are spending on customer service, from $5,000 to $15,000, which would be an increase from 0.5 of 1 percent of sales to 1.5 percent of sales.

That increase in customer service would represent a $10,000 increase in GS&A expenses. Consider that $10,000 increase as a "fixed" cost.

The way to analyze the impact of this fixed cost in our Break-Even Formula, of course, is to add the $10,000 to the fixed cost. Your Break-Even Formula originally was as follows:

$$\text{Break-even volume} = \frac{\$200{,}000}{.35-.15} = \frac{\$200{,}000}{.20} = \$1{,}000{,}000$$

If you increase your fixed overhead costs by $10,000, your formula would then be:

$$\frac{\$210{,}000}{.35-.15} = \frac{\$210{,}000}{.20} = \$1{,}050{,}000$$

Or a 5 percent increase in sales is required to make up for that tripling of the amount of money that you will spend on customer service. (*Note:* Both your sales dollars and sales units would only raise 5 percent, because by not having cut your price, your sales in units increase at exactly the same rate as your increase in sales dollars.)

What would happen if, rather than tripling the amount of time and effort that you spend on customer service, you decided to cut your price by 2 percent? That, too, can be computed by taking a look at your Break-Even Formula.

(continued)

If you cut your price by 2 percent, your Break-Even Formula will be as follows:

$$\frac{\$200,000}{.3367-.1531} = \frac{\$200,000}{.1836} = \$1,089,324$$

These are the numbers that would occur because of your price reduction and its impact on your gross margin percentages and variable expense percentages. By cutting your price 2 percent, your total sales dollars must increase by $89,324.

That is your actual dollar increase in sales. But what tells us how many units of products you must sell? This can only be determined by converting your dollar sales into unit sales. That can be determined by multiplying your dollar sales by your cost of goods sold, which will have increased from .65 of your selling price to .6633 (because of the 2 percent price cut). If we multiply $1,089.324 by .6633, it tells us that your sales volume in units will be $722,549. This means an 11.16 percent increase in your sales volume will be required to make up for that 2 percent price cut.

A simple question is this: Why is it that anybody wants to cut their price, based on the false belief they can make it up in volume? The facts are that if you will spend more money on quality, service, and delivery, and/or devote more time to genuine customer service and/or devote more attention to detail, helping your customer, and otherwise generally doing the job right, it is almost always less painful than it is to try to cut price and make it up in volume.

Situation 4: You're getting your pants beaten off, cutting price is the only thing you can do, the writing's on the wall and there's no place to go.

Solution: Okay. So we don't have answers for everything! It can get so bad, there is nothing else you can do but cut price. But if you must cut price, consider the following: (1) Run a temporary special (if you can survive) to meet your competitor's price—but it had better be *temporary;* (2) Meet your competition if the cut is to be 10 percent or less on a short-term basis. But, again, remember a 10 percent cut on a typical gross margin of 35 percent means that you'll have to double the amount of work you're going to do, the product or service you'll have to sell or provide, and the effort you'll need to expend, just to stay even; (3) Drop the product if the competitor's cut is going to be permanent. If it's your only product or service, try to continue providing good quality, service, and delivery and hope you can last longer than the competition.

At some point, obviously, there is no answer. If your competitor has a ton of money to lose (and substantially more to lose than you do), get out. You will go broke before he does. But if you really understand what we have been suggesting, you will see that there is no reason to be stampeded into taking a price cut to maintain business viability. Most price cutting is a *self-inflicted* wound, because the people who do it don't understand anything other than selling on price. If you can learn to sell your product or service on quality, service, and delivery—and not on price—you'll find your business more profitable and your commission checks larger and more fulfilling.

You must recognize what you do both to yourself and your employer when you cut price. To be comfortable in avoiding price-cutting, you must know what you're doing. That means study, education, and thinking. Many people say study, education, and thinking take time and can be expensive. Well, as the old saying goes, if you think study, education, and thinking are expensive, why don't you try ignorance?

CHAPTER 11

THE TWO CARDINAL SINS
OF SELLING

I don't guess you would want to pay $200, would you?

—Foolish Salesperson

There are two things to avoid if you're ever going to sell at premium prices. One is *wowing*. The other is *cracking*. Premium price salespeople are, albeit subconsciously, aware of these errors and avoid them at all costs. But, unfortunately, almost all the rest of the salespeople are neither subconsciously nor consciously aware of them at all and, therefore, don't even realize that they are committing them. Let's take an in-depth look at these errors to see just how they can negatively affect your sales results.

Let's raise two questions. The purpose behind both of them is to get you thinking about why prospects and customers behave in certain ways toward you relative to your price. More specifically, *how* and *why* do they hammer on you to cut them a deal, give them a discount, or give them a break?

The single best way to do this is to put you momentarily into the role of being a prospect. That is something we're confident you have done at one time or another in your life. But let's be more specific. Have you ever rented a place in which to live? If you have, did you try to negotiate the price, the rent? Only about 10 percent of the people we have asked this question say that they tried to negotiate the rent that they ultimately agreed to pay.

Now, let's ask the same question, but change the subject. If you were going to buy a new car today, would you be willing to pay sticker price for that car? It shouldn't surprise you to learn that virtually everyone we have asked that question says they would negotiate the price of any new car.

Here's the point: Most people would plan to beat up the seller on the price of the new car. But most people will not bother to try to beat up the guy trying to rent them a place in which to live. Why are prospects so pre-disposed to verbally assaulting people who sell cars? Is there something about a car salesperson that just makes people angry?

No. The answer is simple. It's training. And it's yours, not theirs. Car dealers have trained all of us to beat up their salespeople on price. And here's the fundamental point we are trying to make with all of this. If you feel your customers really hammer you for some kind of a discount, or to cut them a deal, or knock something off the price, there's a fairly strong chance that you are inviting and encouraging that kind of activity to hap-pen . . . you just haven't been conscious of doing it.

INVITING CUSTOMERS TO BEAT YOU UP ON PRICE

There are two things that we've previously identified and discussed that salespeople do that invite and encourage people to beat them up on price. One is what we call *wowing*. Wowing occurs when salespeople communi-cate somehow, someway to their customers that they believe that their own prices are too high. If you communicate that to your prospect, you can bet that person is going to hammer you on your price. Almost all salespeople wow to varying degrees. And all of us do at times. But good salespeople break themselves of this habit very, very quickly.

Wowing may be the very simple, seemingly innocent, innocuous things that you say that sound like this: "Are you sitting down?" What kind of a foolish statement is that? You just called on this prospect. He's sitting behind his desk. He has just asked you the price, and you say, "Are you sitting down?" Or "Better buckle your seat belt before I lay this price on you." Or "Man, can you believe these prices?" Or "Think $200 would be too much?" Or "I don't suppose you would want to pay $200, would you?" Or "How do you feel about $200?" Or "How's $200 sound to you?" Or "How's $200 grab you?" And, of course, let's not lose sight of one of the most popular sales lines of all: "Ain't it a crime the price *they* charge for this stuff nowadays?" Think about that. "They" is *you,* isn't it?

If you say any of these things to your prospect, you have clearly signaled that you, personally, feel your own price is too high. When prospects be-lieve that *you* feel your price is high, guess what? They are going to beat on you like a drum because you have told them: "I sell this stuff, and even I think the price is too high. Nobody in their right mind would pay that much money."

Let's return to the car dealer example. The reason you beat up car sales-people on price is that they have trained you over the years to do so. For decades, car dealers have done nothing but tell us they think their prices are too high and that they are willing to negotiate their prices. Next time you are in your car, turn on your radio. A commercial for a car dealer will eventually blast out loud and clear. (This time, however, pay attention to it.) What you're going to hear is stuff like: "Come on in and let's make a deal. We want to sell you a car. No legitimate offer refused. We will meet or beat any competitor's price. We will not be undersold." Translation: Come on in, and let's have a big fistfight over the price of this new car. And every prospective car buyer rises to the challenge.

Not only will you plan to beat up on this guy, you will carefully pre-pare for the altercation. You'll do your homework. Today, you'll even get online to check his profit as well as his competitors' prices. Again, it's all in one word: Training. Car dealers have trained all of us to beat them up on price. Isn't it a shame that their sales training isn't that effective? We guess the difference in the results is the sheer volume of repetitive messages that are sent out in every form of media the dealers can find.

As a salesperson, however, no matter what you sell, you must fully ex-pect that a smart prospect will challenge your price. Wowing can clearly be seen in some of the previously mentioned phrases, such as, "Are you sitting down," "Better buckle your seat belt," and so on. However, big-time wow-ing comes more from something you *don't do* rather than from something you actually do. The number one thing most salespeople don't do, or don't do very well, is talk price. And, if they do, they don't discuss it credibly, comfortably, or confidently. We can prove this to most salespeople by sim-ply asking this question: How comfortable are you talking about the price of your products or services?

Most salespeople don't like to talk about price at all. Based on research that we've been involved in over the past 30 years, we estimate that more than 90 percent of salespeople will not even raise the issue of price with the customer. Rather, they wait for the customer to raise it. Furthermore, al-most half of all salespeople, when directly asked price by the customer, will change the subject and start talking about something else by saying some-thing like: "I'm going to come to that, but let me tell you about how won-derful our (product) (service) is first." They may as well say: "Let me dance around the mulberry bush, babble a little bit at you, and maybe price will go away." You *can* deftly defer price, and there is a reason for it. But you must do it with confidence, and at the right time. We call it handling pre-mature price questions.

Don't be afraid of premature price questions. Expect them. In fact, they are far more common than you think. Most prospects really do want to know the price. In fact, they really need to know it in order to make a purchase decision. However, if you are not in a position to quote a price because you haven't had a chance to create value in the mind of your prospect, you must learn how to delay quoting a price with confidence. The best way to do this is to tell your prospects that you will provide the exact price, based on their specific needs, requirements, volume, and parameters once you and they determine exactly what they need. Alternatively, give them the range in which most purchases fall. We'll talk more about this option later.

Our research also shows that a full one-third of salespeople *never* say the price out loud. That is a little odd—you'll have to verbalize your actual price sooner or later, won't you? Not really, you say? Your reason? Is it that you don't ever *have* to say the price? That you can always find a pencil and paper? (That way you can write it down, and then point at it.) Is it that you can say to your prospect, "There, you can see what the price is"? That way you believe you'll prevent your vocal chords from doing what? Wowing. But here's your trap. Can your prospect hear fear? Can they also see fear? Of course, they can.

Has it ever occurred to you why one of the first things lots of prospects do is to purposely attack you with a premature price question? Why do they do that? Because they're getting a read on you. They're trying to find out if *you* believe you're going to get your price. It's a credibility check. Remember: If your prospect thinks that you really don't believe you're going to get your price, you are wowing. You must learn to deal with this whether it is a legitimate price question or a purposeful ploy.

Prospects know that by attacking you with price questions, they can make you feel uncomfortable. Prospects know that if you thought your price was any good, you would be more than happy to talk about it. Remember, we indicated earlier that more than 90 percent of all salespeople will not raise the issue of price with the customer. So who are the distinct minority who do raise the issue of price themselves? Price sellers! Verify that tonight on your drive home. Go through some retail district. Who's advertising price? Price sellers. Watch television tonight. Who's advertising price? Read the paper tonight. Who's advertising price? Prospects know instinctively that if you really believed your price was any good, you'd be more than happy to talk about it. If you can't deal with price credibly, comfortably, and confidently, you are wowing bigtime.

The second major bumbling error is *cracking*. What we mean by cracking is when the salesperson, perhaps under intense pressure to give the prospect some kind of a discounted price, cracks under that pressure and communicates or signals to the prospect that he or she might be, or indeed is, willing to negotiate the price.

If you communicate to your prospects that you are at all willing to negotiate your prices, guess what? They are going to try to negotiate the price you ask. And guess which way the price is going? If you crack, you're done. If you tell someone that you're willing to negotiate your price, you're going to have to negotiate your price downward.

Cracking almost always results when salespeople say things that sound something like this: "Now, you know I want to work with you on this, George." What kind of a foolish statement is that? George just happens to be the dumbest guy who has ever walked on the planet trying to buy anything from anyone, he just innocently asked you your price, you tell him, and he hiccups that, "your price sounds a little high." So you quickly say to George, "you know I want to work with you on this, George."

But, perhaps you don't say that. Maybe you say things like, "George, you know you're one of our most valuable customers, and we really want to do business with you again this year." Or, "Let me sharpen my pencil and see what I can do for you." Or, "We'll work something out here that will be easy for you to live with." Or, "Let me talk to the boss and see what we can do for you." Or, "What'll it take to get your business?" Anything sound familiar? Salespeople don't even need to be trained to say these stupid things—they simply come up with them on their own in order to *create* a path of least resistance. And, here is the best gem of all, "Tell me where I need to be to get your business."

Let us translate that one for you: "I don't even know my price. In fact, come to think about it, I guess the boss doesn't either. In fact, I guess the reason they sent me over here today is to find out what you think we ought to charge for this stuff. I don't know. I just sell it." Any salesperson who says something like that is telling his or her customer, "I always negotiate the price. Beat me up."

Don't crack. Got it? Well, okay, what do you do? We'll tell you what you've got to do. You've got to hang in there, baby. Let us give you some profound insight into selling at prices higher than your competitors. If you want to sell at prices higher than your competitors, you have to ask prices higher than your competitors. And, having accomplished that, then you have to hang in there or, put more eloquently, you have to learn to acknowledge the reality that your prices *are* higher than your competitors' and proceed with the full expectation that you'll make the sale at that price.

Acknowledging that your price is higher than your competitors' must be done tactfully and diplomatically. But it must be done. The alternative is to crack, and as you saw, if you crack, you're done.

ADVERBS AND ADJECTIVES

Most salespeople have a favorite adverb or adjective that they use to signify they're cracking. Adverbs and adjectives are the words you use to clarify, modify, or specify what it is you're talking about: the "red" ball, the "blue" car, the "wet" seat, the "dry" pavement. We're talking about a "little" kid. Compared to what? A "big" kid. We're talking about a "smart" kid, compared to a "dumb" kid. We're talking about a "wiry" kid, compared to a "strong" kid or a "stout" kid.

Adverbs and adjectives give you different mental images. In fact, creating those images with words is the main use we have for adverbs and adjectives. What's that got to do with your price? Listen. What are you really saying to a customer when you say something like this: "Well, our *usual* price is $200"? What does the word *usual* mean? It means beat me up . . . now!

If you have a usual price, guess what? You must have an unusual price. *Any* word you put in front of *any* price, other than the word "the" has the propensity to do that to you. Let us just run a few of the more common adverbs and adjectives by you that we have heard used over the years: "Our *normal* price is $200." "Our *regular* price is $200." "Our *list* price is $200." "Our *base* price is $200." "Our *catalog* price is $200." "Our *published* price is $200." "Our *standard* price is $200." "Our *asking* price is $200." "Our *quoted* price is $200."

Almost all salespeople have a favorite adverb or adjective that they use. Many even tell us about sitting around thinking up the adverb or adjective they want to use. The reason for that is they deliberately intend to signal to the prospect that they don't think the prospect is going to pay what they were asking, and they don't want to tell the person, point blank, that they are willing to cut the price. But they want to give him or her a signal so that the prospect will come back at them and make some kind of a negotiable counteroffer. How about this wonderful, simple alternative? "The price is $200." You see, if the price is $200, you've always sold it for $200, you've never sold it for anything other than $200, and you fully expect to make this sale at $200. When they ask you the price, you know what you're going to say? "The price is $200." You're not going to say, "Our *usual* price is $200."

While on this subject, something should also be said about *corporate culture words*. What we mean by corporate culture words is that salespeople, especially those in large organizations, tend to infect each other with adverbs and adjectives, the same way people can infect each other with the flu. For example, several years ago, while doing some consulting with the nation's largest manufacturer of cement, one of your authors trained about 500 of their salespeople. While doing this, he found their corporate culture word was "quoted price." For example, a prospect asks, "What do you guys get for this cement?" And the answer was "Our *quoted* price is $82 a ton." We estimated at that time that about three-fourths of their salespeople used the words "quoted price" when giving a price quotation to the customer.

To make this point even clearer, let's look at it this way: You personally have never bought bulk cement in your life, and one day the boss says to you, "Hey, we need 10 tons of cement. Why don't you find out where we can get it and what it's going to cost us?" You say, "Aye-aye boss," and you get on the phone and call this manufacturer:

You: "Uh, we need 10 tons of cement. Who do I need to talk to about that?"
Salesperson: "Well, sir, that would be me."
You: "Okay, my boss said we need 10 tons of cement. What's the price on that?"
Salesperson: "Well, our quoted price is $82 a ton."

Remember, you've never bought bulk cement in your life, and you hear that "quoted price" routine. What's that going to encourage you to say? "What's my price?" "What's our price?" "How much do I get it for?" That adverb or adjective the salesperson inserts signals to the prospect that: (1) the salesperson is willing to negotiate the price, (2) the salesperson does negotiate the price, and (3) the enterprise endorses it. The result? The customer is going to beat up on the salesperson for a lower price. It's just that simple.

NOUNS AND PRONOUNS

While we're talking about inviting prospects to beat you up on price, in the same vein as adverbs and adjectives, don't put nouns or pronouns in front of the word "price."

For example, if a salesperson says "our price" or "my price" to the customer, that salesperson has implied that *others* are charging a different price. Consider, for instance, that a prospect asks: "What do you guys get for this stuff?" The salesperson then responds with: "Well, our price is $82 a ton."

What is the prospect going to think? How about, "What do the other guys charge? I better check around." The salesperson just invited the prospect to go shopping. Never, ever put a noun or a pronoun in front of the price, and absolutely *do not* put your company name in front of the word price, either. Don't say "Digital Pathway's price is only . . ." or "Hardwood's price is . . ." What you should say is, "The price is . . ."

DEALING WITH TRAINED, SOPHISTICATED PROSPECTS, BUYERS, AND CUSTOMERS

Have you ever gone to a purchasing training seminar where they teach professional buyers to do corporate buying? The number one thing that is taught in any purchasing training seminar is this: As a customer, always challenge the seller's price. Always. No exceptions. It doesn't make any difference what it is you're buying. Always challenge the seller's price. And that is taught as blind, religious dogma. "Do not even question this: Always challenge the seller's price." The reason for that rule? All prices can be negotiated.

There is no such thing as a non-negotiable price. Price is just a number. You can define price as if it's a mathematical equation. Price simply means how much money each one (product/service) costs. All price means is this:

$$\text{Price} = \frac{\$}{\text{Unit}}$$

Price is just a number that somebody, somewhere, literally plucks out of the sky and applies to something being offered for sale. Now, you're probably saying to yourself, "That's not true of us, we really work on our price. We do all kinds of studies, and we look at our costs, and we study the competition. We do all that kind of stuff. What do you guys mean price is just a number plucked out of the sky?"

Ultimately, somebody has to say, "Okay, this is the price we're going with." In short, whoever has the final say on price must pick a number. Which number do you want? If it's mine to sell, I have to pick a number. If it is yours to sell, you have to pick a number. We certainly aren't denying that there may be a certain amount of study and involvement in picking that number. Most sellers aren't that cavalier about price. But the bottom line is that when a price is picked, *somebody,* somewhere, did select that price to use. And because of that, *all prices can be negotiated.*

Someone sets that price. That same someone can change the price. All prices can be negotiated. In training, purchasing people will learn that single principle as an irrefutable truth. Always challenge the seller's price.

Now, what's all this got to do with you, the salesperson? It's simple. Any smart or trained prospect or customer is going to challenge your price. So let's start with this single idea: Just because a person asks you for a discount or insists on a discount from you, it doesn't mean you're doing something wrong. It doesn't automatically mean you're wowing or cracking. But if you actually do wow and/or you crack, you have just aggravated the situation. You may have even reminded the prospect who hadn't intended to haggle with you to go ahead and challenge your price. What we're driving at here is simply that a smart, seasoned, or strong prospect or customer **is** going to hammer you, even if you make no mistakes as a salesperson. It's just not that easy to avoid. Anybody who knows anything about buying is going to challenge your price. We guarantee it. Wowing and cracking just encourage more of that pressure to be brought onto you.

So, lesson number one: If a prospect asks you for a discount, you're not necessarily doing anything wrong. But if you actually do wow or crack, you will encourage the prospect's attempts to get a lower price.

Lesson number two: Just because someone asks you for a discount, it does not mean you have to give him one. Most salespeople—we estimate 50 percent of them—fundamentally believe that you have to cut the customer some kind of a deal to get them to buy from you. Unfortunately, lots of these salespeople will offer a discount even if the prospect doesn't ask for it!

Do you want evidence of that? Have you ever put a fairly significant asset of your own up for sale—like a house, car, boat, trailer? When you put it up for sale, did you ask the exact price that you expect to get for it and not ask a penny more, or did you put a little "pad" in there for yourself to negotiate with? Come on, you put a little pad in there, didn't you? Why did you do that? Your answer isn't, "I wanted to give the guy an opportunity to pay too much." Come on, you know that's not why you put the pad in there.

You put the pad in there because you thought, "He isn't going to want to pay what I ask, so I'll add a little bit to it, and then he'll start hammering on me, and I can cut him a deal, and then that'll make him feel good." Unfortunately, we don't have any evidence that cutting prospects a deal actually does make them feel good. What we do have evidence of, however, is that it does make prospects and customers hammer you all the harder the next time if you are involved in repetitive sales.

Evidence: Car dealers, again. None of you believe the sticker price on a new car. Nobody's going to pay that. It's a false price. Car dealers ask more than they expect to get, and then, of course, the prospect comes in and beats up the dealer's sales representative, gets him or her to knock off a couple hundred, or a couple thousand, maybe several thousand. But it doesn't make the prospect feel good. It actually makes that person paranoid, mistrusting, and even resentful. Frankly, these guys are just lucky that people really do need to buy cars. They depreciate, become obsolete, and people need to buy another car. And millions of people need to do this year after year.

Why do we say that it doesn't make the prospect feel good? First of all, most people really don't like to negotiate at all. J.D. Power Associates in *USA Today* (Thursday, September 4, 1997, p. 3B, "J.D. Power to Rate Auto Dealers") states that "We know that 68 percent of customers still hate to negotiate a car sale." Hate! Not dislike. Not uncomfortable in doing so. Not, "just as soon not have to." *Hate!*

Can you sit there with a straight face, and say that you personally love the transaction/negotiation process of buying a car? Very few people can say honestly that they really enjoy that process. That's true no matter the price point, dealership, or nameplate.

The point is, most people do not *like to* negotiate, but most people *do* negotiate. Earlier in reading this book, you probably agreed that you would expect to negotiate if you went to buy a new car. That didn't mean you like doing it. It means you *do* it. And you probably do it mostly out of fear of paying too much if you don't do it. Most people don't like to negotiate, but they will. And the minute they get the idea that the seller's prices are negotiable, they're going to work the seller all the harder. That's how car dealers have trained us to negotiate so strongly when we buy new cars. And that is how many salespeople train, invite, and encourage their customers to beat them up on price when they are trying to sell to them.

THREE INVIOLATE RULES OF SELLING AT PREMIUM PRICES

When working with the retail jewelers' association years ago, we discovered something very interesting about selling retail jewelry. Most of the extremely expensive jewelry is sold by a tiny, tiny percentage of retail jewelers. We're not talking five- or six-figure jewelry. We are talking seven, eight figures. Ten million dollars is not a lot of money for a very high quality piece of jewelry. However, it's still just a piece of jewelry, so we started trying to discover why and how it is that such a very small percentage of retail jewelry salespeople seem to be the only ones capable of selling the expensive jewelry and bringing in huge bucks.

Let's use an example. Look at a new Rolex watch: Let's say its price is $8,000. You can get a new Timex for $40, a new Seiko for $40, a new Casio for $40. Now let us raise this question: Why would you pay $8,000 for a Rolex watch when you can buy a perfectly good Seiko for $40? Besides that, what's the difference between an $8,000 Rolex and the $40

Seiko, anyhow? The answer is, "The Seiko keeps better time." There's no way you're likely to make a two-handed, mechanical watch that is going to be a more accurate chronometer than your basic electronic watch, like the Casio, Seiko, or Timex.

How can someone sell something that is perhaps 200 times higher priced than the competitor's? Is it a better product? So, we started studying this phenomenon, and that study led us to develop the three inviolate rules of selling at premium prices—three things that clearly identify the differing thought and behavior patterns of people who sell at premium prices.

The Rule of Credibility

Rule number one is the rule of credibility. Your prospect has got to totally, absolutely, without question believe you. And that prospect has got to *believe that you believe that you're going to get that price.* They have to trust you in all things.

Studying these jewelers, one of the things we found is that the jeweler who can sell the expensive stuff just drips with credibility. It's just oozing out of his pores. Someone comes in to buy an $8,000 Rolex watch. She asks the price. What do you say? "I don't suppose you would want to pay $8,000 for it, would you?" That would be nuts.

What premium salespeople say is: "The price is $8,000." Then they tell her how wonderful it is. They talk about aesthetic value. They talk about beauty, design, style, color, harmony, balance. If they think she is interested in mechanical things and so forth, they talk about the intricacies of the mechanism. They talk about gemstones—diamonds, rubies, and so on. They will talk about metal—platinum, gold. But they are not going to try to persuade the customer that that Rolex is a better chronometer.

They might even suggest: "You want a good chronometer, something to accurately time something with? Buy the Seiko. $40. It'll tell you what time it is probably more accurately than will a Rolex, and if you really want to know what time it is, call the National Bureau of Standards. Those are the guys who can tell you what time it is. They'll tell you to the nanosecond." But they won't make the mistake of destroying their credibility by trying to suggest that the Rolex is a better chronometer. And if they really are any good at selling, they will sell the prospect *two* watches: the Rolex for a "Dress Watch" and the Seiko for a "Sport Watch."

You must never, ever knowingly misrepresent anything about your product or service. For example, if you want to blow your credibility entirely, try misrepresenting a delivery time or date. Let us give you the bottom line. Nobody pays big bucks for excuses. Why should they? The cheap guy's excuses are every bit as useful as the expensive guy's excuses. If you want to sell at a premium price, you can't have a delivery problem. If you have to deal with delivery problems more often than you'd care to admit, and you're delivering excuses rather than on-time performance, you need to make your delivery problems go away.

Don't ever lie. Don't misrepresent. Don't mislead your customer. If the customer ever finds out that you knew that stuff wasn't going to be ready when you took the order, you not only blow your credibility, but you're dead meat swinging in the wind the rest of your life for that prospect. That's the rule of credibility.

Don't Feel Your Own Price Is High

The second inviolate rule has to do with how you personally feel about your price. Put simply: You can't feel your own price is high. If you feel your price is high, you're going to do what? WOW! In fact, if you sincerely feel your price is too high, we're going to suggest that you go somewhere else and sell something other than what you're selling today.

Unfortunately, many salespeople do feel their own prices are high. How do you feel about your prices? Are they high . . . too high?

Do you want evidence that most salespeople feel their prices are high? A good example happened to us at the Marriott Hotel in South Bend, Indiana. It is a very long, narrow building, all the meeting rooms are on the second floor, and, while there are stairs, most people ride the elevators. The elevators are at one end of the building, and this hotel, on that day, was really busy. Every meeting room had something going on in it, and in preparing to start our seminar, we had our registration table just in front of the elevator doors. We had our sign on the table, designating which meeting room was ours: *How to Sell at Margins Higher Than Your Competitors.*

That morning, six times in less than 30 minutes, we heard the exact same comments from passers-by. Businesspeople would get off the elevator, and one person would see the sign and read it to his or her associate: "*How to Sell at Margins Higher Than Your Competitors.* We ought to attend this seminar today." And on each of the six occasions, their associates responded: "Aw, our prices are already higher than anybody is in the country. We ought to be teaching that course." We have that same scene happen so often at our registration tables around the country that we've actually lost count of the number of times we've heard it. In fact, it has happened so often that it is now far more than just anecdotal evidence. In fact, we believe that it is darn good evidence that most salespeople feel their prices are higher than their competitors'. How about you?

If you feel your prices are too high, you're going to wow. People who sell things at premium prices don't feel their prices are unreasonable at all. They *know* their prices *are* higher than their competitors', but that doesn't mean that their prices are *too* high. Remember, price is just a number. And someone will always have a higher number. What you should be selling is value. Value means what you get compared to the price that you pay. And ultimately, people buy value. They don't buy price. Remember, too, any smart prospect is going to challenge you on your price. You can't wow at your own price, or you are aggravating your problem. So, inviolate rule Number Two: Don't feel your own prices are high. Know you're giving the customer good value.

Respect Your Customer

Inviolate rule number three deals with how you feel about your customer. Put simply, don't believe your customer is stupid. For example, who'd pay a half a million dollars for a fountain pen? A flaming idiot? Bad answer. Do you want to know who would pay half a million dollars for a fountain pen? Somebody who has a spare half a million lying around and doesn't mind spending it on a fountain pen, that's who. And most people who have that kind of disposable money probably didn't get it by being stupid.

They probably didn't get it winning the lotto, either. Most people who have that kind of money—and this may surprise you—*earned* that kind of money. Remember our earlier example about H. Ross Perot. And, again, remember that they didn't earn it by being stupid. In fact, most people who have that kind of money earned it by selling things. You do know that one of the highest paid professions in the United States is selling, don't you? Bar none. And yes, we have considered the athletics and entertainment professions.

A number of years ago Michael Jordan reportedly made $80 million, making him the highest paid athlete in the United States that year. Incidentally, that same year that Michael Jordan made $80 million, he made most of that money selling. It's called endorsements. He reportedly only made $36 million playing basketball. Another point? The same year that Michael Jordan made $80 million (selling *and* playing basketball) there were more than 100 salespeople on Wall Street who earned more than $100 million dollars apiece, selling securities. Interesting thing, isn't it? Michael got lots of money and publicity. Those guys got even more money and no publicity.

Do you need more evidence that selling is one of the highest paid professions in the United States? *Forbes* magazine publishes a list of the 400 richest Americans every October. And as far as we can tell, there has never been a professional athlete who has made enough money in athletics to get on that list (but the people who hire them do). And there have only been four entertainers who have done it, and they have always made the bulk of their money selling. Oprah Winfrey's on the list. She syndicates her shows. Bill Cosby was on the list for a few years. He syndicated his shows. Merv Griffin was on the list several years, but he didn't make his money as a singer and talk show host. He made it selling *Jeopardy*. And the only entertainer who was on there a long, long time was Gene Autry—and he didn't make it singing *Rudolph the Red-Nosed Reindeer* and *I'm Back in the Saddle Again*. He made it selling sports and real estate. Bill Gates sells software. Donald Trump buys and sells real estate. He also sells his image. Got the picture? Selling is a high-paid profession. Giving stuff away ain't. Don't ever forget that.

The people and businesses that are willing to pay premium prices aren't stupid. Whether we are talking about household consumers or business-people, remember that anyone who's paying a premium price almost assuredly *knows* they're paying a premium price. As a consequence, they have a different set of expectations because of that, and you must not frustrate those expectations. Here is the bottom line: If you want to sell at a premium price, you cannot have a delivery problem relative to your product or service. And, the cheap guy's delivery mistakes are every bit as problematic as the expensive guy's ones. Your customer doesn't want to hear about: "One of my guys didn't come in this morning. And another guy forgot to put fuel in the truck, and I've got to go out on the interstate and pick him up, so we are going to be a little late getting there with that stuff." They don't want to hear about that. Do you know what they want to hear: "You need it when? No problem." Inviolate rule number three: Your customer knows he's paying a premium price. Because of that, he has a different set of expectations, and you must never frustrate those expectations.

CHAPTER 12

BUYERS MAKE GOOD
LIARS . . . IF YOU LET THEM

Trust Me

If you're reading this book, you probably want to sell at premium prices. But there is this awkward problem: Customers don't say, "Yeah, I'm ready to pay you that kind of money." Rather, what they tend to say is, "Listen, buddy, I can get the same stuff from somebody else for less money. We buy this stuff strictly on price. Price is the only thing we look at." Then they start preying on your belief that, all things being equal, all people do buy exclusively on price.

Buyers can make good liars. In fact, potentially the most proficient stretchers of the truth are people who are buying things. There are lots of reasons for that, but let's put just two on the table right now.

Number one, most legitimate buyers really do believe they buy on price. Virtually everybody seriously believes that price is the single most important differentiator. But that is not true. Unfortunately, prospects believe it to be true, and therefore, they can tell you a very persuasive falsehood. Do you, too, really think people buy on price? Let's test your belief.

Again, are you wearing the cheapest shirt, blouse, sweater, or dress you could buy? What would happen if the next time a prospect tells you that he or she buys strictly on price, you looked around his or her office and point to computers, office equipment, furniture, business machines, printers, copiers, scanners, and so on, and asked, "Is that _____ the cheapest one you could possibly buy?" Or, asked to tour their plant, warehouse, IT Department, customer service center, or retail store and then pointed at the various pieces of machinery, equipment, and other equipment they use to conduct their business and asked the same question, would they say, "Yes, it's all the cheapest stuff we could get!" You get the point. Businesses are even less likely to buy on price than are household consumers, especially when it comes to buying things they need to earn their living or make their businesses run. (And remember, most household consumers don't really buy on price, either.)

The truth is that people will *say* they buy based on price, but buyers often make very good liars. They believe they buy on price, and they will fervently, persuasively tell you that. But that doesn't mean that they really, really (we mean really) buy on price.

The second reason that buyers make good liars is that when prospective customers lie to you, they do not consider it lying. Instead, they consider it negotiating. Let's examine the fundamental difference between lying and negotiating: You can go to hell for lying, but you get a lower price for negotiating. However, for all intents and purposes, the words lying and negotiating are really synonymous.

If you look up the word *negotiate* in the dictionary, it will be defined as "to confer with others in order to reach a compromise." How could that possibly mean that the words lying and negotiating are synonymous, you might ask? Think about it. When you are no longer negotiating, you have finally gotten around to telling the truth—establishing your true position. While the prospect is still "negotiating," that person is probably not stating his or her true position, but rather, is trying to persuade you (the salesperson) to change something (price) to better suit him or her. Buyers will tell you anything they can think of to get you to do one thing: Cut your price.

INTIMIDATION

Remember, as we have said again and again, price-cutting is a self-inflicted wound. Customers know that. If you studied the tactics used by prospects and customers to beat up sellers on their price, you would discover that everything they do boils down to one of two basic strategies: intimidation or denigration.

Intimidation is the word that best describes frightening, scaring, tyrannizing, pressuring, and bullying salespeople to cut their price. Prospects will engage in all kinds of shenanigans to accomplish this purpose. But this entire set of strategies and tactics boil down to one thing: An effort to make you so fearful that you are going to lose the sale that you lose your composure and/or sensibilities and make some kind of concession on your price. Prospects will try to make personal issues of things to put salespeople on edge. They will feign indignation at things that are said. They will pretend to be angry. They might even throw things (we're serious). They will take offense at anything they can. They will try to make you feel uncomfortable and uneasy. Mind you, not all prospects do this. But most will do it to some degree. Some will be very suave and sophisticated in the tactics that they use. But the bottom line is that most tough-minded prospects just don't want you to feel too comfortable or to take them for granted.

DENIGRATION

Denigration is the fine art and skill of trying to defame, disparage, vilify, degrade, sully, or depreciate the value of the product or service that you are selling. Prospects have no problem tearing apart and demeaning what you are selling to them in an effort to get you to reduce your price. One wonders, sometimes, after all the bad things a prospect may have to say about your product, service, employer, reputation, reliability, performance, people, and even you, why they then actually want to purchase the product or service from you. But, somehow they do.

So what do you say and do when a prospect starts in on you with, "Look, I can get the *same* thing from somebody else for a lot less money" (and perhaps they can). To begin with, it is essential that you understand that prospects will always use the word "same." You don't believe that to be true? How often do you hear a prospect say, "I can get similar stuff from somebody else for less money?" Do you want to know why you don't hear that? Because if a customer told you, "I can get a similar product for less money," you'd immediately start jumping up and down, running around, yelling and screaming, flapping your arms—saying, "Ours is *different,* ours is *better.*" A prospect saying, "I can get similar stuff for less money" would give you an opening to talk about qualitative differences between yours and the competitor's. So, *instinctively* they don't say *similar,* they say *same,* and they play fast and loose with that word *same.* They will use the word *same* when "totally, completely, and entirely different" would be more correct. This is particularly true if you have professionally differentiated your product or service in a way that truly does separate it and you from your competition. It just *can't* be the same.

Prospects will also always try to negotiate with you by using the most powerful and persuasive words they can think of in an effort to intimidate and frighten you into cutting your price. As a consequence, if they can come up with a word stronger than *same,* they will use that. That also plays out when they use the word *commodity,* as in: "You're just selling a commodity," or "We view this stuff as a commodity."

Why do prospects prefer to use the word *commodity*? Let's define it first. The word *commodity* and the word *same* mean the same thing, except commodity means *lots of it.* Same means no discernible difference; you can't tell one from the other. But "commodity" is the same but widely, readily distributed and available for sale. Commodity means: "Everybody and their dog have that same stuff for sale, and now some of their pups are carrying it, too."

When prospects say *commodity,* they're trying to denigrate you, your product, or your service. When they say *same,* they are also trying to denigrate. But the word *commodity* is an even stronger, more demeaning word than the word *same.* "Look—your stuff has no more value than your competitors' stuff, and I can buy it virtually any time or any place from a zillion of your competitors." The implication behind this argument is, "If you want me to buy from you, you're going to have to cut your price." At this point, they are asking you to believe that, "all things being equal, people buy on price, rate, or fee."

As we've stated, prospects can, and do, play fast and loose with the words *same* and *commodity.* Remember, they will say *same* or *commodity* when "totally, completely, and entirely different" would be the more correct set of terms. They are trying to put down your product and service. In doing so, they are both denigrating what it is that you sell and are simultaneously trying to scare, frighten, and intimidate you into believing that what you sell is of no more value than your competitors. The idea behind this is that if it is a commodity and they can get it cheaper down the street, either (a) you had better cut your price, or (b) they're going to actually go down the street and buy it from your competitor.

We suggested earlier that you should actually look forward to prospects telling you about how they can get a product like yours cheaper down the street. Here's why: If prospects thought they could get the same stuff from your competition for less money, they would tell you that in a heartbeat, wouldn't they? They would also be getting it, wouldn't they? So, why is this customer wasting his time telling you about the sweeter deal he has with someone else? He or she might as well go on and get it. Here's the point: When a customer tells you he or she can get the same stuff for less money, he or she is admitting to you that, "I know your stuff is every bit as good—if not better—than the competitors'." Understand the logic: If your prospects are reduced to calling your stuff the *same* or a *commodity* because they can't really say the competitor's product or service is *better,* they have admitted that yours is, in fact, just as good (if not better) than the competitor's. And they are trying to scare you into cutting your price out of the fear that they are about to take their business "down the street."

Logic is on your side. Falsification of the facts or misrepresentation is illogical. Language is logical. Remember, certain buyers *can* make good liars and will stretch facts and/or exaggerate situations. That's why it's to your advantage to learn to listen to the prospect and to look forward to your prospect telling you about being able to get the same stuff from someone else for less money. But you do need to understand one thing. Either your product is the same—no discernible difference—or it's not. If it's not the same, unless the prospect can truly get *better* stuff somewhere else for less money, they're reduced, logically, to saying that your offering is every bit as good (if not better) than the competitors'. And, if they are willing to waste their time talking to you about it, you have to wonder why, don't you? It is easy for prospects to say *same,* but when they do, they get themselves in trouble logically.

So, when it comes to selling at a premium price, there is a fundamental question you need to answer for yourself, and here it is: Is your product or service, in fact, the same as your competitors, or is it not? If it is not, we guarantee you two things: The prospect knows the differences, and the prospect cares about those differences.

Prospects Know the Differences

How can we make those two guarantees? It's simple. Number one: The prospect knows the differences. How do we know the prospect knows the differences? Because you told him. You did tell him, didn't you? Wait a minute—you didn't forget to tell the customer, did you? You did tell him, right? Good. "And did you do so persuasively?" we might also ask. All right.

What's the oldest car collector joke? A guy's just finished restoring his 1928 Packard, and he is so proud that he's about to explode with pride. He puts the Packard in a car show, and he's standing off to the side watching people admire his car. Up walk Hank and Martha.

Hank says to Martha, "My golly, look at this car. Martha, come here and look at this thing." They're just looking this guy's car over. Pretty soon, they *feel* the owner watching them. Hank looks at the owner and says, "Sir, this wouldn't happen to be your car would it?" The owner responds, "Well, yes it is."

Hank then asks, "Really, what year is it?" The owner replies, "It's a 1928 Packard." Hank says, "Really? It brings back great memories. You know when I was a kid, my Dad had one just like it—only it was a Ford."

Actually, that's not a joke. Maybe that's why you didn't think it was funny . . . actually, any car collector has heard those words numerous times. A Ford isn't a Packard. A Plymouth isn't a Pontiac. A Buick isn't an Oldsmobile. A Packard wasn't a Ford. And, today, an Infiniti isn't a Lexus. And a Mercedes isn't a Lexus or Infiniti, either. If there is a measurable, discernible, identifiable, perceivable difference between your product and your competitors'—we make you two ironclad guarantees. Number one: The customer knows the differences (because we know you told them) and number two: The customer cares about those differences.

Before we go to point number two, let's consider the question, "You did tell your prospect, didn't you?" We all too often see salespeople who really do fail to tell their prospect how their product or service really does differ from their competitors'. Salespeople who fail to do that often give away their ability to sell what is the real quantitative or qualitative, differential advantage of their products and services, because in the salesperson's mind, their own products and services are the same as their competitors', when they are not.

Good salespeople will never concede that their products or services are the same as their competitors' if they are not. That is a basic, fundamental principle of selling. But what if your product *is* a commodity? What if there really is no discernible difference between yours and your competitors'?

It is possible to have exactly the same *product* as your competitor. But a good salesperson will never concede the possibility that a competitor has the same *service*. Generally—perhaps. Specifically—never. In reality, any given seller legitimately does have a tough time providing the same general level of service to their customers, day in and day out. It is just plain difficult to maintain the same, consistent level of service 100 percent of the time, even under optimal conditions. There's always something happening. Somebody's off on vacation. There's a big surge in demand. Your supplier fouls things up for you. Your database gets lost. Things get too crowded in your workspace. Your server crashes and so on and so forth. The airlines advertise that they give you great service. Maybe they do if you're the only passenger on the plane that day. But what kind of service do you get when the plane is full—like on the day before Thanksgiving Day?

It is true that you may have the same product, but you'll never have the same service as your competitor. Therefore, never concede that your product or your service is the same thing, if it is not. One more time. If there is a measurable difference between yours and your competitors', your prospect will know the difference, *because you told him.*

CUSTOMERS <u>CARE</u> ABOUT THOSE DIFFERENCES

Of course, once you tell your prospect about those differences, you know that the next line out of their mouths will likely be: "I don't care":

> **Customer:** "I don't care. Yeah, I can tell you the difference between a cup and a glass. A cup's made for a hot beverage—made out of ceramic, got a handle on it. You can pour scalding hot coffee into a cup, hold it comfortably, and enjoy your steaming hot coffee. Glass? A glass is made out of glass. It's made for a cold beverage. You put hot coffee in a glass, it may crack and break, and it's certainly going to get uncomfortable to hold. I know all that, but you want to know something? I don't care about those differences. Price is the only thing I care about. Price, price, price. And if you want me to buy it from you, you're going to have to cut your price."

Do you know how easy it is for prospects to tell you, "I don't care"? They simply say, "I don't care." However, do you know how truly difficult it is to really mean that they don't care? That's different. There was a national case study on whether or not customers cared about seemingly insignificant, inconsequential differences in a product. It started way back on April 23, 1985, in Atlanta, Georgia. What happened on that day? Do you remember? That was the day Coca-Cola changed its formula. Who cared? We didn't care. We drank beer. (Actually, one of us did. The other drank wine.)

But somebody cared, because Coca-Cola decided to (many observers say *had* to) go back to the classic Coca-Cola formula. Let's be more specific. Who really did care? Coca-Cola drinkers cared, that's who! We told you buyers can make good liars. Recognize that the only people in the world who really do care about differences in products and services are the people who buy and use those products and services. The rest of the world really doesn't care. Again, when Coca-Cola changed its formula, we didn't care. We drank beer (and wine). We are here to speak for beer and wine drinkers. We don't think any beer or wine drinkers cared. We asked a few of them. "Do you care?" "No, shoot me another one, I'm dry." That was pretty much the answer we got from that question.

Incidentally, Pepsi-Cola drinkers didn't care either, nor did hot chocolate drinkers, nor did bottled water drinkers. Who cared? Coca-Cola drinkers. But Coca-Cola drinkers cared so much that Coca-Cola had to go back to Classic Coke because the people who cared were the people who bought and used Coke's product every day. They cared immensely.

So let's get back to the basics, and review the difference between price and value. Businesses and household consumers don't buy on price. They say they do, and they often really believe they do. But they don't. They make an economic decision based on what one gets compared to what one pays for, but they don't buy on price. And who knows the differences that exist in products and services? The people who buy and use those products and services. And whose job is it to tell them about these differences? The salesperson's. And the salesperson is you.

HOW TO TELL WHEN THE PROSPECT IS LYING

Can you tell when a customer is lying? You bet. Why is that? Because of logic. Perhaps you have had sales trainers tell you to listen to your customers and find out what they want and need. Then you can sell to those wants; sell to those needs.

We agree with all that. We even teach it. But we're telling you to listen to your customers for something other than wants and needs. If, as a salesperson, you learn what to look and listen for, you can tell when prospects are falsely claiming to be able to "get the same stuff from someone else for less money" or that they "don't care about those differences."

There are three ways to tell when prospects are misrepresenting the truth. One is by observing where your prospects are looking when they are telling you about "that sweeter deal from someone else."

WHERE IS THE PROSPECT LOOKING?

Good salespeople learn to observe their prospects when they are making their sales presentations (assuming, of course, that the prospects and salespeople are face-to-face). These salespeople learn to be keen observers of the prospects' eye movement, in particular. If you were to study neurolinguistic programming, for example, you'd learn that people who are being somewhat deviant or deceitful will seldom look directly at the people they are trying to deceive and will almost never look the person whom they are trying to mislead directly in the eye.

But you don't have to study neurolinguistic programming to understand the importance of this principle. Even the common vernacular of our language recognizes and understands it. How many times have you heard someone say something like, "I don't trust her; she doesn't look at you when she is talking to you," Or, "He's a sneaky-eyed kind of guy," Or, "I don't think you can trust him, he never looks you in the eye."

The opposite is also readily observed by most people, and it's supported by such sayings as, "I looked that guy right in the eye and told him this is the way it was going to be," or, "She looked me right in the eye, said that would happen, and it did."

When people are being honest and straightforward, they tend to look directly at the people with whom they are talking. They look them in the eye. However, when people are being deceitful, they tend to avoid eye contact. For example, has your child ever lied to you? Now, please don't think we are calling your children liars! Virtually every child does get into the cookie jar at some time or other when they have been told specifically not to do so. If you asked your child, "Were you in the cookie jar?" he or she would probably look down to the floor and say, "No." And you would know he or she was lying, because your child wouldn't look at you. Now consider the reverse. Have you ever falsely accused your child? "Have you been in the cookie jar?" The kid looks directly into your eyes (or is it your soul?) and says, "No, Mommy (or Daddy), I haven't been in the cookie jar." And you know the kid is telling you the truth.

Prospects do the same thing. Admittedly, they are adults and have developed more proficiency at lying, but they still have a hard time looking you in the eye when they say, "I can get the same stuff from someone else for less money," Or, "I don't care, price is the only thing we consider when we are buying what you sell." Typically, when being devious in this way, prospects cannot look at you. Rather, they will look down and away, perhaps looking at their hand or their desk, or if standing, at something on the floor. (Or, as one of our clients who is a farm equipment dealer said, they look at that rock they are rolling around with the toe of their boot. This client of ours referred to these people as "Rock Rollers.")

It is also interesting to note that these Rock Rollers will say very threatening things to a salesperson while rolling their rock. Then, once the threat is voiced, they will look up at the salesperson to see how it (their threat) landed on the salesperson.

If your prospect cannot look you in the eye when talking to you, and particularly if your prospect is looking away while making threatening, disparaging, or intimidatory remarks, you can be almost certain that the prospect is "negotiating" about the issue at hand and is not being fully candid with you. Always be suspicious about things said to you under these conditions. It is easy for prospects to lie while not looking you in the eye. But it is far more difficult for them to tell a convincing lie when they are looking you in the eye. (Consider, too, what we wrote about in an earlier chapter relative to you, the salesperson, being able to enhance your credibility—the rule of credibility—by looking your prospect directly in the eye when saying your price: "The price is . . .")

Observing a prospect's eye movement is, however, far from being a perfect science. And granted, many astute prospects have learned to look you in the eye when they are knowingly misrepresenting their real feelings to you. But being aware of a prospect's eye contact is certainly a useful technique to at least be aware of.

The second technique that you can use to determine if a prospect is not being totally honest is to observe when they begin getting personal and start using opinion verbs. This is, by the way, a far more accurate indicator of a prospect's effort to be less than 100 percent truthful with you.

THEY GET PERSONAL AND USE OPINION VERBS

Again, this indicator of prospect deviousness is far more accurate than paying close attention to customer eye movement, so you must learn to use it.

For you to learn how you can use this information about your prospect's efforts to intimidate you and denigrate your products or services, we need to provide you with an example. Let's say you are trying to sell the prospect high-quality, ceramic coffee cups for his cafeteria. But let's say the prospective customer says that he can get the same thing from your competitor for less money. But you know that the competitor's cups are paper cups.

To make this point, let's play out three scenes here:

Scene 1: We have two identical ceramic coffee cups on a desk in front of you. We ask you to look at them. You can see both, and we point at one and say, "This is a ceramic coffee cup," and we point at the other and say, "This is a ceramic coffee cup." Would you argue with those statements? No. Why would you? They are both identical ceramic coffee cups.

Scene 2: Now, we hold up one of the ceramic coffee cups and say, "This is a ceramic coffee cup. Would you argue with that statement?" You say, "No." Then we hold up a paper coffee cup and say, "This is a ceramic coffee cup. Would you argue with that statement?" You say, "Yes. It is not a ceramic coffee cup, it is a paper coffee cup."

Scene 3: We again hold up one of the ceramic coffee cups and say, "This is a ceramic coffee cup. Would you argue with that statement?" You again say, "No." Then we hold up a paper coffee cup and say, "This is a ceramic coffee cup. Would you argue with that?" Again, you say, "Yes." But then we change our posture and attitude toward you, and while holding both the ceramic cup and the paper cup, say, "Well, we classify these as the same. Would you argue with that?" You can't really argue with the statement that "we classify" the two different cups as being the same. You can say we're wrong. You can suggest that we are stupid. But you can't say that we don't classify them the same, because *we just told you we classify* them the same.

What we have done in Scene 3 is to employ the two tactics—intimidation and denigration—that customers use in trying to get you to believe that *they* classify two things that are not the same as being the same. We have done this by making it a personal issue—we said that "we" classify these the same, thereby making a personal issue out of the exchange. And we have said that we "classify" these the same, thereby using an opinion verb, also making it a personal issue and making a statement against which you (the salesperson) can't argue unless you want to offend us by telling us we are stupid, wrong, or something else. Note, too, that we have also successfully denigrated your product (the ceramic cup) by saying we classify (rate, consider, view, perceive, regard) the competitor's paper cup as being the same as your ceramic cup.

What the prospect is preying upon by making it a personal issue and using an opinion verb is that, right or wrong, the prospect is still the prospect. That notion is directly out of the textbook in Salesmanship 101. Don't offend the prospect or customer. Salespeople don't want to get in their customers' faces and tell them how dumb they are, how wrong they are, or be in any way confrontational with them. The prospects know that, and while they may not be cognizant of what they are doing when using this tactic to beat up on you, they instinctively are keenly aware of what they are actually doing. Prospects instinctively know that when they make it a personal thing and start using opinion verbs, salespeople are at a decided disadvantage in their presentation unless they have good people skills and can tactfully and diplomatically carry on the conversation. Good salespeople will (as tactfully and diplomatically as possible) correct prospects. Poor salespeople tend to *crack* (remember that term?) under this pressure and say something stupid like, "You know I want to work with you on this. Let me talk to the boss and see what we can do for you."

But the key thing that premium price salespeople have going for them is that they realize that the prospect is negotiating—remember, we don't call our prospects liars. Astute salespeople are well aware of the implications of prospects' questions. Astute salespeople ask, "Why is the prospect telling me about being able to get the same thing down the street for less money?" "Why isn't this person down there getting the paper cups from my competitor if he really considers paper cups the same thing as my ceramic cups?"

And, remember: The tip-off to this whole thing is that the prospect made it a personal issue and started to use opinion verbs. Recognize that this behavior by the prospect is virtually a sure sign that they are not being entirely truthful with you, if not just flat out lying about having a sweeter deal down the street. Why aren't they down the street getting it? We'll tell you why: They can't get it or they don't want to get it from your competitor (see Chapter 5).

So as a good salesperson, you (now being knowledgeable of all of this) should actually look forward to your prospect saying, "I can get the same stuff from someone else for less money," particularly if you know that your competitor's products are not really the same.

Let's talk about how getting personal and using opinion verbs can lead to the particularly devastating effect of intimidating salespeople. When a prospect says, "I classify," "we classify," "my company classifies," or "the people who use this stuff classify it the same," they are deliberately and knowingly picking a fight with you and are trying to destroy you psychologically. Have you ever thought about how to start a fight? Or have you ever gone to a program where they teach how to stay *out* of fights? Have you ever studied conflict resolution—how to avoid fights?

If you take a course on conflict resolution, one of the first things you'll learn is never to get personal. When you get personal, you start a confrontation. That's what starts conflicts more than anything else—getting personal. Want to see how easy that is? How long has it been since you had a good altercation at home? We are not talking about a "let's break a few plates" fight here. We are talking about a "move out" scenario. We'll tell you how to do it right now. When you get home tonight, walk in and get personal. Say something like this: "Well, I see you did it again." Then, back that up with a statement like, "You are just like your parents," and then throw this one out there for good measure: "In fact, your whole family is that way."

We'll guarantee that you'll get into one of the best disagreements you've had in a long time. And, please notice one thing. You didn't even have a subject to fight about! You do not need a subject to start a fight. All you have to do is get personal. Have you ever seen a barroom brawl start? They always start the same way, someone gets personal: "You got a problem?" "No, you got a problem?" The fight's on . . . and spreads throughout the place.

Prospects will do the same thing. How do they personalize? They must, necessarily, use personal pronouns—I, we, me, our, us, you, they. The prospect says: "I," "we," "my company," "our support team"—and then they go to opinion verbs. The most commonly used opinion verbs are classify, view, perceive, regard, consider. These are all opinions. As a consequence, it's difficult for you to argue against the statements. To make this point crystal clear, read the following six statements out loud: I classify these things the same. I view these things the same. I perceive these things the same. I regard these things the same. I consider these things the same. These are the same.

Notice how much more definitive "These are the same" sounds. "These are the same" is a statement of fact. The rest are statements that reflect a personal opinion. For purposes of recognizing this phenomenon of intimidation in action, smart salespeople learn that, if a prospect cannot use a factual verb and say something very straightforward and factual like, "These things are the same," the customer is "negotiating" with the salesperson. So one principle emerges clearly: The second way to recognize when a customer is negotiating (lying) is when they get personal and use opinion verbs.

If your product or your service are, in fact, in any way different from your competitors', and if that difference is measurable, discernible, identifiable, and perceivable, you can be sure that (1) the prospect knows the differences and (2) the prospect cares about those differences. We guarantee that.

CUSTOMERS WILL USE THE SUBJUNCTIVE MODE OF SPEAKING

Remember, buyers can make good liars, but blatantly misrepresenting the facts can also get them into trouble with smart salespeople. That is because prospects take an illogical position when they're trying to denigrate the value of what it is that you sell when they are trying to intimidate you into cutting your price.

One example: Prospects are likely to exaggerate. They will begin to misrepresent things, fudge their position, and/or use weasel words trying to make you believe you are about to lose the sale. To do this, they almost always go to the subjunctive mode of talking. So, if you want to be a truly effective salesperson, you must learn early on to recognize and/or identify the subjunctive mode. And the glorious part of being able to recognize the subjective mode is that it shows up both in talking and in writing.

Let's imagine that you have never laid eyes on your prospect. In fact, you've never even heard her voice. Your entire relationship has been in writing. Whether it has been e-mailed, faxed, snail mail, or whatever, it doesn't matter. In spite of all of this, you can still determine when a prospect is not being straightforward with you. Why? Because when that person uses the subjunctive mode when you are talking price, she is trying to threaten you. The prospect's problem? She must use the subjunctive mode in order to threaten you.

To master this powerful principle you must first understand the difference between the imperative and the subjunctive mode. Most people know and recognize the imperative quickly. The imperative mode is the command mode. An absolute imperative might sound like: "Halt!" "Stop!" "Move!" or "Go!" Those are *absolute* imperatives. Nobody argues with the imperative. People using the imperative expect you to fully and totally comply with what they are telling you to do.

Let's compare the imperative to the subjunctive. The subjunctive might sound like this: "If you don't stop, you are going to be sorry." That becomes a brain game. You don't have to stop, but if you don't, you are going to be sorry—or so they say. They are using words to try to scare or intimidate you. When they say "Halt!" they expect you to stop. That's it. Just shut her down, right now. But when they say, "You will be sorry if you don't stop," they are trying to scare you into stopping. They know they don't have enough force to *make* you stop, so they try to scare you into stopping.

Okay, what does this have to do with selling? Question: Have you ever been thrown out, run off, kicked out, booted, shut down, or hung up on when making sales presentations? You'd better say "yes," because if you have never been thrown out of a sales presentation, your price has been too low all of your life. You have priced yourself out of somebody's pocketbook, haven't you?

But please recognize one thing. Being thrown out demands mandates and requires that they use the imperative. It all boils down to that. The prospect has to say, "I am not buying from you." It may be that nice. However, it can also be crude and rude: "Out! Out! Out!" "Get out and don't come back!" "Don't let the door knob hit you in the butt!" "Get yourself out of here!" Or it may be very tactful and diplomatic. But, either way, the customer will throw you out.

The authors recall a salesperson in Michigan who said he called on a prospect who was British (or who at least appeared to have a British accent to the salesperson), who worked for the Bendix Corporation. The prospect asked the salesperson about the price. When the salesperson told him the price, the prospect looked at the salesperson and asked, "Is that price negotiable?" The salesperson couldn't negotiate his price, so he simply said, "No sir, it's not." The prospect's proper response to that was: "Goodbye to you." Now, that was a tactful, diplomatic response. But it is no different than if the prospect had said: "Get out of here and don't come back." The result was the same.

You can get thrown out in a lot of different ways, but each one requires the imperative. "I am not buying from you." "You are out of here." Or the prospect simply turns and leaves your facility if he or she came to your place of business. Or the prospect just hangs up on the phone. There are many ways to be shut out. If the prospect legitimately has a sweeter deal, they can and will use the imperative. Remember when a prospect tells you, "I have a sweeter deal down the street," he or she is either telling you the truth or lying. Let's consider both possibilities.

Let's start with the premise that they are telling the absolute truth. If they truly do have a sweeter deal down the street, they don't need you. They not only will throw you out, but they will do so with impunity and suffer no consequences. Why? Because they really do have a sweeter deal. What do they need you for? If, however, the prospect is negotiating (or lying), and he does not have a sweeter deal, but wants you to believe he has a sweeter deal, he can't throw you out. Throwing you out is going to mean that they will ultimately be cutting off their nose to spite their face. So they have to *scare* you into thinking they are going to throw you out. Enter the subjunctive mode. "If you guys don't cut your price, you're out of here." "Unless you guys cut your price, we are not going to do any business." "Either you guys get competitive or we are not going to do any business." Each of those subjunctive statements is designed to intimidate you and scare you into cutting your price.

In the previous paragraph, we carefully chose to use the three most commonly used subjunctive statements that you will hear. As a salesperson, you need to recognize when a prospect is using the subjunctive mode. In order to do that, all you need to remember is that the subjunctive mode is created by the words *if* and *unless,* or the combination of the two words, *either . . . or.* Consider the difference between "Get out and don't come back!" And, "If you don't cut your price, you are out of here." Or, "Unless you cut your price, you are out of here." Or, "Either you cut your price, or you are out of here." When a prospect is using the subjunctive, he is trying to scare you by "explaining" to you the dastardly consequences that will occur to you if you don't cut your price, that is, they will not buy from you unless you cut your price.

It's also important to note that the subjunctive mode always contains hope. Yes, hope! There is always hope. . . . "All you have to do to keep me from throwing you out of here is to pull out your big sharp knife, cut yourself real deep (on your price) and I won't throw you out." Do you hear/see the difference between, "get out and don't come back," and, "If you don't cut your price, you are out of here?" If you can, that is all you need to remember.

To summarize: The three ways to recognize that your prospect is negotiating (lying) are:

1. Observe where they are looking when they are threatening you. Do they "look you in the eye" or do they look away?
2. Do they get personal and use opinion verbs?
3. Do they use the subjunctive mode when communicating with you?

CHAPTER 13

How to "Hang in There" under Intense Pressure to Cut Your Price

You have to stand for something or you will fall for anything.

—Anonymous

We have repeatedly said that if you are going to sell at premium prices, you must first be willing to *ask* prices that are higher than your competitors' prices. But, once you do that in the real world, many prospects will complain that your price is too high. And, at that point, you just have to "hang in there." "Hanging in there" more easily can be described as simply using the powerful, proven strategy of acknowledging that your prices *are* higher than your competitors'.

This chapter is all about the strategies that smart salespeople use to "hang in there." How to be tactful and diplomatic, but nevertheless communicate to the customer, "That is right. Our prices are higher than our competitors' prices, but I fully expect to get the sale anyway," rather than cracking and saying something stupid to the prospect like, "You know I really want to work with you on this. Let me get out my pencil and see what I can do for you." Remember, *cracking* comments typically are made by salespeople who can't handle the heat of battle and tend to crack at the first negative reaction on price.

THE "SO . . ." RESPONSE

There are five solid ways to acknowledge that your prices *are* higher than your competitors' that we have found to be exceedingly effective. The first is what we call the "So . . ." response. The "So . . ." response is exactly what it sounds like. Your prospect says to you, truthfully, that, "You guys are 20 percent higher than your competitors," and your reaction to that is a simple, straightforward, "So . . ." Unfortunately, many salespeople, when told to use the "So . . ." response, say that it makes them uncomfortable, suggesting that saying "So . . ." appears to be confrontational, perhaps even flippant.

The truth is that saying "So . . ." is neither confrontational nor flippant. What *is* confrontational would be to say something like, "You're right. We are 20 percent higher. And I am not going to do anything about it. And what are you going to do about that?" That's both confrontational and arrogant. "So . . ." is just a very tactful, diplomatic way of acknowledging what your prospect has said.

The implication of "So . . ." is twofold. It says: (1) Yes, you are correct and (2) I am not going to do anything about it, even though you don't say it in a direct or confrontational way. You simply say, "So . . ."

Notice the three dots behind the word "So . . ." In printing, those three dots are called an ellipsis. For our purposes here, you can translate those three dots to mean: Shut the hell up! That's three words: Shut . . . the hell . . . up! That's right, three words. Not four. A guy tried to correct us the other day on this. He said that it is four words. No. For our purposes, it is three words, Shut . . . the hell . . . up! That's what dot, dot, dot means when you are using the "So . . ." response. Got it?

We're discussing sales strategy here. We're talking about a maneuver—a purposeful, strategic action. Most salespeople don't even think tactically, let alone strategically. When a prospect says, "You are 20 percent higher than anybody else," you reply to that with "So . . . ," and then you shut the hell up. And then you say nothing, absolutely nothing, waiting for the prospect to reply to your statement of "So . . ." Now, why should you do that? Because the prospect is going to come back at you with a comment that is going to sound something like this: "What makes you think that I am going to pay that kind of money?" Or, "I don't understand why your price is so high." Notice that such replies from the prospect constitute a demand by them for you to make a sales presentation. And that's exactly what you want to do. This is your chance to make a presentation as to why they should pay your price!

Many salespeople tell us, "I try to tell the customer about our better quality, our better service, our better technical help, and our better support. But the customer doesn't listen. All they want to talk about is price. Price, price, price." Well, how would you like to be able to force the prospect to listen to you about the better quality, service, technical help, and support that you offer to your customer? The "So . . ." response will do that for you. And, all you have to do is say "So . . ."

The "So . . ." response actually causes the prospect to demand a sales presentation from you. One more time. When the prospect says, "You guys are 20 percent higher than anybody else," and you say "So . . ." (and shut the hell up), we guarantee that the prospect will respond to you with the likes of: "So, what makes you think that I am going to pay that kind of money?"

And when your prospect responds that way, *bam!* You jump at the opportunity to answer that question. You say something like, "I am glad that you asked that question. Let me give you the answer to that. Let me tell you why people pay us that kind of money. Let me tell you about the technical help, and support, and blah . . . blah . . . that we provide for you." *Now,* they'll listen to you!

We do recognize, however, that you still may not want to say "So . . ." Therefore, allow us to give you some good news. You don't have to say "So . . ." Any curt, abrupt, grunt of acknowledgment will do the trick. What is your favorite grunt? Let us give you some examples of alternatives to use other than saying "So . . ."

A lot of people say, "And . . ." For example, the prospect says, "You guys are 20 percent higher than anybody else." And you reply, "And . . . ," to which the prospect then responds, "And what makes you think that I am going to pay that kind of money?" *Bam!* You come back with, "I am glad that you asked; let me tell you the answer to why we charge the price we do."

Want some more examples of a few grunts? Here they are: "Sounds right." "You bet." "Hell, yes." "We usually are." "Absolutely." "No doubt about it." "Wouldn't have it any other way." "Really?" "That's exactly why you need us!" "No lie!" "Well, duh."

Which of the foregoing grunts you use (among these and the many others that are available to you) depends on your style, how old you are, your prospect's age and persona, and other factors. These days we hear salespeople saying, "Well, duh . . ." because that is what young people are saying to acknowledge the obvious. Remember, what you are doing is grunting an acknowledgment back to someone who has stated the obvious. The prospect has said, "You're 20 percent higher than anybody else," and you have responded with, "Well, duh." And if you shut the hell up, the customer is apt to respond with, "Well, duh. What makes you think that I am going to pay that?" *Bam!* You come back with, "I am glad you asked. Let me tell you . . ." Any curt, abrupt grunt of acknowledgment from you will work.

Don't tell us you can't get prospects to listen to your sales presentation; that they won't let you tell them about your better quality, service, delivery, support, product, durability, or better this or that. All you have to do is use the "So . . ." response. Pick your favorite grunt and use it. Mix and match. Try one grunt with one prospect or customer, another with a different one.

The "Why Not?" Response

A second response to use in acknowledging the fact that your price is higher than your competitor's without *cracking* on your price is what we call the "why not?" response.

Let's say the prospect stonewalls you by saying, "I am not paying that kind of money!" Or, "We are not paying that much!"

Your response to that is "Why not?" Now, we know that a lot of salespeople get nervous about doing what we are suggesting here. Most salespeople don't like to challenge a prospect, because they are afraid the prospect is going to say something disconcerting about their product, company, or service. Don't ever worry about that. When a prospect says, "I am not paying that kind of money," simply ask, "Why not?"

Or, as an alternative if you don't want to put the "not" in there, you might just say "Why?" or "Why won't you?" The real bottom line here is that you must challenge them. Why? Because, once again, we guarantee you that the prospect will come back at you with one of only two types of responses at this point. One is something substantive, like, "Yours is not wide enough, strong enough, or fast enough, that's why not." Believe it or not, that's not a bad response for you to get. Want to know why? If your prospect has a bona fide, legitimate complaint about your product, service, or company, at least now you have an opportunity to sell against their complaint.

Hopefully, they are wrong and you can correct them. Maybe you can say, "Oh, ours is wide enough (strong enough, fast enough). Let me explain to you how it works. Maybe I wasn't clear before blah . . . blah . . . blah." In the unfortunate circumstance that your prospect is correct in his or her complaint, face it, you are not going to get the sale anyway. So, at least, if nothing else, when you hear this objection often enough, you have concrete evidence to suggest that someone go back to the drawing board and come up with one that *is* wide enough, strong enough, and fast enough for that type of prospect. You can't hurt yourself by getting a prospect to tell you what is wrong with your product, service, or company. You may not *like* it, and it may mean *more work* for you to do, but it *will* improve your life if you respond accordingly. Again, ideally, you can sell against the prospect's complaints because they misunderstood you or you hadn't presented it well enough or with sufficient clarity.

The other answer you are going to get to your response of "Why not?" will be something in the subjunctive mode. "I am not paying that kind of money. Why not? I am going to tell you why not! Because your prices are too high. *Either* you guys get competitive *or* we are not buying from you! I told you we buy this stuff strictly on price. Price, price, price."

Now, notice how that is subjunctive. But what does subjunctive really mean? "Either you guys get competitive, or we are not buying from you!" It's *either, or*. Notice, here, that they also are complaining about price. One more time now. They are attacking you about price, but they didn't say there was anything wrong with you, your product, or service. They have told you they can get it cheaper down the street, your price is too high, and that unless you get competitive, you are not doing any business with them. In short, they have gone to the subjunctive mode.

Invariably, when prospects go to the subjunctive mode, they will start attacking you about price and implying (or even clearly explaining to you) that either you get competitive or they are going to take their business down the street.

That is intimidation—clear and intentional intimidation. Period. However, they are not really saying anything substantial. They are just dive-bombing you with price.

So, how do you respond to them without cracking? You respond with something like this:

> I realize that you think that our price is high. We probably are 20 percent higher than our competition. But let me tell you why we get 20 percent more. We not only give you a lot better product, but we are 100 percent committed to delivery dates. When you buy from us, when you place an order with us, we give you a guaranteed delivery date. And let me tell you something else about our technical help and transitional ownership, support . . . blah, blah.

In short, you start selling the prospect, rather than cracking.

When a prospect goes to the subjunctive and can't say anything substantially wrong about your product or service—when the prospect starts dive-bombing you on price and can't use the imperative (i.e., throw you out)—you can bet they really don't have a sweeter deal. If there truly is a sweeter deal and you don't crack, you are wasting their time. And, if they start dive-bombing you—repeatedly going back to price, price, price—they surely are working very, very hard to get you to crack, aren't they? Why is that prospect working so hard to get you to crack? Here's why: One of three reasons will always be in play. The prospect can't get it from your competitors. He or she can't get it from your competitors. Or, the prospect doesn't want to get it from your competitors. (Remember, there really are two "can't get its.") Let's go ahead and look at all three of the reasons in some detail.

The First "Can't Get It"

The first "can't get it from your competitors" is really a throwback to the old joke that we referred to earlier in this book as one of the classic sales jokes. It went like this:

Prospect: "Look, buddy, I can get the same stuff from your competition for less money."
Salesperson: "Well, I'm sorry, but I can't let you have it at that price. I guess you will have to get it from my competitor."
Prospect: "Well, I would, but I can't."
Salesperson: "Why can't you?"
Prospect: "Well, they are out of it right now."
Salesperson: "Oh, you come back to me when I am out, ours are free. We can give you just as great a deal when we don't have any, either."

Remember, we told you that we'd refer to this example again and again. What that prospect was saying in reality was:

> I want that guy's price, but I want your inventory. I want that guy's price, but I want your investment in inventory. I want that guy's price, but I want your investment in machinery, software, and equipment. I want that guy's price, but I want the way that you hire and train your people. I want that guy's price, but I want the way you plan and schedule your operations. I want that guy's price, but I want the way you run your business. Gosh, you know, come to think of it, I guess I want everything about you, I just want that meathead's price.

A smart salesperson's reaction to that sort of situation is, in essence, "Yeah, if you want that meathead's price, go down and get his inventory (or lack thereof), his lousy investment in inventory; his dumb investment in machinery and equipment; the lousy way he hires, plans, trains, and schedules. But if you really want the way we do those things, you are going to have to pay our price."

The Second "Can't Get It"

What do we mean by the second "can't get it?" Oh, the competitor has it, in stock, and can deliver it on time, when needed. No problem. The only problem for this prospect is that your competitor won't sell it to your prospect. Why won't they sell it to him? One reason may be that the prospect hasn't paid for the last stuff he bought from your competitor. Let's take a little philosophical shot at that one. If you are not going to get paid for it either; you may as well charge more. Remember, we have said that the most expensive customer that you will ever sell to is a price buyer. Well, the deeper truth is that the one that is really the most expensive is the price buyer who never pays you.

The prospect who is telling you about being able to get it cheaper down the street may very well be a prospect that your competitor will not do business with anyway. Anyone with sales experience has had this happen at one time or another: You take an order from somebody and, after the fact, wish that you had never met that customer, let alone written the order, because the problems started the very day you turned that order in.

One more time. Remember, when a prospect is telling you about that alleged sweeter deal down the street, and he starts dive-bombing you and explaining to you that if you don't cut the price, he is going to take his business elsewhere, but he doesn't throw you out, you can bet that something about that alleged sweeter deal isn't true. It always boils down to the reality that he can't get it because they are out of it, or he can't get it because they (your competitor) won't do business with him.

The Prospect Doesn't Want to Get It

The third reason the prospect will use the subjunctive mode is that he or she doesn't want to buy it from your competitor anyway. Why might that be the case? Because your competitor is a jerk, a crook, very difficult to do business with, unreliable, or some other reason. Yes, the competitor has it in stock and is more than willing to sell it to the prospect. However, the prospect just does not want to do business with your competitor.

Have you ever known that you could get something for a little lower price, but you didn't do so because you didn't want to do business with the seller? Perhaps you didn't like the way the seller does business, or you didn't like the seller's credit and collection policies, or there was all the nuisance of filling forms out . . . blah . . . blah . . . blah. When your prospect elects to use the subjunctive mode and is persistent in telling you about that sweeter deal he has down the street (when you haven't cracked), he likely doesn't have—or won't take—that sweeter deal. Something about it is not to his satisfaction.

The sum of all of this? Don't be so quick to cut your price. The simple truth is that one of the biggest problems many salespeople have is that they prematurely and unnecessarily cut price, because they don't understand the dynamics of customer negotiation strategies. Never, ever forget that price-cutting is a self-inflicted wound. It is something that you do to yourself. So, one more time, when prospects stonewall you with statements like, "I am not paying that kind of money," just ask them, "Why not?" And listen to their answer. If their answer is in the subjunctive mode, almost assuredly that customer is negotiating with you. Don't crack.

"Keep on Selling" Strategy

What we mean by the "keep on selling" strategy (the third way to "hang in there" in acknowledging that your price is higher than your competitors') is: When the prospect says, perhaps accurately, that, "You are 20 percent higher than anybody else," you just point-blank acknowledge the fact, perhaps by saying, "That's right, we are 20 percent higher, but let me tell you why we get more for what we sell."

Many salespeople flinch at doing this, because they find it a difficult thing to do. Often they fear that by admitting that their prices are 20 percent higher than their competitors' they will immediately lose the sale. Unfortunately, such an attitude shows a lack of the fundamental understanding that people who do sell at premium prices actually learn to *use higher pricing to their advantage*. People who do sell at premium prices learn to stand tall, chest out, and say things like, "You bet our prices are higher. Let me tell you why we get more money. We get more money because we give you a better product, better service, better technical help, blah . . . blah . . . blah."

To understand this point, let's repeat a disarmingly simple, yet profound idea that has appeared throughout this book. Here it is again: Price makes a statement. It makes a credibility statement. A low price makes a negative, derogatory, diminutive statement about a product or service, while a high price makes a positive, salutary statement about that product or service. Remember the earlier example of the new Rolls Royce parked out front? We told you that we would sell to you for $87,000, and we suggested that you'd ask, "What is wrong with it?"

The second thing we suggested that you'd ask was, "Do you have title to it?" Because you couldn't believe that we would be willing to sell you a new Rolls-Royce for $87,000 unless something was wrong with it or we stole it or it was a drug dealer's car or something. But, remember that if we told you that we had a new Rolls-Royce parked out front and we offered to sell it to you for $600,000, we knew what your reaction would be. "What kind of Rolls-Royce have you got that is worth $600,000? I don't think any Rolls-Royce is worth $600,000. I have to see this car. Show me, tell me, explain to me, sell me on why I or anybody else would pay you $600,000 for a new Rolls-Royce." When you tell somebody with your bald face hanging out, credibly, comfortably, confidently, that, "Yes, that is our price," and that, "Our prices are higher, but let me tell you why we get more money than our competition," you trigger that "the hell you say" reaction in the customer—a variation of the attention-grabbing technique addressed under the "So . . ." response outlined earlier in this chapter.

By openly acknowledging that your prices are higher than your competitors', you trigger one of the most open, responsive, receptive frames of mind in your prospect that you could ever imagine. Openly acknowledging that your prices are higher than your competitors' prices will actually trigger a demand for you to make a sales presentation.

Remember the reference we made earlier in this book about going to the lowest price brain surgeon? Let's look at another, similar example. Would you be willing to go out for the low-price bid for your child's (spouse's, mother's, father's) medical treatment? Why won't you go out for the low-price bid? Two reasons: number one, and most important, you are afraid of a cheap doctor. And, number two, you blindly assume that the more expensive physician is a better doctor, even though you don't have any support for either of those two suppositions.

Let's start with the first one. You are afraid of the cheap doctor. Why are you afraid? Because he or she is cheap. Price makes a real statement here, doesn't it? What is the second oldest medical school joke? What do they call the person who graduates number 100 out of a class of a 100 in medical school? "Doctor!" Yes, they call every one of them "doctor." The person who graduates last in his or her class is still a doctor. They have had the same training, the same experience. What makes you think they are not any good just because they are cheap?

Does their skill have anything to do with their price? What makes you think a cheap doctor is less skilled than an expensive doctor? It is kind of like watching a ski race and some guy loses by a tenth of a second. Clearly he can't ski as fast as the winner, because he lost by a tenth of a second. Every time they run the Indy 500 automobile race, one of the drivers comes in last. Does that mean he doesn't know how to drive a race car? Of course not. Let's face it—you've got no reason to believe that a cheap doctor is not a good doctor. Not all doctors are money-grabbers. You know there are a lot of people who go to medical school, get out of medical school, and then go into medical missionary work or work for an insurance company and never, ever charge for their services. These are perfectly competent people, but they don't charge anything directly to patients for services.

The other reason why you won't go for the lowest price is that you believe that the expensive doctor is a better doctor. But you really don't have any support for that position, do you? What is the oldest medical school joke? "Doctors bury their mistakes." Just because a doctor is expensive doesn't mean that he or she is good. Do you know what it takes to be the highest priced neurosurgeon in the United States? You have to ask the highest price (and really be a neurosurgeon). You don't have to be the best. We recognize that you might be sitting there saying to yourself: Okay, I got the point. But I am not selling neurosurgery. That's a stupid example. Okay, let's prove the same thing to you by talking to you about tires for your car. That's not neurosurgery, either. You have probably bought a tire or two for your car, haven't you? Same question, different subject.

Have you ever purposely gone out to buy the cheapest tire in the store that would fit on the car you're planning to drive? Very few people who buy tires will buy the absolute cheapest tire they can find for their car. Want evidence of that? Go to your local tire shop and ask the tire dealer what percentage of the tires they sell are the cheapest tire they stock in their store.

Not only do most people buy better stuff (e.g., tires) for themselves, most people will buy better stuff for themselves, even when they know they don't need it. Let's prove that to you. Have you ever been to Hawaii? It is not a very big place. Oahu, the island where Honolulu is located, is where maybe 80 percent of the state's population lives. It is roughly 20 miles wide, and maybe 40 miles long. In fact, the entire island is not as big as most major U.S. cities.

One of your authors was in a major hotel in downtown Honolulu, right on Waikiki Beach. He asked a group of local residents how many of them had bought the cheapest tire they could find in the store the last time they had bought a tire for their personal vehicle. Not one person indicated they had. Nobody in the group raised a hand. He asked twice, just to be sure. Again, nobody raised a hand. So, then he thought he should ask the obvious question, "Where are you going?" Then, each one looked at him with an uncomprehending look and asked, "What do you mean where are we going?" So he expanded the question, "Are you going to drive out to Yellowstone Park in Wyoming this summer or what? Did they finally finish that bridge? I know they have been working on it a while."

The point is this: If you lived on the island of Oahu, why would you buy good tires? You could walk home if you had to. Similar example: This same coauthor has a buddy in Colorado who works for a farm and ranch supply store. Based on the principle that people don't tend to buy the cheap stuff, especially for themselves, his company stocks one cheap tractor tire in each of their stores to use as a shill, to help sell the more expensive tractor tires. Their reasoning is that farmers will not buy a cheap tractor tire because they are all apparently afraid of high-speed blowouts. Where do they go on these tractors that they need such good tires? Farmers and ranchers will tell you that they buy on price, and they do. High price, not low.

Would you like a little more evidence? How about this letter one of your authors received after conducting a public program in Chicago on the subject of selling at margins higher than your competitors'. It went as follows:

> Dear Larry:
> Just a brief note telling you how much I enjoyed your seminar on January 22 in Elk Grove Village. I have been involved in sales most of my life, both in France and America, and I am very pleased and proud to say that I do embrace your philosophy and guideline every time I try to make a sale. Fortunately, it has worked very well for me throughout my business life of 41 years. I thought I would share a story with you and perhaps you will want to bring it up in one of your future presentations.
> I grew up during World War II in the South of France in a family of six children—in what I will consider a low income category. To make ends meet, my father had a large garden and all of us would sell fresh vegetables at the local open market on weekends. We always had for sale two baskets of tomatoes from the same garden and of the same quality, but at two different prices. Guess what? The higher price, without exception, sold first. So, we kept adding the tomatoes from the lower priced basket to it.
> Thank you again for a most enjoyable and refreshing day.
> Your French Audience [name withheld]

Now, you don't think that people really buy the more expensive tomatoes, do you? Ever tried it? It is an old retailer trick that smart retailers don't share with everybody. If you take two articles that are identical, stick them on a shelf, put a higher price on one, and represent it as a little different, almost every time the higher priced one will sell first. But you may be a little fearful to try it if you don't know how to sell things at premium prices.

Still don't believe what we are saying here? Let's quote the *Wall Street Journal* (July 21, 1995, "Hot, Cool Spots: Phoenix in Summer, Alaska in Winter"):

Hot, Cool Spots: Phoenix in Summer, Alaska in Winter
Here is an alternative to crowded beaches—the sweltering desert.

Phoenix tourism officials are inviting the traveling public to visit their 110-degree environs this summer. It is a ploy to smooth out their market's seasonality, and to the surprise of many observers, it's working. Occupancy at Phoenix-area resorts stands well above 70 percent this summer, up from barely 50 percent three years ago.

More surprising yet is how Phoenix did it—partly by raising prices. "For years, we tried building demand by giving rooms away, and that only made people think it must be awful here in summer," says David Radcliffe, chief executive of the Phoenix and Valley of the Sun Convention and Visitors Bureau. "So we made the decision to raise rates and stop apologizing for the heat."

The article went on to say that the same thing was done in Alaska, but in the wintertime.

Please understand, again, that price does make a statement. Price makes a credibility statement. And a low price makes a negative, derogatory, diminutive statement. You can charge a price so low that you hurt your sales. By raising price, you may find that your sales volume actually *increases*. It won't necessarily, but there is a good chance that it will, especially if you learn to present your price credibly, comfortably, and confidently.

Testimonial or Corroboration Selling

The fourth strategy that premium salespeople will use in acknowledging that their price is higher than their competitors' is "testimonial or corroboration selling." To do this, you must learn to use testimonials and corroboration of your claims by others. One of the most persuasive things you can do to get someone to pay you a premium price is to get a strong testimonial, verification, validation, or corroboration of your claims by others.

Why is this so effective? People don't mind paying premium prices, but they don't like to think they were the only ones dumb enough to pay the premium price. It's not the price that is the issue. It's the embarrassment of paying the higher price. How do you get over that bump in the road? By letting your prospect know who some of your other customers are and have been. Name-dropping is essentially a testimonial. Written testimonials are fine. If you have them, use them. But we are not necessarily talking just about written testimonials.

Incidentally, even if you do testimonial or corroboration selling poorly, it can work to your advantage. Here's why. We estimate that fewer than one in four salespeople actually use this as a consistent selling strategy. We don't know why they don't. They just don't. But because so few do, it is extremely effective for those who do use it. It is also simple and easy to employ. All it boils down to is, essentially, (1) acknowledging that your prices are higher than your competitors', (2) dropping the name of a customer you sell to, and (3) explaining why that customer buys from you.

For example, you might say:

I know you feel our price is high, and we probably are 20 percent higher than our competitors. But, let me tell you who some of our other customers are, and let me tell you why they buy from us. For example, we sell to ABC Corporation [insert any well-known, well-positioned, and respected customer/client here]. Why do you think *they* buy from us at these prices? Because they are stupid? No. You think they don't know that they can get it cheaper from our competitors? Of course, they know that. In fact, our competitors are constantly trying to sell to them. But they buy from us and they have been buying from us for the past 10 years. You want to know why they buy from us? Let me tell you why. Because of our guaranteed delivery program. As I told you earlier, our president, when he took over our company 10 years ago, said we will not have service or delivery problems. And we don't. I can guarantee you on-time delivery. How can we do that? I will tell you how. Before I can take your order and promise you a delivery date, I have to do two things: (1) I have to check with our programming department to be sure that we have enough available programming time to get the application reconfigured and to your programmers by the time you need it; and (2) I have to check to be sure that our most experienced programmers are available to work exclusively on your application. I have already done that. You've said you have to have everything by the fifteenth of the month. We have the available time, and we can dedicate our most experienced programmers to you. If you order from us, you are going to get it by the fifteenth of the month. And that guaranteed delivery program that I am giving to you is the same reason that ABC Corporation buys from us.

Then, perhaps, you continue with a second testimonial. Maybe it goes as follows:

Now, thinking about your business reminds me of DEF Corporation [a second, well-known and respected customer in their segment and industry]. They buy from us, too. You think they don't know they can get it cheaper from our competitors? Of course they do. You want to know why they buy from us? Some of it is the guaranteed delivery program I just mentioned, but it also has to do with our quality assurance program. Let me tell you about our quality assurance program blah . . . blah . . . blah.

And then maybe you throw in a third testimonial: "Oh, that makes me think about GHI Corporation [a third well-known customer]. They are customers of ours, too. Why do you think they buy from us? It is because blah, blah. . . ."

The way to do testimonial or corroboration selling is to pick two or three names to have in mind *before* you make your sales call. Then, in your presentation, you are prepared to drop the names and explain why it is that those customers buy from you. Do a little thinking before you make your sales call. Don't use all of the same customers' names all of the time. Some of your prospects will be more impressed with some of your customers than they will be with others. If you have a prospect that is in the automotive industry, maybe the best examples you could use would be automotive-related. If you have somebody in software design, the best example to use might be somebody in that business segment.

Incidentally, in doing testimonial or corroboration selling, don't be intimidated about dropping the name of your prospect's competitor who is buying from you. That can, in fact, be one of the most effective testimonials you can give. If your prospect respects that competitor and finds out that competitor is buying from you, he may begin to wonder why that (highly respected) competitor uses you as a supplier and he doesn't. Often, the most effective testimonial you can give to prospective customers is that you are selling to their competition. If your prospects have a particularly high regard for that competitor, you have a leg up on everybody else. And in making your testimonial presentation, don't forget to stand tall, chest out, and establish the fact that your prices *are* higher than your competitors' prices.

Look Hurt

A fifth method to use in acknowledging that your prices are higher than your competitors' prices is the simple act of "looking hurt." Hurt. Pained. Perhaps even mildly offended. Get that pained look on your face. Think about saying something like, "How can you say that to me? There is no argument on my part that our prices are higher than our competitors'. I've never denied that. But that doesn't mean that our price is too high. After all, our product is better . . . blah . . . blah . . ."

The strategy of looking hurt can be employed in many different ways, but it simply comes down to communicating in some way to the prospect that your feelings are really hurt. You aren't angry. You are just hurt. Learn to use your own inimitable style of expressing hurt feelings. Don't ham it up or go overboard. Just look hurt and express it by using some mild statement that indicates your (hurt) feelings and then continue expressing why your higher price is justified.

In sum, there are five proven ways for you to "hang in there" and acknowledge that your prices are higher than your competitors'. Whenever a customer claims that "your price is too high," you should be prepared to use all five. Mix and match them. And don't forget that the purpose of "hanging in there" is to avoid *cracking*. And remember, too, that if your customers go into the subjunctive mode of talking, they are clearly telling you that they don't have a better alternative, but that they learned in "attacking the salesperson school" that they should always challenge a seller's price; that they should repeatedly challenge the seller's price; and that, "If you don't ask for a discount, you won't get one." But you, as the seller, have five different ways to respond to the customer in acknowledging that your prices are higher than your competitors' and not *cracking*. Remember: If they have a sweeter deal, they can and will throw you out with enthusiasm. They will use the imperative mode. If they can't use the imperative, they are negotiating with you. There is no need to cut your price.

CHAPTER 14

INDICATORS THAT YOU
ARE UNDERPRICING

Nobody goes to Toots Shor's anymore—it's too crowded.

—Yogi Berra

Baseball players say interesting things—or, at least, interesting lines are attributed to them. Supposedly, one of Yogi Berra's most famous lines was, "It ain't over 'til it's over." That's something you always seem to hear from loser after loser on election evening. Yogi is supposedly credited with a couple of other favorites like, "If people don't want to come out to the ballgame and watch it, I can't stop them," and, "Much can be observed by just watching." Let's see how Yogi's legendary wit plays out when it comes to selling at premium prices.

IF PEOPLE DON'T WANT TO COME OUT TO THE BALLGAME AND WATCH IT, I CAN'T STOP THEM

Much of the need for the material in this book is based on the insights of those last two statements. Many salespeople think the statement, "If people don't want to come out to the ballgame and watch it, I can't stop them," is silly. Yet, many a salesperson has told his or her sales manager, "If people don't want to buy our product, I can't stop them" (or something to that effect). Well, you sure *can* stop them if you learn to sell—in contrast to taking orders. Selling is about getting people to buy things they might not otherwise buy because they lack knowledge or information. Many salespeople say they feel their prospects don't buy because their products or services are too high priced, when in reality, they haven't learned to explain to their prospects why buying their product or service at a fair (high) price is going to be beneficial to them.

MUCH CAN BE OBSERVED BY JUST WATCHING

The intellectual treasure, "Much can be observed by just watching," runs in the same vein as the, "I can't make them buy it," line. There is a lot of truth to the statement that you can see a lot—if you'll just look. And one of the things you can see is that your prospects and customers will alert you when you can charge higher prices, because they will tell you when your prices are too low. They will tell you, accurately and honestly, if you will just pay attention. They will tell you in the way they behave, the things they say, and the things that they do. But you do have to be paying attention in order to pick up on these clues.

When was the last time you worried that your prices were *too low*? If you are a typical salesperson—and especially if you are one who is paid some sort of commission on the dollar volume you sell, the answer is *probably never*. Very few salespeople ever worry that their prices are too low. They are so afraid of overpricing that they never even imagine that their prices could be too low. And *they virtually always end up under-pricing because of it.*

One of your authors once met a contractor who specialized in installing railings on balconies in high-rise buildings. He asked him about his product liability problems, wondering about people falling over or through the railings. The contractor's response was thought provoking, "What problems? Nobody ever tests the strength of those railings. They are so afraid of going over the edge that the most they'll do is stand two feet away and give them a little shake with their extended hand. The only reason a railing has to be strong is to withstand high winds. People will never deliberately test how strong a balcony railing is with their bodies."

The same thing holds true for testing prices. Virtually nobody will ever test to see if their price is high enough, always being afraid of going over the edge. It is for that very reason that we are not nearly so concerned about indicators of prices being too high (although it is possible for prices to be too high and we've listed those indicators in the next chapter). The latent propensity in most salespeople is to charge too low a price. Remember our previous examples of how airlines reacted to deregulation so long ago? Incidentally, that is the exact same thing that happened when the trucking industry was deregulated.

IF YOU EVER MAKE A PRICING ERROR, YOU SHOULD MAKE IT ON THE HIGH SIDE

If you ever want to sell at a high price, you always want to make any mistake in your price on the high side. There are several reasons for that. The first is that if your price is too high, it's easy to lower it. The second is that if your prices are too low, it is tough to raise them. People will almost always resist a price increase, even when warranted, wanting to know why and how you can justify it. However, they will respond warmly to a price decrease. The third reason is that overpricing isn't nearly as hazardous to your business health as is underpricing. As we pointed out in the section on volume swings, you can work your heart out and go broke underpricing. But if you go broke overpricing, at least you won't be as tired. And, frankly, if you are a business owner, your business probably won't die any faster if you are going broke overpricing. The real fact is that most businesses survive a lot longer with *no* business volume than they do with *unprofitable* business volume. With the understanding that if you are going to make an error, it is more logical to overprice, let's think about what the indicators are that your price just might be too low.

Your Gross Margin Is Getting Smaller on the Same or Rising Sales Volume

If your gross profit margin begins to decline, especially on rising sales volume, you probably have too low a price. (Incidentally, the reverse of that is also true. If your gross margin begins to climb on decreasing sales, your prices are probably too high.) If you want to talk about how to fine tune to the right price, start by monitoring your gross margin *by product line or service offering.* If you only have one product line, that's easy. However, if you're a wholesaler, distributor, or retailer with thousands of line items, you aren't going to like that advice. However, it is really the only way to determine the right price. And, frankly, if you use a computer, it isn't really that difficult to do. Learn to use your information technology system for one of the things that it was originally designed to do—crunch numbers.

If you want to be successful and sell at a premium price, it will certainly never occur as a result of a series of propitious accidents. Being successful at anything is a function of knowing what you're doing. And that takes effort—effective effort. Everybody we know who is in a highly profitable business carefully and consistently monitors gross margins.

Your Net Profit Is Going Down

Net profit decline is not *necessarily* a sign that prices are too low, but it *may* be a flag to that effect. If your gross margin is going down while your sales are going up, you have a pretty serious indication that your prices are too low. Again, we can't over emphasize how important gross margin is in determining if your prices are too low—or too high. You should price to achieve a constant, profitable gross margin on increasing sales brought about by selling good quality with impeccable service and, of course, on-time delivery.

Prices Are Below Your Competitors'

If your prices are below your competitors' (unless that is a deliberate, conscious business intention for a specific reason on your part), your prices *are* probably too low. Remember price does make a statement—a statement about not only the *quality* of your product or service, but also the *advisability* of doing business with you. As we said several times, if you were offered a new Rolls Royce for $87,000, you'd ask, "What's wrong with it?" or, "Do you have title to it?" You'd think that it was somehow defective, damaged, or stolen. If you tell someone your product is cheaper, they'll believe you, in every sense of the word. Low price makes a statement: a diminutive statement. High price also makes a statement: a positive, salutary statement.

There Is a Lot of Talk by Your Customers about How Good or How Much Better Run Your Organization Is Compared to Your Competitors

If your customers start telling you about what a fine business operation you have, you're leaving something on the table. The only time your customer will tell you what a fine job you're doing and what a great organization you have is when they're trying to encourage you to keep on doing what you've been doing—*underpricing*.

Have you ever bragged to anybody about what a great job he was doing—*to his face*? The only reason you ever brag about someone *to his face* is if you're trying to pull off *positive reinforcement* (that's what they call it in the psychological literature). If you let someone know how wonderful you think he is doing something, he likely will keep on doing it.

Just as an example, have you ever taken your kids out to a nice restaurant for lunch or dinner? Fancy place, you know, waiters in black suits, the whole thing. Your daughter's eight, your son's six. Nobody cries, nobody spills any milk, nobody kicks anybody, and nobody fights. (This is a fairy-tale.) At the end of the meal when you are driving home, you say, "Hey kids, I was really proud of you." Now why are you bragging about them to them? *Because you want them to keep on doing it!* Now, next week, same kids, same restaurant. While they only spill one glass of milk, you are most upset because your son punched your daughter, resulting in a loud, ear-splitting response. Later in the meal, your daughter, determined to get even, throws a spoonful of mashed potatoes at her brother and hits the lady at the next table. Are you still bragging about your kids on the way home?

The only reason your customers are going to tell you about what a "fine business" you've got is if they're trying to keep you doing what you've been doing. Now, to be sure, once in a while somebody might say, "Thanks, I appreciate what you did," and not be trying to con you. That's reasonable and realistic. But if you ever have too many customers telling you what a fine operation you've got, your prices are probably a little too low. The truth is, you really don't need to put up with that kind of talk. Raise your price and see how fast it stops.

General Absence of Any Complaints about Price

If nobody's complaining about price, your prices are too low. You're leaving something on the table. There ought to be somebody gasping and choking at your price. People who teach negotiation skills teach buyers to flinch. Some will flinch no matter what. If *nobody's* flinching, your prices definitely are too low.

Your Price Has Not Been Changed Over a Long Period of Time, Particularly during Known Inflationary Periods

If you cut your price X percent (say 2 percent), you have to do Y percent more volume just to make up for the 2 percent price-cut. If you don't raise your prices for a year, and inflation is 2 percent, what have you done? You've taken a de facto 2 percent price-cut. And we have not had a period without some form of inflation in the United States since the late 1920s. What does that mean to you? It means you really do have to raise your prices regularly.

If you are just too lily-livered to raise your price during inflationary times, you are, in essence, taking a price-cut. Very few people, if any at all, who will be reading these words were even alive during the last known period of deflation in the United States. Just remember, if you want to stay viable and make some money, you'd better be prepared to be a little bit aggressive on price. This means you really do have to raise your price on a regular basis.

Prospects Buy without Haggling Price, or Even Asking about What Is or Is Not Included in the Price, or Don't Even Ask the Price at All

If prospects contact you and just say, "Ship me a couple of these," or, "Why don't you send over four dozen of those," or, "I want to order this," your prices are too low. But what is a "fair" price? For most people, a "fair" price is the price they paid when they felt they got a great deal. If your prospects *know* you charge a "fair" price, your prices are too low.

If you really want to know what a "fair" price is, we'll tell you. It's the price that is charged when both people feel they got taken. If there is ever a "fair" price, both sides will figure they "got took." If your prospects know you're going to be fair with them, that surely means they feel you are leaving a lot on the table. When a prospect says, "Oh, I know you'll be fair," you should really take that as an insult. If your prospect feels they don't have to ask the price, and they can trust you to be fair, you are known as a low-price vendor. They should at least be concerned enough about your price to inquire about it—perhaps not paranoid, but at least reasonably alert to what your prices are; just enough to "keep you honest" as they say, just distrusting enough to ask, "Now what is that going to cost me?"

You're Getting Many New Customers for No Apparent Reason or Effort on Your Part

If you suddenly start getting lots of new customers, and you haven't been out there beating the bushes, advertising, promoting, marketing, and prospecting—they're just kind of swarming in through the door—*your prices are too low.* That's the "thundering herd beating a path to your door" syndrome. That's the better mousetrap at work.

The world is not going to beat a path to your door because you have a better product or offer a better service. The world is going to beat a path to your door *because the price on your product or service is too low.* Did People Express Airlines have a better product (service)? Or did they just have too low a price? Did Laker Airlines have a better product (service), or too low a price? When the "thundering herd is beating a path to your door," try raising your prices. They'll go away and leave you alone when you get your prices high enough to be "fair" to you.

You Have a Sudden Upsurge in Business Volume, Particularly from New Customers

If you suddenly start getting new customers and/or if old customers suddenly start buying from you, that tells you that the word is out that they can get a good deal from you—probably too good a deal. Think about it! The only reason you are going to get many new customers for no apparent reason—or that several customers who have been buying from you for a long time (but who use more than one source) would start buying *more* from you—is that they're probably buying less from your competition because your prices are too low.

Your Customers Insist That if There Is Faulty or Defective Product, You Have to Make the Product Work or Replace It, Rather Than Refund Their Money

One of the things that almost assuredly will indicate that your prices are too low can be discerned from the way your customers behave when there's a services problem or a defective product. There is one fundamental principle that is virtually never violated by any customer. If people buy something, and *feel they received a really good deal,* but they find something wrong with it, they will want you to repair, replace, or exchange the product. After all, "A deal is a deal, and you have to make it right." But if they buy something, and then find that maybe *they paid too much,* they will usually want their money back. "No, it's not any good, but another one probably isn't any good, either. Just give me my money back."

Do you want to develop a substantive way to determine if and when your prices are too high or too low? Try this strategy. Whenever you receive a customer complaint about your product or service, write down the name of the customer, the product, and what the customer *demanded* that you do about it. Here's why. Price-buyers tend to do the most complaining. You can identify products and/or services on which your prices are too low just by keeping such a log and periodically evaluating the frequency that certain items appear on it. Also, by keeping track of the customers who complain, you can start paying attention to what they buy. This is particularly valuable if you sell for a wholesaler, distributor, or retailer who sells a large variety of products. You'll find that the customers who begin to assemble in the "complainers group" will tend to buy only some specific items, but never buy other items. What does that tell you? That the products they are buying are probably priced a little low.

Remember, you also want to keep a record of what your customers demanded that you do about their complaint. Their demands can be classified into one of two varieties: (1) money back (discount, refund, credit memos, etc.), or (2) replacement (repair, exchange, etc.). When a customer wants money back, it's virtually always because they feel they've paid too much. Your prices may be too high on those items. But when they want you to repair, replace, or exchange it, your prices are likely too low.

Once you log customer complaints, you will begin to notice that a pattern inevitably begins to emerge. If you keep such an ongoing record and analyze it, you'll find that your customers' behavior will tell you when your prices are too high or too low on various products and services.

Labor and Materials Costs Have Increased without an Increase in Your Price

If your labor or materials costs begin to increase, especially if you're a manufacturer (but even if you're a retailer, wholesaler, distributor, contractor, or whatever) and your prices don't go up, obviously your margins will begin shrinking. That means you are going to have to raise prices, or your enterprise will probably begin to have trouble meeting payroll and other expenses. Remember, maintaining gross margin is an absolute necessity if any organization is to remain in business.

A Known Price-Buyer Starts Buying from You

You should always try to identify a few known price-buyers. The good news is they are almost always easily identified. They are the ones that really hammer you on price. If a known price-buyer starts unilaterally placing orders with you, your prices are probably too low on those items or services being ordered. So, you occasionally want to aggressively *try* to sell to a price-buyer—not because you really expect to get an order, but to make a price check. Please understand this: If you do get an order from a known price-buyer, you have found out that your prices are too low!

As we have suggested, price-buyers tend to take vast amounts of your sales time. Here's some advice worth repeating: If you're trying to earn a good living at sales, don't spend much time making calls on price-buyers. Just head on down the road when you've got the pure price-buyer who is doing nothing but wasting your time. But remember this, *once in a while,* you really need to try to sell to a price-buyer in order to do a price check.

Here's the way to do that. Don't call on known price-buyers very often. And when you do call on them, don't ever give them a better price; just give them your *real* price—the same deal that you're giving anybody and everybody else. Do this just to see if they'll buy at those prices, because if *they* buy, it will tell you that your prices are too low on what they buy.

This effort at checking the correctness of your price should not be considered unethical, and you shouldn't feel that you are merely using someone or taking advantage of their time. After all, most price-buying customers will willingly waste *your* time and effort. They will ask you for a quote or a bid just to do their own price check—perhaps just to keep the supplier they're intending to buy from "honest." They don't feel that there is anything wrong with that—even when it costs *you* thousands of dollars in time and effort to work up your bid or quote. They feel that's just part of your "cost of doing business." Therefore, you ought to be able to make a price check just as well as your customer. Shouldn't you?

We know a sales pro in Phoenix who amusingly refers to price-buyers as "bird-dogs." He both operates and sells in a ladies clothing store. We were in his store one day looking at some displays he was having installed and a woman came into the store. When he saw her he said, "See that lady over there? She's one of our bird-dogs."

We thought he was going to tell a joke, so we asked, "Oh, yeah, how's that?"

He said, "Yeah, she's one of our pointers."

Still not catching on, we asked, "What are you talking about?"

He said, "I'm sorry, that's just what I call some of our shoppers. She comes in here all the time. Never buys anything. I'm pleased she's here."

We asked, "Why would that please you if she doesn't buy anything?"

He said, "If she ever came in here and pulled anything off the rack and carried it over to the cashier to pay for it, we would have incontrovertible evidence that our price on that item is the lowest price to be had anywhere in the world. And we don't even have to pay her to do that research. In fact, she works at it almost full time and has never made a mistake."

You Have a Big Backlog of Demand, Particularly if That Demand Exceeds the Average for Those in Your Industry or with Whom You Compete

If your customers have to wait longer to receive a product or service from you than to receive the same products or services from your competition, your prices are probably too low. Look at it like this: If your prospects or customers are willing to wait three or four weeks to get something from you, and are willing to do so when they could get it from your competitors in a week and a half, what does that tell you? *Everybody* wants it yesterday. If your prospect or customer is willing to wait longer to get something from you when they can get it quicker from your competitor, it is because your deal is too sweet. Your prices are too low.

You might be offended at what we've just suggested, and say, "No, it's because our quality is that much better." Well, if your quality is so much better, why don't you charge more? To be sure, you don't want to drive off all your business, but willingness to wait for late delivery of "better quality" may very well dissipate when the price of that "better quality" goes up a little bit more. You see, if your customer prefers to wait longer for you to deliver, that waiting time is already a premium that they're willing to pay because you're so much better (cheaper). We'll bet that if you raised your price just a little more, some of that willingness to wait might likely go away. Again, this is a way to test your price. Check your backlog of orders compared to your competitor's backlog of orders, in terms of time, and it will tell you if you are too low. Relative to time, your order backlog should never exceed your competitor's order backlog.

How can you find out about your competitor's backlog? It's easy. You or a customer can just call them and say, "Hey, how long would I have to wait to get a shipment of whatever (or service on whatever)?" You'll find that they are most happy to give you the information. If you sell for a manufacturer, getting such information is particularly critical, but it is also important for those who sell services, are wholesalers, distributors, or even retailers, depending on what you're selling.

Customers Buy More than They Need, and You Know It

What does it mean if your customers buy more than they need? There are only a few reasons why this would ever occur: (1) They can't pay for it and want to load up before you find that out. (2) They are afraid they won't be able to get it in the future. (3) They are afraid your prices will rise, and they want to get it on hand before they do.

The way to handle all three of these reasons is simple. Raise your prices! Look at it this way: (1) If you are not going to get paid for it anyway, you may as well charge more. (2) If prospects or customers are afraid they are not going to get it and start hoarding, you can stop their hoarding by raising your prices. (3) If they are buying more than they need in anticipation of rising prices, they have just told you they think your prices already should be higher.

Your Organization's Bad Debt Collection Procedures Are Increasing in Activity

If you suddenly start spending more time collecting money that is owed to you, it could be that your prices are too low. Here's why. If your average day's receivables begin to increase, it may be because you have become attractive to price-buyers. And there are really only three reasons why your average day's receivables will ever increase. One is that the economy is turning sour, and nobody's paying any of their bills as fast. If that's the cause, you'll see it all over television, on the Internet, and in every newspaper. The second is because whoever does your credits and collections has gotten lazy. Let's assume that is not tolerated in your business. It isn't, is it? If that's the case, that leaves us with the third reason. You've gotten attractive to people who are slow payers; that is, to price-buyers.

If the economy hasn't gotten sour, and if you are just as aggressive on collecting your receivables, and if your daily receivables begin to increase, we'll bet that you have probably gotten attractive to price-buyers. If that's the case, what do you want to do? First, you want to take a look at your *new* customers. Because your new customers, in all likelihood, are the price-buyers who are running up your average collection time. Once you've identified them, look at what it is that they buy. In that way, your price-buyers (bird-dogs) will clearly point to those items on which your prices are too low.

Now, you might be saying, "My job's selling. It's not to monitor receivables." We understand that, but that's why it's necessary to learn how to work on the development of your career—not just your job. And your career isn't to operate as an island or in a vacuum. Your career mandates that you have to operate as an integrated whole with everything else in your organization. Many salespeople think, "My job is to go out there and get orders. I'm not concerned about receivables unless it's on sales I made (and then I'm only concerned if I'm not going to get a commission until they pay)." Astute salespeople aren't so shortsighted. As a sales professional, you need to learn to be concerned about receivables, because they can certainly identify areas where your prices are too low.

You're Getting Someone Else's Credit Cut-Off Business

If this is happening, your prices *are* probably too low. Price-buyers are not only slower payers, they often become *no* payers. If other suppliers have refused credit to customers who then come to you as prospects, you need to raise your price. If a price-buyer comes to you after he or she has been cut off from credit elsewhere, you may not have the lowest price in town, but you're probably next in line. There's no point in taking an order from somebody who isn't going to pay his or her bill. If you are getting your sales volume increases from customers who are struggling to stay in business, you aren't going to be gaining any profitable sales.

You Know Your Customer's Gross Margin Is Getting Bigger and Your Product Represents a Significant Portion of Your Customer's Cost-of-Goods-Sold

We have continually emphasized the role of gross margin throughout this book. The reason? Because gross margin is the most basic signal of the lifeblood of any organization, just like your pulse indicates some basics about your body. No pulse, no life. No gross margin, no wages, salaries, commissions, or profits.

If you sell to other businesses, you should learn to monitor *their* gross margin because that will tell you when to raise *your* prices. Unfortunately, few salespeople ever think this strategically when it comes to pricing, especially when it comes to raising (or lowering) prices. There is a propitious time to raise prices, and that is not necessarily (or even usually) annually or every spring or "whenever our costs go up." It is a function of doing it at the right time. And that right time is *always* when your customer's gross margin and sales volume are increasing—when he's getting fat, when he's making money. What is the sure-fire indicator that he's making money? His gross margin is increasing, particularly if his sales volume is increasing.

We saw this phenomenon several years ago in the automotive industry. Remember when they were making those embarrassingly high profits? When all the big auto companies were giving those million-dollar bonuses to their executives? The automotive manufacturers knew they were prime targets for price increases, so they said, "Absolutely no price increases." They stiff-armed their vendors, many of whom said, "Oh, okay. You will tell us when we can raise prices, won't you?" And they answered, "You bet, but not now, not now."

But the people who knew what they were doing simply passed along a price increase anyway. They knew that the automotive manufacturers would never tell them, "Okay, now is the time to raise prices—stick it to us." There is never a right time for you to raise prices in the eyes of any customer. Therefore, those who made money looked at the automotive manufacturer's gross margins and knew they could raise their prices. Automobile sales volume was increasing and the auto companies' gross margins were going up. This was the time to give them a price increase.

Like Yogi is reputed to have said, much can be observed by just watching. Pay attention. There is a time to raise prices, and your customer will tell you when that time arrives *if* you watch his gross margin and sales volume. The difference between a pro and an amateur in anything—sports, selling, or whatever—is that pros really study what they're doing. It doesn't make any difference if it's their golf swing, baseball swing, backhand, downhill skiing, or the prices they are charging. If you are really a pro, you *know* when you can go after the price increase.

Gut Feeling—You Just Simply Don't Feel Your Prices Are Too High

If your gut feeling just tells you "maybe we can do better," we'd recommend that you raise prices. Intuition does play a role in pricing. Some people seemingly just have a feel for knowing when they can get away with a higher price. But a lot of salespeople *don't,* because it has never even oc-curred to some that their prices may be too low, being (dis)content in the knowledge that their prices are *always* too high.

Your Request for Quotation Activity Increases Dramatically

This point is particularly important for anyone who works in a bid sit-uation, because if you want to sell (through bidding) at top dollar, you will need to keep a careful record of your requests for quotations (RFQs). If you are asked to bid six times in a normal week, and you suddenly find that you're asked to make eight bids per week, one of two things is happening: (1) either the economy's picking up (which, again, you'll read or hear about in the media), or (2) your prices are too low and the word's out on the street. If your RFQ activity is increasing, and everybody else's is too, your prices aren't necessarily too low. But don't forget that when business is booming and demand (necessarily) is high and climbing, you should be aggressively raising prices when the time is right. If your RFQ activity is increasing, but nobody else's is, there seems to be a genuine preference on the part of prospects to buy from you rather than someone else—and there's a good chance that it's because your price is too low.

Your Success Rate on Winning Opportunities You Bid on Significantly Increases

For example, if you normally get one out of four opportunities that you bid on, and all of a sudden, you find that you're getting one out of three, you can suspect that your prices are too low. A good example of this can be seen by studying those contractors who have survived in the construction business. Those who have continuously made money invariably look at the win/lose percentage of the contracts that they bid on. And when their success ratio begins to increase, the first thing they check on is whether they are making mistakes in estimating. Did we forget the other half of the roof, or something like that? Then they'll check out the take-offs, the estimates, and so forth. And if they don't find mistakes, they deduce, "Our prices are too low. We are winning more than our *fair share.* Maybe we have been sharpening our pencils a little *too* much!"

Incidentally, an unusually strong and critical parallel can be seen here for people who don't sell in bid situations. A lot of salespeople are terrified of losing a sale—*any* sale. However, if you want to sell at premium price, you'll have to learn that you must lose some sales, because you will never know your prices are high enough until you lose some. And the only way to do that is to *test* your prices. The nice thing about bidding is that you can test your price *every* time you submit a quote. When one sells off a price-list, it can get a bit expensive testing prices because just printing new price-lists every day can be expensive.

Incidentally, while we are talking about losing some sales, a word to the wise about market share. If you have a 25 percent market share, that means you *better* lose, on the average, three out of four jobs that you bid (assuming that all four jobs were the same size). When you strive to increase market share, there is a chance that your organization may be tempted to do that by "buying" the business. And that is not always a smart thing to do. Improving market share through sale of the right quality stuff, delivered on time, and backed up with good service will be profitable. But increasing market share at the expense of declining gross margin just might put you on the track of becoming the biggest player in your business to file for bankruptcy. (See Chapter 1 for the names of several of the world's largest companies that have recently accomplished that feat.)

You're Tempted to Sell at a Higher Price than You Are Asking or Quoting

Temptation is an interesting thing. A lot of people fight it. But one temptation that you ought to succumb to is your temptation to raise prices. If you are tempted to do so, give it a try. The worst thing that can happen is that you lose a sale. *You'll never know if your price is high enough until you test it.*

There is one reason why we would far rather sell in a bid situation than off a price-list. That is because we can test our prices with every job we quote, every day, and judge what percentage we win. That information tells us something, and puts us in an environment where we can test our prices every day and know what we're doing, rather than have to live with a flawed price-list or catalog for six months to a year or more. Trust us, you do your homework in a bid situation, you're going to know how you're doing all the time!

Remember, as we said at the outset of this book—*you* cut your price, *you* write those numbers down, *you* slit your throat. Your competition isn't the one that quotes your price, *you* do. If you are too low, too often, only one result—sooner or later—is going to happen. That is why you must *test* your price.

Your Prospect Tells You He Would Like to Work for Your Organization as a Salesperson

This one is thrown in just for fun. But there is some truth to it that merits consideration. We know of some situations where prospects have asked salespeople if their employer is hiring salespeople. Translation: "Anybody can earn a great living (for a while) at the prices you guys charge. It may not last forever because the company will probably go broke pretty quickly, but in the near term you must be picking up some pretty easy commissions." One more time, your prospect will alert you to the fact that your prices are too low.

Your Competitor's Salespeople Start Complaining to Your Customers about You and How You Do Business

If your competition starts complaining about you and the way you do business, your prices are probably too low. Why? Look at it like this. Have you ever complained about a competitor who charges higher prices than you do? If your competition starts complaining about the way you do business, you're hurting them. But you are also hurting yourself. You're leaving a lot on the table. We don't recommend getting any satisfaction from that.

A Potential Distributor for Your Products Is Already Bootlegging Your Products and/or Your Regular Distributors Are Charging Far Higher Prices than They Were Supposed To

If you've got a product that you sell to someone who, in turn, resells the product to the end user, and you find out that someone who is *not* an authorized distributor is selling your product, guess what? Your prices are way too low. The only way this can occur is that this unauthorized distributor is able to obtain your product, pay the bootlegger (who is probably your customer unless employees are stealing it from you), and still sell at a competitive price to the end user—and presumably make some money at it.

We know of a couple of incidents where this has happened, but the most telling example comes from a story told by the late Fred Wacker of how, as a manufacturer, he discovered that his price was too low. He was selling a product that had to be used in pairs. He sold the product strapped together in pairs to his distributors with a suggested resale price of $150 a pair. He discovered that his very best distributor was only hitting about 70 percent of quota, while most were hitting quota, or even a little better. Even those with a poor track record were hitting quota. So he went and talked to his best distributor, only to discover that the distributor thought that the price of the product was $150 *each* and they simply came strapped together in pairs because the user had to use them in pairs. He was selling them for $300 for the pair—and he was hitting 70 percent of quota. Guess what Fred did? He raised the price.

A lot of things can happen in a distribution channel. And if you sell to wholesalers and distributors, and/or you are a wholesaler or distributor, you're in that channel. Study the other distributors and wholesalers. What do they sell? Where do they get it? Look around. If an unauthorized distributor is bootlegging a product and competing with you, how can they do that financially? Consider what you can learn from the implications of what they are doing—as well as thinking in terms of taking legal action against them. (Make sure to check relevant state laws and get good legal counsel.)

Competition Bows Out and Can't Compete with You Because They Went Broke

"Hot dog! Ran those guys right out of business." Don't ever come bragging to us about how you ran a competitor out of business. If you ever get any satisfaction from running your competition out of business, you probably are making two major mistakes: (1) If you ran a competitor out of business, you're likely leaving a lot on the table. That's bad enough, but the other mistake is worse. (2) If you ran your competitor out of business, you have probably financially set up a *new* competitor to come into *your* business—a competitor who can and will compete with you on a lower price basis.

This is especially true if you use any sort of dedicated machinery or equipment in your business. Here's why that's a problem. When your competitor went broke, his assets were probably sold off in liquidation. That means somebody bought that machinery or equipment at liquidation value, and now you've just set up a new competitor to come in with far lower costs (and, subsequently, prices) with that newly purchased machinery or equipment.

For example, an airplane is a dedicated machine. Once you build an airplane, you may as well use it for an airplane. Today, who's flying the airplanes of airlines that went bankrupt since deregulation? Or did they just throw all those airplanes out in the ocean when those companies went bankrupt? We'll tell you who is flying them. Some of the old, existing carriers who snapped them up cheap, and some of the startup airlines that sprang up subsequent to airline deregulation. Admittedly, many of those airplanes from the late 1970s and early 1980s bankruptcies are now obsolete and are no longer flying (at least in the United States) but new airplanes built, bought, and put into service since then have experienced the same fate if they were bought (leased) by the newer startup airlines that have failed.

So, remember, if you run a competitor out of business, you have likely left something on the table in the process; but worse yet, you very well could have caused them to sell off any dedicated machinery or equipment that they had. This machinery or equipment could likely be put back into competition against you, which means that you're going to have even more price competition. It's not unlike an attacking army having its own artillery turned on them by the enemy. It's not good! So, don't ever price to try to run competition out of business. The only time that strategy works is if you are certain that you can buy that machinery or equipment from him—but if you ran him out of business, wouldn't it be pretty unlikely that he would let *you* get your hands on it?

Your Customers Quit Buying from You, But Then They Come Back

This is the absolute, most difficult concept for most salespeople to grasp, yet it is essential to understand it if you are ever going to sell at a high price. This is especially true if you are ever going to slam-dunk a sale. Again, here is the principle. *If you ever lose a customer, but then he comes back to you, your prices are too low.* This is particularly true if there was a bitter final scene. For example, he said unkind things about your mother's nocturnal habits, referred to you as the south end of a northbound horse, and then said with great glee he would *never* buy from you again.

If you ever lose a customer, but then he comes back to you, your first question should be: *Why* is he coming back? The answer is usually because he went and checked everybody he could, every vendor he could find, and he found out that you have the best deal. Your prices are lower than any-body else's (compared to the quality, service, and delivery you give). This tells you it's time to raise those prices.

The Principle of Shane

Back in ancient Hollywood history, there was an extremely well-known movie titled *Shane*. It was a classic western in which the late Alan Ladd played the title role. The most famous scene is the last one in the film, when Shane is riding off into the sunset and the little kid is chasing after him yelling, "Shane, come back, Shane!"

What's that got to do with selling? Plenty. Don't ever chase a prospect. If you ever have a prospect "walk" on you—"I can get it down the street, cheaper"—*Let him go!* Chasing him, yelling, "Shane, come back, Shane," is a stupid waste of time. *Let him go!* If he is a pure price-buyer (like he says he is), and he buys strictly on price (like he says he does), the only way you will stop him from going out the door is if you give him a price so low that he feels there is no point in shopping other sources; that is, a price so low that he knows he can't possibly do any better—the *lowest* price in town.

Let him go. Because when he goes, he will be doing *research* for you. Absolutely thorough, methodical, and accurate research concerning the value of what you have to offer compared to the value of every competitor of yours that he can find. The principle of Shane is this: If Shane ever comes back, *your last quote was too low.* If Shane comes back, he is saying (no mat-ter what he actually says), "Sir, Shane reporting in. I just went out and checked every deal I could find from your competitors and it looks like yours is the best deal. Is that last quote still good?" The answer to that is, "NO! Since we last talked that price has gone up (10 percent, $200, whatever)."

You—The Salesperson—Grab the Lunch Check, Pay Cash, Do Not Need Any Receipts, and Don't Want Any More Commission Checks This Tax Year

This one is a bit facetious and you may not even see the humor. But the point is a good one. If salespeople are getting fat and making tons of money while their employer's not making any money, prices are too low. We know that most of the people reading this are in sales, and you'd like to get real fat, and confidentially, you don't really care if your employer makes any money. Again, you may feel that way *until* your company files for bankruptcy.

Then, not only do you have to look for another job, you probably won't get any commissions that are still due you. Commissions aren't wages.

When you have a bankruptcy, commissions usually don't get paid. That's when you might learn the difference between 1099 income and W-2 wages. Of course, maybe you will make a lot between now and the time the organization goes belly up. But you can be assured that if you're getting fat at the expense of your employer's operating profits, the slack will come out of the chain. They will either wise up and cut your pay or commissions, or they'll file for bankruptcy.

A Competitor of Yours Wants to Buy from You and Says He Can't Make a Shipping Schedule and Wants You to Private Label, Especially if Producing the Product Requires Extensive Cost and Effort on Your Part

Can you afford to sell to a competitor? If you have a competitor who can afford to buy from you (at your prices) and resell to someone else, you have a sales and marketing problem, and/or your prices are too low. We occasionally run across businesses who sell to their competition, but in most cases, we can't figure out why. It's understandable if you're selling to a competitor who can sell in a market that you're excluded from (because of a law or something). But we can't understand how an organization can possibly sell to a competitor who's selling to a customer that is fair game in the marketplace. If you're prohibited from selling in Noplaceland, and you have a competitor who's authorized to sell in Noplaceland, you might sell to them. That makes sense. But if you sell to a competitor who sells to customers you can and should be selling to, your prices are too low or you have a sales/marketing problem. Why can't you reach that customer? And/or how can the competitor who buys from you and can afford to pay your price still (presumably) profit by selling to a (should be) customer of yours?

The Prospect Comes to Your Office with a .357 Magnum, Points It Squarely between Your Eyes, and Says, "You Have to Quote This Job Because I Want You to Have It"

If a prospect makes it too easy for you to sell to him, your prices are too low. If a prospect comes to your office and insists on you making a bid or a quote, your prices are too low. There may be even other, more sinister reasons that they want a quote so badly from you. But if they're waiting on the curb for you to come to work in the morning, or if they're climbing in over the transom when you're closing up at night saying, "Hey, you know, we didn't get a bid from you yet, and we need one so you can get the work," it's because they know your bid will be lower than anyone else's.

The Prospect or Customer Asks, "Is This Price List Still in Effect?" or, "Is This Quote Still Good?"

The answer is "no." That's right, "no." Whenever a prospect or customer asks, "Is this price list still in effect? Is this quote still good? Is this bid still good?" the answer is, "no." The only reason anyone would ask you if this quote is still good is because they *cannot believe* that this quote is still good. But they will ask on the off-chance you're really dumb enough to say, "Yes." They reason that they may as well take a shot at it. Putting it that way is far better than saying, "I'm sure this price isn't in effect any more, is it?" and thereby alerting you to the fact that they think your prices are too low. Know how to fix this and prevent it from happening in the first place. Always place the time frame inside of which your price is still valid—for example: "Prices good for 30 days or 45 days."

CHAPTER 15

INDICATORS THAT YOU
ARE OVERPRICING

Question: "What are you going to say when they ask about your price?"
Answer: "Look hurt."

—Sporting goods salesman in Texas

It is certainly possible to overprice any product or service. But overpricing is a far less common practice than is underpricing. The fundamental reason for this is that most people are so terrified that their prices are too high that they never even come close to pushing their prices as high as they really ought to be. As a consequence, they rarely, if ever, test their price in any meaningful sense. Virtually always, they're so *certain* that they'll lose all their sales that they won't even sample the waters and try raising their price.

Interestingly, many people have discovered, albeit inadvertently, that their sales volume actually increased as a consequence of raising prices. To be sure, when you do raise prices, you usually do lose some sales. But as we have stressed, you can afford to lose some sales, because you still will make more money by raising prices. The question is not so much whether you will lose sales volume. Rather, the question is whether you will lose so many sales that you'll lose profitability to the organization and income for the people who work there.

We all know that printing errors occur in books, magazines, newspapers, advertisements, catalogs, published price-lists, and even on the Internet. So what happens when someone makes a mistake and publishes *too high* a price in a direct-mail catalog? There is no real opportunity to correct that price short of publishing an errata sheet. And if the erroneous price is not caught before the catalog is distributed, there is no way to correct the price at all. You just have to live with it. Yet, people in the catalog and direct mail business give numerous examples of where the wrong price was printed and the price was entirely too high compared to what the price was supposed to be—and yet sales volume, in many cases, actually increased over what was projected. And in even more cases, even though there was no gain in sales, the normal sales volume was maintained. No loss. Zip. Zero. Nothng.

We need to make one more critical point relative to worrying whether your prices are too high. Many businesspeople feel they have competitors who are always 2 percent below their price. And they've noticed that when they lower their price 5 percent or 10 percent or whatever percent, their competition lowers their price the same amount and still manages to be 2 percent lower than they are. Yet, these same people don't seem to realize that if they would raise their price, that competitor who is 2 percent lower than they are almost always raises its price by the same amount . . . and is *still* only 2 percent lower. In the final analysis, the only sure-fire solution to obtaining a reasonably high, profitable price for selling your products and services is to be willing to test your price to see what happens when efforts are made to sell at that higher price. The ability to sell at a higher price is a function of your selling skill, because there is no *right* or *correct* price.

BUT I REALLY THINK MY PRICES ARE TOO HIGH

Yes, there is certainly a possibility that your prices *are* too high. And just as there are indicators that your prices are too low, there are indicators that your prices may be too high on your products or services. Perhaps a brief look at some of the major indicators of overpricing is warranted for purposes of completing your understanding of this whole pricing issue.

Your Competitors' Prices Are Lower Than Yours

If your competitors' prices are legitimately lower than yours, it is possible that your prices are too high. Remember that the basic thesis of this book is that you should fully expect your competitors' prices to be lower than yours. But just because your competitors' prices are lower than yours does not necessarily mean your prices are too high. And even if everybody's prices *are* lower than yours, it is still not necessarily an indicator that your prices are too high. Certainly, however, if you have other competitors whose prices are as high as or higher than yours, it is doubtful that your prices are too high. But if ALL your competitors' prices are lower than yours, yours could be too high.

Your Gross Profit Percentage Is Growing— But Your Sales Are Not

A second indicator that your prices may be too high (or perhaps have gotten too high with your last price increase) can occur when your gross margin or gross profit percentage starts growing but your sales volume begins to decline. As we've pointed out, your gross margin or gross profit is that percentage of the sales dollar that is left after you have paid for what you sold. The only way gross profit can decline is if your sales price is too low relative to those costs. Likewise, the only way your gross profit can increase is if those same costs are low relative to your price. Therefore, increasing gross profit or gross margin percentages can be an indicator that your prices are too high. But this increase in your gross margin had better be the result of higher prices *coupled with a decline in your sales volume.*

If you raise your price and you actually sell more, you'll not only be experiencing an increasing gross margin but increasing sales volume, and there'll be a whopping increase in your organization's operating profit and its ability to pay the people that work there—including you. This is not an unheard-of phenomenon, particularly when people have been charging too low a price to begin with. Therefore, if your gross profit percentage is growing, and your sales are not declining, and/or if your sales actually are increasing, this would definitely not be an indicator that your prices are too high. However, it could be possible that your prices are too high if you experience an increasing gross profit margin with declining sales. Just be sure that the declining sales are more than offsetting the increase in gross profit dollars, which could still cause your firm, and the people working there, to realize as much or more profitability on the declining sales.

You Receive a Significant Number of Customer Complaints (or Inquiries) about What Is or Is Not Included in Your Price

Naturally, customers will tell you that your prices are too high, and salespeople (including you) will also complain that your prices are too high. However, neither of these is a valid test of overpricing. In fact, many experienced sales managers will argue that the one sure-fire indicator that a business's prices are too low is when the salespeople *quit* complaining that their prices are too high.

You should take it as a given that your customers and salespeople around you will complain that prices are too high. But an indicator that prices (perhaps) really are too high is when those making inquiries about the price directly ask what is or what is not included in the price. For example, if your customer thinks your prices are too high, they will often ask, "What does that include?" Many times people will hear a price that they think is extremely high, but will almost always assume that the price is reasonable and, therefore, try to justify it. What they are trying to do is to validate in their own mind the reasonableness of the *seemingly* too-high price.

You should analyze these inquiries very carefully to determine that the customer is, in fact, trying to validate the *correctness* of the price. For example, if a travel agent says that a trip to a vacation spot is $2,000, the customer might ask, "Does that include lodging?" or, "Does that include airfare?" or even, "Does that include meals?" If someone is buying a coffee mug and the clerk says the price is $20, it would be doubtful that the customer would inquire, "Does that include delivery?" or, "Does that include all taxes?" but they might ask, "Is it hand-painted?" or "Is this made by a local artist?" The point is, when a price is perceived as being high, customers will try to verify the many dimensions of the price in trying to ascertain that it is a *reasonably* high price.

Your Dollar Sales Volume Is Declining

Another potential indicator that your prices are too high is if and when you begin to experience a decline in sales volume. However, as we all know, sales volume can decline for lots of other reasons, too. One of those reasons is lack of sales effort. A second reason, of course, can be lack of promotional and advertising activity. Yet, a third reason can be the economy, and still

Higher Prices, Higher Sales

Many CEOs are scared to death of pricing their products higher than those of their competitors—even if the competing products aren't of equivalent quality or usefulness. Walter Riley, who heads G.O.D., Inc., knows the feeling. But his own experience with pricing strategy has taught him that you shouldn't be afraid to charge more if you're confident you're offering more. At G.O.D., an overnight freight business, a price boost was the key ingredient in a mix that led to meteoric growth. From its founding in 1983 until three years later, Riley kept his prices competitive with other truckers' prices. "We were toe to toe with them," he says, "and we still weren't getting any new business." In 1986, the company began pricing at a 5-to-7 percent premium, and the price change, along with a small acquisition, brought sales from $3.8 million to $12.7 million in one year. Charging a premium price, Riley says, meant instant credibility. It also differentiated G.O.D. from its competitors. "Raising our prices startled purchasing agents into seeing that we weren't just like our competitors. And they were willing to pay extra for overnight delivery." Did he spot a trend?

another reason can be a set of new competitors in the marketplace. There are many other reasons, too.

So, just because your dollar sales volume begins to decline, it does not mean that your prices are too high. However, one should look at timing relative to this question. If you raise prices and your dollar sales volume begins to decline, it may indicate that your prices are too high. This is especially true if you are studying the other marketplace indicators that impinge on the sales volume that you might be expected to do, and nothing has changed.

In the absence of any other reason for your sales volume to be declining, and given that you simply raised prices in the reasonably near past, there may be grounds to believe that your prices are too high.

Your Competition's Share of the Market Is Increasing

If your competitors' market share is increasing, it is highly possible that your prices are too high. Or it may be an indicator that they're trying to "buy in" to the market. Many people believe that market share ensures success in the marketplace. However, history really shows no such correlation and is replete with examples of the largest single competitors in a marketplace filing for bankruptcy. For example, the world's largest retailer has filed for bankruptcy; the second largest convenience food chain in the United States once filed for bankruptcy; the largest public transportation company in the United States filed for bankruptcy; the largest retail grocery chain filed for bankruptcy; the largest bus company filed for bankruptcy; the largest cement manufacturer filed for bankruptcy, and so on. Unfortunately, the pursuit of market share has been touted as a source of success in business in many of our nation's leading business schools and most respected journals. Consequently, many people believe that market share, per se, is the secret to success in business and blindly pursue it, assuming that profitability will necessarily emerge.

Let's face facts: If market share ensured success, General Motors wouldn't have the problems they have faced for more than 20 years. In the 1950s and 1960s, General Motors' main concern was that they had *too much* market share and the Justice Department would break the company up. Today, they worry about sustaining even a viable market share. A lot of good "owning the market" did them. Don't be so concerned about losing market share to your competition, particularly if your competitor is a fool, blindly trying to increase their share of the market. Remember, it is better to be profitable at whatever volume of business you're doing than to go broke while being the largest guy in the business. You're just a bigger bust if you're the biggest in the business when you do go bust.

From a strategic standpoint, you should also think in terms of your share of the market relative to business volume. Almost always when business is turning down in a recessional cycle, companies gain market share. Likewise, when business is improving, they will almost always lose some market share. The reason for this, of course, is that in a business downturn many companies either abandon a product/market or go out of business and, consequently, those who stay in business find an increasing share of the market. Conversely, when business is expanding, more players enter the marketplace and, as a consequence, most *all* competitors in the marketplace lose some percentage of market share.

You Are Receiving Many Price Complaints

If you are receiving too many complaints about your price, it is highly possible that your prices *are* too high. However, once again, be very cautious about simplistically believing that the number of price complaints you receive is the *sole* indicator that your high prices are too high. Many sales-people receive price complaints *because they invite and encourage price complaints*. As we have pointed out, many salespeople encourage and invite price complaints by the way they handle the very issue of price itself. Lines such as, "Isn't it a crime the price they charge for this stuff?" or "Do you think eight bucks per unit would be too much?" invite price complaints from customers. It may be that your prices are too high. And, of course, if your prices really are too high, you probably will get a lot of price complaints. But be sure you are not inviting or actually causing those price complaints to occur yourself.

Whenever There Is a Request for an Adjustment because of a Faulty or Defective Product or Poor Service, the Complaint Is Actually a Disguised Price Complaint

When a customer has bought something from you, and the customer is not satisfied with that product or service, he or she likely will register a complaint. By studying these complaints, you can determine if, in fact, you are receiving a truly faulty or defective product or service complaint, or if it is a veiled complaint about price. Such a determination can be made with surprising ease. Almost always when people complain about something that they bought, and they feel that the price was fair to them (meaning reasonably low), they will simply want you to repair, replace, exchange, or somehow make good the product or service that they bought, believing that "a deal's a deal." However, if people buy something and then discover that they could have bought it cheaper from someone else, they almost always tell you that they want some kind of credit memo or a refund.

If you are sincerely interested in determining whether or not you are charging an adequately high price, maintain a record of all complaints about allegedly faulty or defective product or service you receive from your customers. You should not only record what the product or service was, but also record the *demand* made by the customer to make it right. Such demands can be categorized as either some form of, "I want my money back," or, "I want you to repair/replace/exchange the product (or service)." If most of the complaints you get are about someone wanting their money back, your prices are probably too high. On the other hand, if most of the complaints you get are for repair/replace/exchange, your prices are definitely not too high. In fact, they are probably too low.

Your Wholesaler Asks Quite Seriously, "Is This the Retail Price?"

If you sell to someone who resells your product, those people may indicate to you that your prices are too high. The way they do that is by seriously asking if the price you're quoting is the retail (resale) price. If that customer who is going to resell your product is absolutely dumbfounded at your prices, this may be an indicator that your prices are too high. However, again, a warning is necessary here. If the customer is going to resell your product, he will probably feel that the more he can beat on you in an effort to get a lower price, the more that will facilitate his ability to resell the product at a lower price. Therefore, you need to be careful in interpreting the veracity of such statements by customers who intend to resell your product.

As a Salesperson, You Begin to Ask, "If I Take Less Commission, Can I Sell at a Lower Price?"

Sometimes salespeople in the field do face a situation in which their prices are too high. And it is not unusual for salespeople to offer to take lower commissions in an effort to get a sale, because they simply know that they're not going to get the sale at the price that they are currently asking. This situation most commonly emerges in large volume sales. One situation comes to mind concerning a company that sold furniture to hotels. The salesperson had a lead on a sale for 500 rooms of furniture to a new hotel under construction. She decided that, at the prices they were currently asking, her company would not get the order, but if the company "got competitive," they could get the order for the entire 500 rooms of hotel furniture. She approached her boss and suggested that she was so certain that she could get the sale that she would be willing to give up half her commission in order to lower the price to get the sale. This practice was successful and probably did accurately indicate that the company's initial price was too high. It is less likely, however, that such tactics would work in a very small order situation. But a reality check here. How often do you go to your sales manager and offer to take a smaller commission in order to cut the price and "get the sale"? If it's too often, you're on dangerous ground.

Customers Are Calling the Office and Inquiring about Your Prices or to "Double Check" Your Prices

Many times when people receive a price that they believe to be outrageously high, particularly in a written quotation format, they will check with someone else to be sure that the quotation was accurate. Again, when such inquiries occur, whoever fields those inquiries should be extremely cautious about automatically assuming that this is an indicator that their prices are too high. However, it is a distinct possibility.

You Have a Tough Time Explaining Your Prices

If you find yourself negotiating and you have a tough time justifying your prices compared to your competitors' prices, it is possible that your prices are too high. Again, however, it is possible for you to invite and encourage price complaints and/or to be so stupid, lazy, unthinking, or naïve that you cannot adequately explain why it is that your product or service does warrant a higher price because of its superior quality, your service, delivery, spare parts, customer service, or some other quality. Simply having to answer questions as to why your price is higher than your competitor's price is not an indicator that your prices are too high. In fact, high-performing salespeople who sell at high prices view that as an opportunity to suggest to the prospect the very reasons why their prices are higher, and why the prospect should buy from them at that higher price. However, if you seem to be unable to explain why your prices are warranted when they are significantly higher than your competitions', it is possible that your sales prices are too high.

In summary, it *is* certainly possible to have prices that are too high. The reality checks outlined in this chapter might indicate that your prices are not only higher than your competitors' prices, but *are* too high. However, always keep in mind that it is very difficult to charge too high a price. Your price only becomes too high when you don't think it is warranted, and/or you cannot justify the reasonableness of your higher price because of your superior quality, service, or delivery. You should also keep in mind that if you are going to be a viable competitor in the marketplace, you probably *must* charge a higher price than your competitor. The reason for that is that, ultimately, most businesses that go broke do so by cutting prices or failing to raise prices when they should. Therefore, there is a high degree of probability that if you are in a viable business, your prices must be higher than some of your competitors' prices. The businesses that fail are almost always those that charge lower prices—not those that charge a higher price.

CHAPTER 16

HOW PROSPECTS WILL ATTEMPT TO GET YOU TO CUT YOUR PRICE

How can you advertise your product as being the finest quality if you buy cheap stuff?

—Supplier to Automotive Industry

Several years ago while working in Tampa with a group of professional purchasing specialists, one of your authors was intrigued when they started talking about how they purposely beat up on salespeople. The purchasers actually were trading secrets on "tricks" they used to get salespeople to cut their prices. The author's initial reaction was one of resentment, since he has always been extremely sales-oriented. It was as if they were talking about his family in front of him, but they didn't realize it was his family they were talking about—and they certainly weren't saying very nice things. He became a little uncomfortable and was about ready to leave, when he realized that he could shamelessly become the "fox in the henhouse": He could write some of this stuff down and use it to help some of his sales buddies. In fact, that's when he first conceived the idea of developing the material in this book on the subject of pricing and profitability.

LEARN THE TRICKS AND COMBAT THEM

We certainly haven't recorded all the myriad tricks that tough, smart, aggressive prospects can use to beat you up on price, but any veteran salesperson has encountered many of these maneuvers at one time or another. This chapter is certainly not intended to be a divine revelation. Instead, its purpose is to shed some light on what you can do when some of these situations occur. Many of these points will be ones mentioned earlier in the book. However, we wanted to revisit them for emphasis, put them all in one place, and deal with each in more detail.

They Stiff-Arm You

This is accomplished by simply saying, "I can't pay any more," or, "I can only pay X amount." This tactic is designed just to get you to knuckle under, as if the amount had been decreed from heaven.

The way you foil this trick is to say, "Why not?" or, "How did you come up with that figure?" When you respond with that, they're going to say, "Because (somebody) said so." When they say, "Because so and so said so," they're clearly identifying the person with whom you can most effectively do your selling.

Any highly successful salesperson knows that you sell to *decision makers* and people who *influence* decision makers in the real world. However, it is sometimes difficult to uncover who those people really are. When your prospect says, "Because so and so said so," he or she is telling you who the real decision maker is.

Your job, of course, is figuring out how to get to that decision maker, because until you do, you can't really sell the quality, service, or whatever it is that you feel is your competitive advantage. Remember, however, that you really do need to know what your competitive advantage is in order to sell it. A business-to-business buyer's job is often just to beat you up on the price once they've made sure they will get the right stuff—on time. If you can deliver the right stuff—on time—and especially if your competition can't, you have to get to the decision maker in order to explain that to them. That's all part of salesmanship, and remember, that's known as back-door selling. So don't just lie down and die when your prospect says, "We can't pay any more." Ask, "Why not?" and find out who it is you should have been selling to in the first place.

They Imply (or Flatly State) That Your Competitor's Quality, Service, and/or Delivery Is as Good or Better Than Yours

When your customer says, "I can get the same exact thing from your competitor, and cheaper," your internal reaction to that should be, "Then why are you talking to me?" Now, don't actually say that out loud, of course, but *ask and answer* that question silently to yourself. Think: If my prospect says to me, "I can get just as good a deal (or better) down the road," why doesn't he do it? The answer is because he can't, doesn't want to, or had better not. If, in fact, he could get a better deal down the street, he wouldn't spend any time telling you about it! He would just run you off and place his order with your competition, wouldn't he?

How do you handle this maneuver? Waste some of your prospect's time (professionally, of course). Why should you do that? Look at it this way: Your prospect's time is valuable to him. If he knew of a better deal, he'd just take it. But by spending time telling you about a better deal, somewhere else, he is actually signaling you that he (1) really can't get a better deal—he's misrepresenting price or the other vendor can't deliver on time or is refusing to sell to him (perhaps because he hasn't paid his last bill); (2) can get the deal, but really doesn't want to (which means he prefers to buy from you and the grounds for that preference, of course, warrant a higher price to you); or (3) can get the deal but had *better not,* because so-and-so told him not to do it.

Even when your prospect is telling you the truth—that he *can* get just as good a quality, service, and delivery from your competitor at a *lower price*—it doesn't mean he *will* buy from them. It just means he is trying to get you to cut your price. What that prospect is really saying, even then, is, "I want you and everything about you. I just want your competitor's price."

Your reaction to that should always be, "If you want everything about me, you will need to pay my price. If you want my competitor's price, then you get him and everything about him: his lack of inventory, trained support staff, investment, parts, experience, his inability to deliver, his lack of warranty or guarantee, and everything else." Remember what we have continually stressed throughout this book; often prospects WILL lie (or at least exaggerate just a little) about the other guy's deal. And also remember, they are often told *what* to buy and/or *from whom* to buy it. For a multiplicity of reasons—and who knows what those reasons may be—that person may have to (or badly need to) buy from you. But he is still apt to say, "I can get it cheaper down the road," in the hope that you will be obliging and cut your price.

As we emphasized earlier, if your prospects really spend a lot of time talking to you about the better deal they can get from someone else, they not only may *want* to buy from you, they may *have* to buy from you. Why? Because your competitor *won't sell to them!* Maybe your prospects haven't paid their last bill, or they are just too difficult to do business with, or pay but it is just too much trouble to get paid, or it is troublesome just to comply with their silly rules or paperwork.

They Say, "Let's Write It Up at a Lower Price This Time—We'll See if We Can't Pay More Later When We Know How Well You Can Perform"

Let's analyze this one. This argument by your prospect is a simple admission that he does pay more for good quality, service, and delivery (why else do you have to be at a *lower* price than the vendor he is buying from *now* unless he is tacitly admitting that *proven* better performance is worth something more to him) and, therefore, that this reaction is likely a ploy.

Look at it this way: If you can do it once (sell at a lower price), you can do it again, and again, and again. Don't ever fall for lines like, "You can get your foot in the door," or, "We can get things rolling." These old ploys prey on a notion that economists call *marginal pricing, incremental price,* or *going after the marginal customer.* Remember what we have said about not messing with price-buyers? Reason 4 was, "They will tell your other customers how little they paid you."

Marginal pricing will work only when your customers *can't* (be careful not to read that as "don't" or "probably won't") talk to each other. The word is *can't* talk to each other. Because we'll assure you that if they *can* talk to each other, *they will.* Federal and state governments make it illegal for vendors to fix prices, but that certainly doesn't discourage buyers from comparing prices. If your customers can talk, be assured they will.

The theory of marginal or incremental pricing is a great academic concept. There's only one thing that economists forget to tell you when they advise you to do it. Customers are likely to compare notes. And when they do, your price-buyer (for whom you cut this great deal) will tell other prospects and customers about that deal, and in the process, end up training them to go after the same, lower price. Let us give you an example or two.

Purchasing agents talk to other purchasing agents. Buyers talk to other buyers. Owners of companies also talk to other owners of companies. Physicians talk to one another. Network administrators talk to one another. And mortgage brokers talk to one another. It really makes no difference who your prospects or customers are. People almost always talk to people in *their industry*. Contractors talk to contractors, manufacturers talk to manufacturers, and retailers talk to retailers. But, even more specifically, retailers in the clothing industry talk to retailers in the clothing industry, and people who manufacture concrete blocks talk to people who manufacture concrete blocks.

Your customers almost assuredly will talk to your prospects and other customers—and it only takes *one* contact for the word to get out. Let's say you sell electrical supplies and equipment, and you sell to 27 electrical contractors in your territory. But let's say you're not selling to the other 49 that do business in your territory. So, to "get your foot in the door" with a new customer, you cut your price.

You are going to slit your throat if you do that. Do you know what's going to happen to you? If you sell to a new account for $18, and you've been selling to your other accounts for $20, you can bet that, sooner or later, that new customer is *going* to talk to someone from one of your older accounts. And you know what they'll say. They'll start talking about business. And the new account guy will say to the old account guy, "Hey, you buy from those yo-yos?"

"Yeah, sure do."

"What do you pay for (copper, outlets, switches, etc.)?"

"We pay $20. What do you pay?"

"Well, you better learn to buy smarter. I'm only paying $18."

"What?"

"Yep, $18. You better learn something about buying."

"You can't be buying those for $18."

"Am too, am too! In fact, I will fax you a copy of the invoice on my last order from them, along with a copy of the canceled check to go with it."

And the word will spread from there to all your old accounts. Now, what have you just taught the old accounts? You've taught them to come and ask you for what price? $18? No, they don't want $18. They want $16 to compensate for having been taken advantage of in the past. That's what happens in the real world. And it makes no difference what you sell or do when you sell it. Remember, every type of prospect talks to others like them. They get together, they have conventions. And even when people change jobs or lose jobs, they seldom change industries. They just change employers. And they're going to remember what they were paying over there. Never forget, you end up *training* your customer to beat you up on price.

They Say, "We Don't Care about Quality, Service, or Delivery—It Doesn't Make Any Difference; Price Is All That's Important"

When this happens, tell your prospect, "Okay! We'll have it to you in four years." But then he'll say, "Oh no, no, we need it next Thursday." Then say, "So, you do care about delivery," to which he will reply, "Well, yeah, but quality's not important." Say, "Okay, then we'll send you nothing but rejects." But then he'll say, "No, no, it's got to be top quality."

When your prospects say they don't care about quality, service, or delivery, they are really trying to negate your competitive advantage. They'll say, "We don't care about this, we don't care about that, all we care about is the price." But they are saying that in the hope they can get you to cut your price and still get better quality, service, and delivery from you. If you push them, every time they'll say, "No, we have to have it by _____," or, "We can't take seconds."

They Change the Quality, Service, or Delivery Requirement Once You Have Struck Your Deal

Here's the way this one works: They say, "We have to have top quality, top service, immediate delivery. In short, we want a 10 on a scale of 1 to 10."

Of course, you'll say, "Then the price is a 10. You want a 10, the price is a 10." But they will say, "No, no, no. The price has got to be 5."

Now wait a minute—why is it *always* and *only* your *price* that's negotiable? Why isn't anything other than your price negotiable?

One thing you must remember is that *everything* is negotiable, not just price. Keeping that in mind may enable you to drive a hard bargain—and strike a deal. But that is not the end of it. What this ploy amounts to is that *after* you have struck a deal—let's say you promise an 8 on quality, service, and delivery, at a price of 8; then they *raise* the quality, service, and delivery back to a 10 *after* the deal is struck. And they almost always do it the same way—they call you and you hear this silly, nervous laugh and it then goes like this, "Hee, hee, um, uh, guess what? You know that training session for our programmers we set up for three weeks from now? Well, hee, hee, my boss said we've got to have them trained by next week. That won't be any problem, will it?"

If you say, "Oh, that won't be any problem," you are crazy! Because what they are trying to do is maneuver you into an earlier date—at the three-week delivery price! That is, they want your ability to have the training staff, materials, equipment, and facility available, regardless of your filled calendar—at your competitor's price!!

How do you handle that? If you are smart, what you'll say is, "Oh, yeah, I think we can do that for you, *but let me find my water-cooled calculator* so we can figure out how much *more* that will cost."

On these deals, you must always use your "water-cooled calculator." You can't use a standard electronic calculator because it will overheat. That's because any changes of this nature require the use of big, wide numbers, and you have to keep hitting the "X" bar so many times that any conventional, high-tech calculator will blow it up! The principle is this: If your prospect ever wants to change *anything,* you must raise the price. That is true whether he or she wants to change things up or down, whether he or she wants more or less, sooner or later. And if you don't believe that is done, look at what the oil and gas industry did in the United States. When we said we wanted lead in our gas, they said, "That will cost you extra." But when we said we *didn't* want lead in our gas anymore, they said, "That will cost you extra." And the oil and gas industry is only one example. Another comes from the construction industry. In fact, the typical contractor has a word for it. He calls it a "change order." And any shrewd contractor will tell you confidentially, "You bid the job close and make your money on the change orders." In fact, a lot of contractors *live* for change orders. Example: Let's say you're building yourself a little cottage on the lake. And you're out there looking around while the walls are going up. You're in what is to be the master bathroom and you decide that the closet looks a little dinky. You think, "Maybe we could move that one wall just a little to make the closet a little bigger."

So you explain the problem to the builder. And the first thing he'll say is, "Oh, my goodness." Then his eyes roll back up into his head, and then they will refocus on you. Then he will say, "That's a load-bearing wall," to which you will say, "That's not a load-bearing wall. There's nothing below it. There's nothing above it. What do you mean, that's a load-bearing wall?"

To which he responds, "You don't understand. The *particular* wall that you want moved happens to be the *physical stress center* of the entire country! Oh my, if we have to move that wall. . . . Oh, we're going to have to rip out everything we have already put in. We're going to have to tear out the foundation. We're going to have to push that mountain back about 40 feet. . . . Oh my! We can't do it. Well, maybe we could, but we'll have to have an additional $200 million to do it. Well, we'll see if we can do it, for another $200 million." Of course, this is an absurd exaggeration, but you get the idea. Changes in the original deal automatically up the price.

Let us provide you a real-world example of how an association executive tried to pull this, "Let's change the quality, service, delivery at the original price," ploy with one of your authors. This gentleman called, wanting to know if the author would be available to present a workshop for a couple of days at his trade association convention. He could, and the agreement was signed for two mornings, back to back. That was in June. In December, about a month before the meeting, the author's phone rang. The trade association executive identified himself, and then he said, "Hee, hee, hee . . . ."

Immediately, your author thought, "Here comes the change order. Get out the water-cooled calculator, change order coming."

The trade association executive continued, "Hee, hee, hee, guess what? My board has decided to do an afternoon session in addition to the two morning sessions at our convention."

The response? "That's great. *Who* are you going to get to do the afternoon session?" Well, the association executive wondered aloud, could they maybe get *you* to do it?

You don't think your kind, caring author stuck it to him, do you? Well, he did. You're right. But only because he's a consummate educator—not because of greed. You see, he felt it was his moral duty to teach the association executive about the hazards of a change order. It had nothing to do with any pecuniary gain. Hee, hee.

The honest truth is, if the executive had been honest up front about how much he wanted the author to work, the author might have agreed to do the additional program at the same price for the two mornings and the afternoon as for the two mornings. Frankly, your author would rather work with the group then lie by the pool. But when the executive came back with that "hee, hee, hee," it was obvious that he was trying to get a half-day of work for free. So your author used his water-cooled calculator on him. You will almost always know when they're working you, because you'll always hear that "hee, hee, hee." If they have really made a mistake and gotten themselves over a barrel, they don't say, "hee hee hee. My boss said . . ." Instead, they'll say, "Hey, I'm bleeding to death. I'm hurting. I have to have this stuff by Thursday. I don't care what it's going to cost me. Can you get it here?"

You Are in Your Customer's Office, the Big Boss Stops By, Interrupts Your Conversation, and Says Intimidating Things Like, "Are You Still Buying from These Guys?"

Why do they do that? Well, with an inexperienced sales type, if someone important says, "I thought we decided to quit buying from these guys," the salesperson will often panic and think, "I can't believe it, I'm about to get thrown out of here."

You think that's not planned? You think that's not intimidation? You think they don't orchestrate that? The whole purpose behind it is to scare the salesperson who's never been through it before. By saying, "I thought we decided to quit buying from these guys," they hope that they can scare you into thinking, "I better go to the lowest price I can think of right now, or I'm going to get thrown out of here." Don't fall for that. Remember, you didn't just happen to sneak through the system for no reason. If you're there, they're interested in buying from you. And, now that they're working you, hammering on you, and beating on you, all they are really telling you is that they *want* to buy from you—but they want to see if they can get you to cut your price.

They Buy on Their Own Turf

This trick is purely psychological. They know that they can probably work you on this point. They can rig all the props. They can shape all the events. They can even put your competitor's literature on their desk to show you that they are talking to your competition. They can do all kinds of things. If nothing else, even secretaries can be asked in advance to come in and bring them little notes saying such things as, "Mr. X, the representative for (your competitor) called to ask if his appointment tomorrow is for 10:00 A.M. or 10:15 A.M." Or they say, "I just received a telephone call from (your competitor), and she says that her price on those (products like yours) is only . . ." There are all kinds of shenanigans that can go on. Remember, some customers will go to any and all lengths to stampede you into cutting your prices.

They Assert You Have to Meet Certain Requirements, Such as, "We Can Pay Only X Dollars per Unit"

This is just another variation of the stiff-arm. When they say, "My boss said that we have to do this for less than $15 per unit. I don't care how you get to that price, but that's what it's got to be," they are just trying to get you to knuckle under. There is a particular way in which they work this one. Let's say you're selling something that has three components: A, B, and C. And you're asking $16 per unit. They say, "No, no, my boss said $15 per unit. If you can get it in there at that price—the three of them adding up to $15 a unit—we can do it. I don't care how you do it, but we can't pay any more than $15 a unit."

Often, when they do that, the next thing they'll say is, "You were asking $16. How'd you come up with the $16?"

If you fall for that question by answering it, you're in trouble. Because if you say, "We're figuring $5 on A, $6.50 on B, and $4.50 on C, and that's how we got our $16," they'll say, "Come on, surely there's some fat in there. How about A? Could you maybe get that down a little bit? How about $4.50?"

You say, "Well, I don't know. Maybe I could go to $4.75. And over here, on B, I might be able to get down to $6.25; but C, $4.50, that's the best I can do on C, so still it's got to be $15.50."

So you are hoping they will pay the $15.50. Boy, are you naïve! The dumbest thing you can do is itemize your cost build-up; because the minute you do that, you have said that the *real* fat is in Items A and B, but there is none in C. You've just been cherry-picked!

You know what they will say then? It'll probably go like this: "Tell you what. We'll buy C from you at $4.50, but we'll look for this other stuff from somebody else. We'll put it together ourselves." That's called "shooting yourself in the foot," or identifying where the fat is in your own pricing. Negotiation seminar trainers call it "unbundling." Whenever they say, "We have to meet a certain price per unit," *never* itemize any cost breakdown, or tell them how you build your price. If you begin to itemize your price on units that go into the product, you will inevitably identify where the slack is to your customer. The principle is this: If you talk in terms of a package deal, then only have a package price. Never, ever allow yourself to be unbundled. Period.

They Criticize Your Quality, Service, or Delivery

"You guys are terrible. You guys are always fouling up. We didn't even get one completely satisfactory shipment from you last year. And on and on. . . ."

It is a most interesting phenomenon how customers (who are price-buyers) can so accurately and with great precision remember all the things that went wrong last year, the year before last, the year before that, and on and on. We know of one salesperson who swears he had a customer who was 24 years old and could remember when his company got fouled up by the salesperson's company in 1980. We think that's incredible—that a 24-year-old prospect can remember what happened before he was even born!

When you hear, "Remember back in 1938 (1948, 1958, 1968, 1978, or whatever) when you guys let me down?" you say, "Yeah, that's right (if it's true). We did. But you know what? It's now been nearly _____ (insert the number) years and we've not failed you since. And we aren't going to fail you for another _____ (insert the same number) years." Never argue with them; never disagree with them (particularly if they said something that was true). Turn it around. Use it as your own tool. Say, "You're right, but since then, we've been perfect, haven't we? We've done this and that, and our delivery has been outstanding, our service has been faultless, you've never had a problem, and so on." It's amazing the way little things can be criticized, but you can use these criticisms as an opportunity. And remember, the only reason they're criticizing you is to get you to chop your own price.

They Fudge on How Much They Are Going to Buy

We know this observation may not be much of a surprise to you, but we still have to make it. Have you ever noticed that when they fudge on how much they are going to buy, that they always err on the high side?

When you have a prospect who says, "We're going to buy 150,000 of these puppies," and the most they've ever bought from anybody is 3,000, you know something is up. Something BIG. Like they're really going to buy 150,000; they're going to get 50 times bigger, right?

There are three ways to handle these people. One way, with the real four-flusher, is to do this (incidentally, we don't normally recommend this, but if you've got a master "fudger" that you need to control, do it) say, "You need a quote on a hundred and fifty thousand, huh? Ohhh. I'm so-o-o-o glad things are going so well for you. I'll tell you what, let me get out my order pad here and let me write that down. Hundred and fifty thousand units, right. Hummm. Boy, that is great. Tell you what, why don't you take this pen and sign this purchase order for the hundred and fifty thousand units and then I'll write in the price as soon as you sign it. And then, if you like the price, you've got me. If you don't, just tear it up."

Your prospect will probably say something to the effect of, "Well, I really wasn't thinking we'd order the 150,000 right off. I mean, I really wasn't thinking we'd order . . . that is, that our initial order was going to be 150,000."

So then you ask, "How much was it going to be? 5,000?"

"No."

"3,000?"

"Yes."

"Oh, well, then let's get a different purchase order and we'll write down the 3,000."

This foregoing dialog, of course, is a bit contentious. That kind of talk *might* get you into trouble. However, it won't with a price-buyer who is trying to take advantage of you. The only time you want to use it is with an absolute liar.

But, there are a couple of other, better ways to play it that are a lot smoother and far less confrontational. For example, Alternative A is: When they say "150,000," you can say, "Great, let me write that down. Now our price, when you order 150,000 of these, is $10 per thousand. But I must warn you, that's only if you order 150,000 through the course of the year. You don't have to start with that quantity. You can order as little as 1,000 if you want to. But, if you order less than 150,000 at a time, you have to pay for them according to this schedule. It's $20 per thousand when you order only 1000; if you order 5,000, it's $18 per thousand; if you order 25,000, I can get it to you at $16 per thousand, and if you order 50,000, you can have it for $13 per thousand. Now, the point is, this price of $10 a thousand is good for 150,000; but I will have to bill you at these smaller quantity prices if you order smaller quantities. But, *if by the end of the year,* you've ordered 150,000 total units, we'll *credit* you what you overpaid when you paid in these smaller quantity prices."

The advantage to this strategy is: (1) they have to order 150,000 or no rebate is due, (2) even if they order 150,000 and they do get the rebate, you have the use of their money during that period of time, and (3) rather than rebate to them in cash, you can give them a rebate in the form of a credit memo against yet future purchases. In this way, you keep and get the use of their money, and you've got a locked-in sale toward the future when they spend off their rebate.

Alternative B, which isn't quite as good as Alternative A, is the same deal—only with a slight variation. If they order a hundred and fifty thousand, the price is $10, and you charge the same for the smaller quantities as above. But then you tell them that once they have paid the sum of money they would have paid for 150,000 units (in this case $1,500,000) in total, that you will then ship them the remaining balance of the 150,000 units. Same deal, only not as good for you as Alternative A.

They Say You Can Use Their Name as a Reference with Other Potential Customers

Of course you can. You can always disclose your customer list if you want to. But why should you cut your price because you can use their name? You can use their name anyway. Unless you sign some form of formal contract saying that you would *not* disclose them as a customer, why can't you use their name? If we tell you we sell our services to XYZ Corporation, and if that isn't a lie, why can't we tell another prospect—unless we agreed with XYZ Corporation that we would *not* disclose it? When they tell you "you can use our name," of course you can. But you shouldn't have to cut the price just because you can use their name.

They Keep Stalling, Looking for Concessions

All the studies we've ever seen show that the longer a prospect drags out a purchase decision, the greater the pressure on the seller to make an additional concession on price or some other kind of benefit such as improved delivery, quality, or service.

Remember, time pressure is virtually always greater on the *seller* than on the *buyer.* Consequently, when the buyer starts dragging out negotiations and then dragging it out some more, they are trying to pressure you into hustling to close the sale. If you do that, you will almost assuredly make unwise and overly generous concessions. Don't do that! Remember, time pressure is virtually always the greatest on the seller *until* the buyer has used up his slack. Then the time pressure flip-flops and pressure is far greater on the buyer. Don't let yourself be pushed into finalizing the transaction. Be patient. Let them burn their candle.

Ultimately, they will have to order, and when they feel that pressure, they won't be so demanding.

They Insist That the Users—The People Out in the Field, in the Office, or in the Plant That Use Your Product—Don't See Any Difference in Your Products or Services from Your Competitor's Products or Services

When they say that their users don't see any difference between your product and/or service and those of your competitors, that is your open invitation to do back-door selling. When they say that, you say, "You mean the people out in the field don't see why we are superior? I can't believe that. Would you mind if I go talk to them?"

When they tell you that, "the people who are using that stuff say yours is no better than anybody else's," they're pointing the finger at a decision maker or someone who influences decisions about what to buy. And you should *sell* to decision makers and people who influence those decision makers the most, not people who handle paperwork or perform perfunctory duties. Pursue your opportunity to talk to "those people" who say you aren't any better than anyone else.

They Do Their Homework, and They Know about Problems Your Organization Is Having

When they use this strategy, they are trying to scuttle your confidence by kicking dirt in your face. But a lot of times, they are merely on a fishing expedition and are really trying to get you to rat on yourself. For example, if they are fishing, they can't be precise. There is a big difference between these two statements: (1) "I hear you are having problems," and (2) "I hear you are having problems delivering those Ocotol units out of Philadelphia on time because of the breakdown in your supply of Phramis bands."

If they are *specific and correct* about your problems, they know. But if they only refer to general "problems," then they are fishing. Don't fall prey to the fishing trick.

If it is true that you have problems, and they obviously know the specifics, you need to acknowledge it—but don't let them beat you up. Hopefully, you have the problem covered, and you can say, "Yeah, we do, but don't worry about it, because your stuff isn't coming from the Philadelphia warehouse. It's coming from the warehouse in Atlanta." Hopefully you've got a good and honest answer if they have done their homework. But don't air your dirty laundry by saying such things as, "Gosh, how did you know about the problems with the Phramis bands," when all they said is that they *heard* you were having problems.

They Appear Busy and Can't Give You Time to Sell, Thereby Forcing You to Just State Your Price

Here, again, they're trying to get you to stab yourself in the heart. Your prospect says, "Hey, look, I don't have time to listen to all this garbage about quality, service, or delivery. Just give me your price."

He might be telling you the truth here, but if he doesn't have time to listen, you can't sell. And if he is a genuine, viable prospect, he will want to hear about what you have to offer. So simply test this statement by offering to come back *when he does have time*. Say, "Oh, I didn't realize this was an inopportune time for me to call. When will you have some time? How about tomorrow afternoon, or could I come back on Monday morning? Let's make an appointment."

When prospects say, "I don't have time to listen," they are really trying to stampede you into cutting your price by preventing you from selling your quality, service, or delivery. If they are successful at this, they have been able to put all the emphasis on price *because you let them.*

The way for you to parry this thrust is to make an appointment for when they will have time. If they won't make an appointment, they aren't going to buy from you, anyway—at least not at a profitable price.

They Use the Old "Rock-Bottom Price" Ploy

The prospect says, "Look, I don't have time to make an appointment on Friday or on Monday. In fact, I'm leaving here in 10 minutes. I'm going to go on vacation, and I won't be back for six years, so I've got to have your absolute rock-bottom price if you want in this game. If you want this order, you'd better give me your best price, and you'd better give it to me *right now,* because this whole decision is based on price."

When a prospect does this to you, you go for the slam-dunk. You go for the sale. But first, you need to understand the logic behind this. If he knows all about your quality, service, and delivery; and your competitor's quality, service, and delivery; and he knows your competitor's price—and the only thing he doesn't know is your price and all he needs to know is your price—and nothing but your price—and this purchase decision is to be made on price—and price alone; then he must be *ready to sign* when he gets your price. So you simply reply, "Great, tell you what. Get your pen out. Get ready to sign your purchase order, because I'm going to give you my best price. But this price that I'm going to give you is only going to be good for *two minutes.* I want you to know that before I give you this price." (If that is a little rough for you to do, just say, "Hey, great, that means you can commit to the order right now if my price is the best price. Right?")

In this situation, you must absolutely go for the business. The reason? Because if the prospect *knows* everything, and his decision is strictly a price decision, you don't really have a sale to lose, do you? If the decision is going to be made strictly on price, and if your price is too high, you were never in the game in the first place. You never had a prospective sale to lose. But you might *gain* a sale—even if your price is *higher* than your competitors. (That is, if your prospect is willing to pay you a little more than your competitor, and you can be convincing about the two-minute limit on the decision.) Always ask, before committing your best price, if the customer is ready to buy *right now.*

For example, you're asking $18, and the prospect says your competition is asking $17. You think your prospect is willing to pay you 50¢ more than your competitor, but not $1. So now, the decision is yours. If you want in the game, you have to give them your "best price." So test your price by first asking, "If I give you my best price, *right now* (as they are demanding), can you *commit* right now?" Then you can give the prospect your best price—but it is only good for two minutes. Put the same pressure on him that he's put on you.

So, let's say the prospect then says, "Okay," and you say, "Okay! It's what I told you: $18." By doing this, you have now initiated a price check.

Understand that when you give your "best price," you will force an answer of "yes" or "no" from your prospect. If the answer is "yes," write up the order. But if the answer is "no," take a walk. Why is that? Because the prospect can now buy from your competitor at $17. Unless, of course, he or she was stretching the truth about your competitor's price (or was telling the whole truth *but* is not willing to pay you more than a 50¢ premium over your competitor's price). He or she can still go talk to the other salesperson and say, "Hey, you know, you're going to have to get your price below $17 or I can't do business with you." And, maybe your competitor will cut further, but maybe not. And if your competitor won't cut further, what happens if your prospect comes back to you? *Your last price was too low!*

If the prospect comes back to you and says, "I'll tell you what. We talked it over and we can pay you $17.75." They have just acknowledged that you are worth more, but maybe not a dollar more. Now you have the sale at $17.75, or you can still test your $18.00. That is your choice. But remember, you will never know your price is high enough *until you lose a few sales.* You must test your price if you ever want to sell at top dollar. You do that by using the slam-dunk technique. Give your quote, but make it good for only *right now.* You have to learn to get the business—and you need to experience the thrill of a slam-dunk. You can gain both of those by forcing a price check when they demand your best quote and they have to have it *right now.* And the best way to make a price check is with a price-buyer. If that type of prospect buys at your "rock-bottom/two-minute" price, you know your price is low relative to your competition. And if he or she says, "you lose," looks around, but then comes back with a counter-offer, you have at least learned that your price is competitive in the eyes of a price-buyer.

But what if the buyer says, "I can't commit right now—your two-minute price isn't fair. In fact, you know I can't commit right now. I simply need your best price *right now* so we can bid on a job we are trying to get. We won't know if we can actually commit to buy from anybody until we get the contract. But we need to know our costs—which is why we need to know what the price to us will be so we can work up our bid." The solution to this ploy is to get the customer to *commit to commit,* in writing. That is, ask for a *contingency contract;* one that states, "If we get that contract, you have the order at your (two-minute) price." Recognize, you don't have to hang a price out there for the customer to shop around with for six months. You can bet that you would be expected to stick to your price when the company got the contract in six months, even if your costs have gone up; but if it is known that your costs have gone down in the interim, you would be asked to offer a better deal. There simply is no reason for you to commit to a price in the future, if they can't (won't) commit to buy it at that price in the future. It is always possible to *commit to commit* (in writing) if they really can't commit now because of the contingent nature of the business. Never give a firm quote until your prospect can commit. In fact, "When can you commit?" is a good question to ask in any selling situation, particularly when a prospect tries to stampede you into giving your absolutely best price, "right now."

They Act Unreasonably and Do Crazy Things

This is one of our favorites. You may recall an earlier statement we made about some professional buyers whom we heard talking about doing crazy things to make salespeople feel unsure of themselves. One actually told us, "You know what I like to do? I keep an old stack of papers on my desk, and when the salesperson gives me their price, I say, 'What? Are you crazy?' and throw the paper up in the air. You'd be amazed at what a bunch of paper floating around in the air will do to terrify a salesperson."

Another one said, "You know what I do? I pick up my phone and throw it in the wastebasket. You can't break a phone. You ever try to break a phone?" Another said, "I always toss their business card in the wastebasket."

When your prospects do crazy things, always remember that the more bizarre the behavior, the higher the probability they *have* to buy from you. Why are they going through these histrionics unless they have to buy from you, or at least are under a lot of pressure to do so? The entire United States saw this acting crazy phenomenon played out in spades in *world-class* negotiations years and years ago. You likely weren't even alive when this happened, yet you can finish the sentence. While speaking at the United Nations, Nikita Khrushchev actually started beating on the table with his shoe when he said Russia would bury the United States. And he won with that strategy with world-class negotiators.

Doing something crazy is a strategic move for the prospect if the salesperson is not aware of the tactic. Just be aware of it, and learn how to foil it. Remember, if they do something really off-the-wall, the higher the probability they really need to—or have to—buy from you. Why else are they going to all this bother? So when they take paper and throw it in the air (or throw the telephone in the wastebasket), how do you react? Totally nonplussed. When they throw a stack of paper in the air, you say, "Hey, that's great! I'm glad you did that. It looks like fun. But you know, I'm here to get your order. Why don't you sign this order, and then I'll help you pick up that paper."

They Hit You with Terms to Their Advantage and Use False Breaking-Off Points

In this situation, they are both stiff-arming you and testing your resolve. They say, "Look, that's it! There's no point in talking about it. If you can't come in at $500 per session, you're out in the cold."

When this happens, you always want to test them. You break away from the table (but leave the door open) with a statement like, "Well, we can't really do that, so I suppose I shouldn't waste any more of my time—or yours for that matter. How about if we both think it over and see how it goes for you with those other guys. I'll make it a point to call again in a few days (weeks, months) to see how things are going."

In negotiation, you have to learn to use false breaking-off points. And never be afraid to walk, because they will probably come back around. But remember, you've got to learn to lose a few sales if you want to sell at top dollar. You can't make every sale. Again, you will never know if your price is high enough until you lose a few sales. Remember market share, almost by definition, means you aren't making every sale. You should have some idea of the percentage of your sales calls, bids, or quotes that you really should win. If you are meeting that closing ratio, you should be content—especially if you're making money and your employer's making money. Low price (or high price) is not the only reason anybody buys anything. And, remember too, if the customer buys from your competitor, but he will talk to you again, he's giving you a clear signal that all is not well with the new vendor.

Sometimes They'll Use a Shill to Negotiate with You

This is just a buyer's variation of the turnover game used by the police. One prospect starts hammering on you and hammers down your price until another one takes over and starts beating on you some more. The whole idea behind the turnover game is that the first one talks in big quantities ("We're going to buy 100,000. Give me your best price") and negotiates you from $15 to $13. Then, the next one takes over and says, "Well, now. We're talking about $13 and so on and so forth, and we want this and we want that," but conveniently forgets that the number is 100,000 units. Now the talk is about an order of 3,000.

The whole purpose behind the turnover game is so that they can *forget* what they want to and *remember* what they want to. And what they'll remember is *your* lowest price and the things *they* want to remember. What they'll forget is how much they're supposed to order.

Remember, the price of a product or service is not just the dollar value per unit or service offered. It's the total agreement. The terms of payment, the freight, to whom (and where) it is shipped, to whom it's billed, warranty coverage and commitment, any delivery charges, any changes in the contract, and any specific volume of business. What they do in the old turnover game is to conveniently forget what they don't want to remember.

The only way for you to handle this is: When they have a new player on the field, you go right back to your old price. And when they say, "But Joe said you'd agreed to $13," you say, "Yeah, but he didn't buy then. Are you buying?" (Notice the set-up for the slam-dunk?) You come right back out with, "You buying? I'll give you the same deal he had, but he wasn't buying at that price and that deal. I'll give you that deal at those terms and quantities. But if you want to start talking different terms and quantities, we're going to have to go back to the beginning and start talking again about the terms of payment, service levels, who's going to pay the freight, training costs, where it is going to be delivered, how many job sites it's going to have to be delivered to, and so on." You're just spring-loaded. You go right back to your original position whenever a new player appears on the field.

They Ask for Throw-Ins

This negotiation gambit is called *nibbling*. We always like nibbling ourselves, as buyers, and the people who teach negotiation skills teach people to nibble and have done so for years and years. We knew of one instructor who was teaching a group of purchasing professionals. He said, "Let's suppose that *you, yourself* are buying this new red Porsche convertible for $120,000. You've just negotiated the best deal you can on the price, so now you say to the salesperson, 'I'll buy, where do I sign?' But just as you go to sign, you pull the pen off the contract and you ask, 'Now this car will come with a year of free car washes, won't it?' "

What salesperson has got courage enough at this point to say, "No"? Who is going to jeopardize the sale of this $120,000 Porsche over a few car washes? Virtually none will. But you, the salesperson, had better learn to handle this situation. If you are the salesperson, you've got to say, "No." Because if you don't say, "No," the buyer is going to own your family farm. If you say, "Aw, sure, I'll wash it myself," the buyer will surely then say, "Great, great. Now, where was I? Oh, yeah," and he will go to sign the contract again, but then will *again* pull the pen off the pad and say, "Oh, yeah, one more thing. My wife wanted me to be sure to ask if we get the upgraded floor mats with the car? We will, won't we?" And you'll say, "Upgraded floor mats. Yeah. Sure." And he'll say, "Great. I just wanted to be sure. Now, let's see, where was I? I was signing it." But then he'll say, "Oh, and my daughter wanted to ask, will the washes include waxing?" And you'll say, "Sure," and then he'll ask if you will throw in the dealership. And the last request will be for your family farm, and *then* he will actually sign the deal.

You have to say, "No." It's not a question of *if* you say no; it's a question of *when*. A good nibbler is going to own your family farm if you don't say "No." The logic here is that when you say no, you've given that person the very problem he thought he gave you. When you say, "No, it doesn't include a year's worth of free washes," then he's got this problem: Is he going to jeopardize the purchase of this $120,000 red Porsche convertible over car washes? Come on now. *Just say no.* He is really committed to buying the car from you at this time. He's not going down the street over water, soap, and car wax.

But what if you can't say no? Baby needs shoes; you need a sale today. You just *can't* say no. If you just can't say no, then use the slam-dunk. When he says, "Now, this will come with a year's worth of free car washes, won't it?" you say, "Yes, but only if you can sign the contract right now." Translation: "Yeah, you get the washes, but don't even think about upgraded floor mats. You try for the floor mats and you are going to lose car washes."

Another gambit is to make a demand of the prospect. For example, a seminar participant told us that his wife was a buyer for a retail chain and she loved to nibble. He said they were out buying themselves a mattress and she got into nibbling. And just as she went to sign the contract, she said to the salesperson, "Now, you will throw in a couple of pillows if we buy this mattress, won't you?" Without batting an eye, the salesperson looked her squarely in the eye and said, "Yes, but only if we can have a photograph of you in the bed with the pillows that we can use for promotional purposes in the future." He said his wife's jaw dropped . . . and then she took her pen and signed the contract. He said he thinks that permanently broke her of nibbling.

Understand, if you can't—just can't—say no, then handle the nibble by saying, "Yes, but no more." "Yeah, I'll throw in the tank of gas, but only if you sign right now." Or make a demand of the prospect. Also, remember that the first nibble is almost always the smallest nibble, thus the cheapest and least painful to concede. So learn to *ask for the order on the first nibble*. If you don't squash it at that time, they are going to go for your family farm.

They Say, "We Could Buy at Any Price if Only . . ." or, "My Boss Said We Could Pay Anything if You Could Only Get It Here by Thursday"

How to handle this? Slam-dunk! Ask for the order. Because if you say, "Oh, yeah, we can get it by Thursday," then they will start hammering you on price again.

Never make a concession without asking for something (like the order). Don't say, "Sure, we can get it by Thursday." Instead, try this response, "Let's suppose we could get it by Thursday, could you sign the contract right now?" Or better yet, say, "Let's suppose we could get it by Thursday, what are you willing to pay?" Force them to come up with a price or to acknowledge that you will have to ask for a higher price in order to comply with their special request. Don't give away your competitive advantage (which, in this case, is Thursday delivery). When they're talking to you, making demands, and they're saying, "Hey, my boss said we could pay anything if we can only get that by Thursday," put a price on Thursday delivery. Say, "Let's suppose we can. What are you willing to pay?" or, "That will cost you X dollars." That clarifies, front and center, that you are negotiating the value of *delivery on Thursday* to them (which is what they're really trying to buy and may be the real reason they know they will or must buy from you).

They Walk Out on a Deal Occasionally—Just to "Teach You"

Once in a while a prospect is going to take a walk just to "teach you." We've actually seen them walk out on deals where the price they were walking *from* was a *lower* price than the one they were walking to, just to teach the salesperson a lesson. Here's their point of view, "Look, I told you—you have to do better, and I can prove it." These prospects who do this (pay more to your competitor) often view this as an *investment* in beating you up now in order to secure lower *future* prices.

You can (and will) lose some sales on those transactions. They will go down the road and pay somebody else more money now to teach you that later when they say, "You have to do better," they mean you have to do better.

In coping with this tactic, you have to remember two things: (1) It often costs them a lot of money to change vendors, and (2) your statistics on how much business (market share) you have to gain if you cut price to sell something, which normally makes cutting price a really stupid thing to do.

You can't make every sale. And you probably don't want every sale—at least not to price-buyers. Furthermore, they'll frequently counter your offer with an alternative (lower) price just to test you. And some of them, no matter what your price is, will adamantly tell you they just can't pay that much or need a lower price.

Many people who study and teach buying and negotiation will tell their trainees to counter any offer—no matter what it is. You need to recognize that when somebody comes back with a lower price, it doesn't mean it's the most they're going to or can pay. And, again, when they come back with a lower price, you just test it by saying, "Well, that's interesting, but have you considered what you'll be losing if you don't buy from us? You're going to lose our quality. You are also going to lose our service, access to our spare parts, our knowledge and expertise, our complete line, and on and on." Don't give them a guilt feeling—just say, in a straightforward way, "Hey, do you know what you'll be losing?" and run it right back around to the subject of your superior quality, service, and delivery.

They Negotiate Trivia

Again, this is another variation of nibbling. They start talking about who's going to put the gift wrap on it or the markings, or who should pay for the special handling, or whatever else it might be. Handle it like nibbling, because *now* the cost to you is *trivial*—"If I could do that, could you commit to the order right now?"

They Learn to Get Tougher at the End of Negotiations

Any good negotiator will invariably get tougher toward the end of negotiations. Unfortunately, studies show that salespeople, in their efforts to fi-

---

Price as a Competitive Advantage

Price usually means:

$/Unit

- Terms of agreement
- Terms of payment
- Freight
- Who shipped to
- Who billed to
- Warranty
- Delivery
- Changes in the contract
- Specific volume of business
- Service levels required
- Training commitment required

---

nalize transactions, will tend to make far more *concessions* toward the end of negotiations.

The principle that emerges here is that when you sense you have a deal, quit making concessions, because that's when you really are apt to shoot yourself in the foot. When your prospects start to take tough stands, you should quit making concessions and use up (actually, burn up) their time. Remember, at that point, when they've decided to buy and they start getting tough, their wick's burning in melted wax. They have probably wasted all their slack and now time pressure is beginning to be greater on them than on you.

They Say, "We Need to Reduce to Only Two Vendors—If You Want to Be One of Them, You Will Have to Cut Your Price"

This technique is known as *whipsawing* because if you say, "I can give you this price," they'll now go to your competitor and say the same thing. "My boss said we have to cut to two vendors. And these two have both cut their price. If you want to be one of the two vendors, you have to be one of the two lowest." And then they go to another vendor with the same line. And they just keep whipping all of you back and forth until finally somebody says, "I can't do it."

How do you handle this? When they say, "We have to reduce to two vendors and if you want to be one of them, you have to give us a better price," you come back with the old, reliable slam-dunk: "Could you commit if I give you my best price right now—or do you have to go shopping? I'll give you my best price, but it's only good for two minutes." You must put the same heat on them that they are putting on you.

But what if they misrepresent their intentions by saying, "Yeah, I can buy right now" and then once you've given them your "best price," they say, "You lose." They then take your best price and shop. No problem. Remember the *Principle of Shane*? If they "trick you" out of your best price and then go shop it, they are doing *research* for you—checking your deal against every one of your competitors. Remember, if they come back, your last quote was too low or why would they have come back? Had they found a better deal, they simply would not have come back. This is also true if they actually buy from your competitor and then come back to you.

They Say, "I Need a Reason to Cut Off This Long-Term Vendor—So in Order for Me to Do So, You Must Be Below Their Price"

This is just like the aforementioned scenario. If you say, "Okay, I'll do it," they'll go to their long-term vendor and say, "Hey, you know this other company? They're below your price. We'd like to keep you as a vendor, but for us to do that, you will have to be below their price." Again, they just whip you back and forth.

You handle this the same as the aforementioned as well. You ask them to buy right now, and you tell them your price is only going to be good for two minutes. Remember, even though they know your price, and they can say no and walk out (or throw you out), if they come back (or let you in again) that will tell you that *your last price was too low*. If they had found a better deal while shopping your "best price," they would have taken it.

They Sit So That a Light or the Sun Is Blinding You So You Can't See Their Faces

It really is essential for you to have visual feedback when selling. Whenever you are partially blinded, you can't do that effectively—so the customer has a definite advantage. Why is that? He can see you far better than you can see him.

Whenever this happens, remember these two words: *acknowledgment and encroachment*. Acknowledgment is, "Oh, boy, that light's really blinding me," and encroachment is, "You don't mind if I pull these drapes, do you?" or, "You don't mind if I turn this light off, do you?" or, "You don't mind if I turn this lampshade, do you?"

The reason for acknowledgment is really to say, "Hey, I'm wise to your game." The reason for encroachment (turning the light off or pulling the drapes) is to say, "and I'm in charge."

You can't lose by using acknowledgment and encroachment. If they did it to you on purpose, you've got to say, "Hey, I'm wise to your game and I'm in charge." If they did it inadvertently, you can't make them angry by doing the same thing, can you? If they didn't *realize* that the sun was blinding you, and you say, "Hey, that sun's really blinding me. You don't mind if I pull the drapes, do you?" What are they going to say? Maybe, "Oh, I'm sorry, here let me help you." If they didn't do it on purpose, they don't want the sun blinding you. They want you to be comfortable. But if they did do it on purpose, you scuttle their efforts by both acknowledging and encroaching. It can all be done politely, using the same words.

They Say, "We Need a Prototype," or "Let's Get a Working Model," or "Let's Get Some Renderings—We'll Worry about the Price Then"

This one has cost a lot of salespeople a lot of money. If you are ever in the position where you are going to *give away* your ideas (in no matter what form) on the chance that you *might* get a sale, you better learn to charge for those ideas. Many a large customer has broken a smaller business by saying, "We're not sure you can make it. Why don't you give us a working prototype. Once you've proven you can do it, then we'll negotiate the price."

Whenever a prospect says, "Why don't you give us a proposal (or design, or drawing, or prototype, or plan, or outline, or working model, or sample, tangible or intangible) and we'll look it over," charge for it. We'll guarantee you, once they get your drawings, your ideas, your concepts, or your working model, they will walk it down the street and give it to somebody else to bid on. You can bet a pure price-buyer will take your ideas and run down the street to "El Cheapos" to see if he can't get "El Cheapos" to sell it to him at a lower price.

The way you learn to charge for your ideas (or prototype, rendering, drawing, or proposal) is to say, "Yes, we'll be glad to build your prototype (or submit a proposal or give you our drawings), but you need to know, we do charge X dollars for this developmental activity unless, of course, it is not going out for bid. Of course, you know that we do copyright and register our drawings (designs, documents, plans, etc.) to be sure they are not expropriated by other people." You'd be surprised what a copyright bug will do to cut down thievery, especially by *large* corporations (their lawyers know that others do know that their company has "deep pockets," and they don't want any legal hassles). Also, the prospect of being accused of theft might seriously slow down your overambitious executive (buyer) who thinks you are too naive to protect your ideas. Be sure to copyright your ideas—all that is required is the copyright notice © on the first page, plus the date and the name of the copyright holder. Just be sure to keep the original document so you can prove it was your idea first.

If you are really timid and feel you just can't say that you will have to copyright your ideas or get paid before putting them on the table to be stolen, then another way to say the same thing is, "Hey, sure we'll be glad to submit those ideas. But I must warn you, we charge X dollars for this. Of course, that price is *applied* to the purchase price if you do buy it from us. Otherwise, we'll have to be paid for our copyrighted materials because, as you know, they are the very essence of our business." All it takes is guts enough to say, "Hey, this is valuable. You know it and I know it. We're going to charge you for it." Or, "We're going to charge you for it. However, if you do buy from us, it's applied to the purchase price." This second option, of course, takes any "sting" out of you asking to be paid—if they're honest.

If they're not honest and were planning on stealing your ideas, they're going to get indignant and say something like: "Huh, what do you *mean?* If you can't trust us, why we just can't do business." If they react that way, you know you are dealing with the south end of a northbound horse. All they were trying to do was lift your ideas anyway, and there probably wasn't any sale for you to lose in the first place. Just walk away from it or say, "Well, we can't give away our ideas, but we would be glad to bid on the other guy's drawings (proposal, etc.)." If they say you can't bid on *theirs,* ask if *they* can bid on yours. If they say you can't bid on theirs unless you submit yours, again tell them you will submit yours—for a price. Or you will submit yours first next time. However, this time, you will submit yours *after* they have submitted theirs, because you don't see any need to participate in a contest for the best drawings or designs. Presumably they know what they want done and are only interested in bidding it out. In short, find out how badly they want your ideas. And remember that the difference between professionals and amateurs is that pros get paid. If your ideas, concepts, designs, and drawings are as good as you say they are, they deserve to be sold at a fair value. And if your prospect says, "The others don't charge," always reply that this doesn't surprise you because you have "wondered how professional and/or competent their people are."

Admittedly, this is a game of strength. But that contest (of strength) should be won by you if your engineers, programmers, technicians, actuaries, curriculum designers, and others are as talented as you say they are. What you will find is that you will often be paid when you do this, and that your competitors never really put in a proposal, design, drawing, or other document. Perhaps they weren't even asked to submit one, because your prospect knew you were the best and wanted your ideas—they just wanted them for free. Ideas are very valuable. And if you don't think copyrights (and patent) laws aren't tough—and enforced—ask any author, artist, musician, or advertising agency how they can generate ideas and still get paid for them. In fact, all an advertising agency has to sell is an idea!

They Play the Power Game Relative to How the Furniture Is Organized, Where to Sit, and Even on What to Sit

Situation: Your prospect asks you to sit down. But the only place for you to sit is the couch over in the corner a hundred miles or so from where he is sitting—and you want him to see your samples or presentation materials. Or, you come in and sit down—but your prospect seems to be sitting on a throne. That person is sitting on an elevated chair (it's called the *Mussolini technique*), or he has cut two inches off the legs of the chair you're sitting on, so when you sit down on the chair and you look up, your nose is just looking over the top of the desk and you're holding your samples up over your head trying to show them. Or you are asked to sit down, but the only place to sit is over behind his potted plant.

How do you handle any of these maneuvers? Just remember those two words we mentioned earlier: *acknowledgement* and *encroachment*. If your prospect has cut the legs off your chair just acknowledge it: "My, my, this chair is uncomfortable. You don't mind if I stand, do you?" Or, if you had "strong pills" for breakfast, you stand and look at the legs and say, "Look at that! Somebody shortened the legs on this chair. You don't mind if I stand, do you?" Then you encroach—you make your presentation while standing.

Whenever you feel that you are seated in a compromising location or position, we recommend that you just stand up and take command. Simply say, "Gee, this is really uncomfortable. Do you mind if I simply stand here and talk to you?" In a way, the customer has really kind of forced you to flip-flop the situation, because when you're standing there, unless your customer is really big, you're going to be taller no matter how short you are—and the high ground is working for you. After all, it's a power game. Understand it for what it is, and play it. Remember, when prospects pull these tricks, you merely acknowledge the ploy and then you encroach back. If you let your prospect walk on you, either you're not going to get a sale, or you're going to give away the product and get nowhere.

The Power Lunch Game

This is a pure psychological game. You are invited to a big, fancy lunch. Society has taught us that if someone takes us to lunch, we owe him or her something. Just play stupid, enjoy your lunch, and never feel guilty—or obligated to cut them a deal. If you do, it could be the most expensive free lunch you ever had.

They Have Your Competitor's Literature on Their Desk So You Can See That They're Also Talking to Them

Experienced salespeople love this one. For one thing, good salespeople love to read upside down. In fact, veteran sales pros have often lost their ability to read right side up. However, most can read an entire desktop upside down in three seconds and commit it to memory—from 20 feet away, in poor light, and through bifocals!

Second, it again gives you the opportunity to *acknowledge* and *encroach.* You say, "Ah. I see you're talking to our competition. I'm so glad you've talked to them because now you know you want to buy from us because of our quality, service, and delivery." Then you just lay your literature right down on top of your competition's literature and keep on talking and selling. If you're *real* strong, you might even say, "I'm glad you've been talking to these guys, because now you know that you want to buy from us. In fact, you won't even need this." So you pick up your competitor's literature and throw it in the wastebasket—or put it in your briefcase and carry it out with you. Got the guts?

They Try to Split Up Your Sales Team

If you use a sales team, they'll often say, "Hey, your compatriot said we can get that for $18." The only way to handle this tactic is to say, "You'll have to talk to my partner about that, because I'm not authorized to offer that."

Incidentally, if you are exposed to a lot of dividing and conquering, rely on the electronic age and learn to use digital recorders. Record any conversations when your partner isn't there so he or she can review what was said, or at least review the salient points. Be sure to ask your prospect for permission to do this, however. This divide and conquer technique can be devastating. You've seen it done in retail stores. A customer comes in, pulls a jacket off the rack with $300 marked on it, and says to the clerk, "I was in here yesterday and they said I could have this for $260."

What are you going to do? The only thing you can do, other than sell it for $260, is get tough. You can say, "Oh, yeah? Who said that?"

"Why, the clerk."

"Oh, well, what was the clerk's name?"

"I don't remember."

"Well, was it a male or a female?"

The answer you might get at this point is, "Oh, they all look alike to me."

When they use this "somebody else said" ploy, you must keep pushing, because they will stretch the truth or misrepresent to some degree what they heard. You've got to say, "Hey, we've got to get that salesperson in here," or, "I'll have to check that with Jan." Otherwise, simply say, "I can't make that concession; you'll have to talk to her."

"I'm a Really Great Customer"

"We pay our bills on time, every time." "We listen to your ideas fully and fairly when they have merit." "We provide feedback to you in regard to the serviceability of your product." "We share information on production schedule changes and information on new and upcoming products." "We don't dump unnecessary rush orders on you." "We wring the fat out at our end." "We adapt to your (the vendor's) order/shipping procedures." "We tolerate—and don't exaggerate—occasional performance lapses on your part." "We educate ourselves about your products and the technology associated with it."

When your customer starts bragging about what a great customer his or her company is, remember this: You don't have to cut your price simply because *they have done what they said they were going to do (and ought to do) as a good customer!*

When they say, for example, "we pay our bills on time, every time," you say, "Yes. That's right and we really appreciate it, and it's because of that good record that we've been able to give you this favorable price (that I just quoted you)." Don't say, "Oh, yeah, we'll cut our price because you pay your bills on time (like you agreed to)." Just because they did what they *promised to do* doesn't mean you owe them a price cut. The same goes for all the rest of their bragging about what a good customer they are. When they say, "We give you feedback with respect to the serviceability of your product," you answer, "You bet, and because of that, we've been able to give you the kind of product, help, and service that you need." And when they tell you, "We educate ourselves about your products and the technology associated with it," you respond, "Yeah, and you know we appreciate that. And since you've done that, we've been able to also do a good job for you." Don't go cutting your price just because they start telling you about what a great customer they happen to be. They are *supposed* to be a good customer, just as you are *supposed* to be a good vendor.

If they weren't good customers, you couldn't sell to them, or you'd have to charge an even higher price. Isn't that true?

All of these strategies are described in a very concise, easy-to-use format in the Appendix, entitled The Premium Price Seller's Ready Reference Guide (p. 233).

CHAPTER 17

HOW TO FINALIZE A TRANSACTION WHEN YOU'RE FACED WITH PRICE RESISTANCE

> When in doubt, raise your price.
> —Zachary Raphael

It is an absolute certainty that you will get price resistance from some of your prospects and customers. This does not mean they will not buy from you, even when your price is higher than your competitors'. But you must know how to contend with the pressure. There are no 100 percent foolproof methods for foiling every effort to get you to cut your price, but some of the following strategies (which rely very heavily on the foundational ideas already presented in this book) should give you ideas to reflect on and actions to take when you get price resistance.

DEALING WITH RESISTANCE

The following techniques are useful when dealing with price resistance.

Know Your Competitive Advantage and Use It

We talked about competitive advantage in Chapters 3 and 4. Remember what your competitive advantage is—if it isn't price, it *has* to be quality, service, advertising, promotion, salesmanship, or your ability to deliver. You need to know exactly which one or combination of these is your strong suit. If you've got the right quality and your competitor doesn't, emphasize quality. But if service is your strength and your competitor has the same quality, learn to sell service. Likewise, if delivery is the key, as it often is, learn to emphasize your ability to deliver. Obviously, however, the more closely aligned your competitive advantage is with the stated needs and buying motives of your prospect, the greater chance you'll have of sales success.

Sell to Users and Decision Makers

Talk to and sell to the people who make the decisions, not to functionaries who merely collect brochures and prices. Not all people in purchasing jobs are functionaries, but a lot are. There is no point in talking to someone who is only collecting information.

Remember, too, that you must sell to people who influence decision makers. They may be the people who use the product, or run the plant, or work in the IT department that makes things work. Better yet, they're the ones that own the place. Always look for power and influence in the prospect's business. Analyze and study its structure, processes, and procedures to get this information and get to the power source early. Find the people who both own the problem and have the resources to fix it.

Finally, don't be afraid to do back-door selling when you have to do so. Just learn to be tactful and diplomatic about it. Never forget that you will not be given permission to do it, so you must do it discreetly after determining who makes and/or influences decisions in that prospect's business. The truth, though, is this: If you enter the account high enough, you never have to do *any* back-door selling, and you can avoid that risk altogether.

Use the Old but Still Good FAB Strategy: The Features, Advantages, Benefits Technique

People don't buy products on features, nor do they buy on advantages. They buy when they understand what the benefits are that they will receive from the use of the product (or service). Most people don't need a diamond-tipped (feature) drill. They may not need a lightweight (advantage) drill. They do, however, need a hole in the wall (benefit) and don't want to have to work too hard to make it. The features and advantages of the product will help them gain the benefit they really want—a hole in the wall obtained with speed and ease. It is always a good idea when facing price resistance (or at any time in selling) to emphasize how your products' or services' features and advantages translate into benefits for your customer—especially if your competitor's offerings have those very same features, advantages, and benefits.

Do Classification Selling

Remember, some items are more important to prospects than others. Fuel is far more important to a gas station's business than is coffee for travelers to purchase (although not as profitable). Don't forget that the importance of price in making a purchase decision is, essentially, inversely related to how necessary the item is to the buyer. When the item is not very important to the buyer, more emphasis is placed on price in the purchase decision. But when the item is critical to the customer, price pales in importance.

Feature Any Price Objections

If somebody says, "Hey, your price is high," say, "Yes. You bet. Our price is high. In fact, let me tell you why it's high. It's because we provide you this quality and this service and this delivery," and so on and so forth. Never be ashamed of having a high price. One more time: Your high price makes a statement. A *statement that your product is better.* Tell your prospect you are cheaper, and he or she will believe it in every sense of the word. Tell your prospect you cost more and he or she will wonder why: "How do you get off charging more than your competitors? Tell me (sell me on) why I, or anyone, would pay you more money for this?" Remember, the fact that your price is higher than your competitor's will trigger a "the hell you say" mentality, which will spawn the most receptive, responsive frame of mind in your prospect for buying.

Understand the Magic Square

We have discussed this concept before. However, it bears further review. If your customers want a "10" in quality, service, and delivery, they must pay you a "10" in price. And if they say the price has to be "P-1," then you say they're going to get "QSD-1." They have to pay for what they want to get. They want a "10"; they pay a "10." That is just a question of conditioning in negotiations.

Don't ever hesitate! When your prospects say, "We can only pay X dollars," then tell them they can only get X amount in quality, service, or delivery. By doing that, you authenticate your asking price. By suggesting they can only pay less if they receive less, you clearly establish the price of your product as a "10."

Use Testimonials

Those who sell at high prices know that one of the most effective ways to do so is to be willing to tell your prospect who else buys from you. In fact, many sales experts will tell you that the testimonial or corroboration selling we described earlier is the single most important tool to use in selling at a price higher than your competitors'.

You really can never hurt yourself by telling your prospect who your customers are. Even when your prospect is of a mind that, "If you sell to them, you can't sell to me," you won't hurt yourself, because it is better that he or she learns up front that you sell to the competition *before* they buy from you anyway. Otherwise, you may lose both of your customers. Customers respond well to knowing who else buys from you, because most don't like to feel that they are, "the only ones dumb enough to buy from you at these prices." Testimonial or corroboration selling overcomes this fear.

Point Out the Services That You Provide to Them That Cost Money

One way to sell at a high price is to remind your customers of everything they actually get for that price. Ask them, "Hey, do you know that we do this for you?" Many times, prospects don't know what benefits may come to them by buying from you that they won't get from your competition. If you don't tell them, *nobody* is going to tell them for you, and they aren't likely to figure it out by themselves. Never assume that your prospect knows anything substantive or esoteric about you, your organization, your product or your service. Don't speak down to them, but do ascertain what they know, and tell them what they should know that they don't.

Use Unique Selling Points

Learn to use unique selling points. Uniqueness sells. Differentiate your product. Anything that makes your product different from your competitor's can be construed as an advantage. Remember when 7 UP was an uncola? What, exactly, is an uncola? We don't know, but they sure raised a ruckus about it in their advertisements, and we understand it was a very successful campaign for them. There was another, similar strategy used in beer ads. Miller Beer said they were, "Draft beer in bottles and cans." Their evidence was that the beer was not pasteurized—which they said made it different. Here is the principle: Anything you have that makes your product unusual or different can be used to get people to buy at higher prices.

That is what makes the market for "collectibles." That's why one of your authors collects rare automobiles and another collects historical signatures and documents. But you'd better get out there and honk your horn about it, or nothing is going to happen. It is unlikely that your prospects will observe or discover it all by themselves.

Get Personal: Tell the Prospect Insider Information

Salespeople who use this technique find it very successful, because the prospect often thinks he is somehow ahead of the pack. When you say, "Hey, confidentially, if you order from us, you'll be way ahead. Why, next month we should have our updated server online and we're going to be able to do (this) for you, and we'll be able to give you same-day order turnaround, and . . ."

Make the Prospect Beholden to You

This technique is designed to get the prospect to feel indebted to you. These are the special things, the thoughtful things that you do for your prospect. This is when you remember his comment that he, "just loved those chocolate chip cookies at that place in Springfield," and you just happened to be in Springfield and thought of him and bought this small box for him (assuming, of course, they can take such a token gift). These are the little, thoughtful things that you might do—not bribes, but genuinely thoughtful things. Remember, though, be sincere about these things. Programmed or "no brainer" gestures of this nature will always blow up on you sooner or later. And remember, the more business-related or oriented the thoughtful action is, the better. Don't ever forget that people buy from people.

Ask the Prospect What You Can Do for Him or Her

Prospects will tell you that you never seem to care about their problems. They'll say that what most salespeople worry about is whether or not they're going to get a sale. To employ this sales strategy, you need to ask your prospect, "What can we do for you *and your organization*?" "How can we design things or do things to really help you with the problems that you are trying to solve, or the problems that your customers are addressing?" Salespeople who show genuine concern will tell you that you will get a far more favorable response from otherwise indifferent customers if you really try to help them accomplish the things they want to do or overcome problems they are having.

Call at the Right Time

Unless you are cold calling (not a good idea, by the way), don't ever "drop in" for a sales call. Always have a prearranged appointment or a preset schedule. If you just drop in on your prospect, the implication is that your prospect doesn't have anything to do (and, frankly, neither do you) and can just drop everything to talk to you when you feel like showing up. Remember how you have felt about people who have just dropped in on you? It is an insult to anyone with a job to think they can drop everything whenever you show up.

Also, under the heading of "call at the right time," remember to always be on time for your appointment. If you must be late, call and say you will be late and ask if it is okay to come anyway, or if you should make another appointment. Also, make them honor your appointment. If the prospect doesn't see you on time, ask his or her assistant how much longer it will be before the person can see you, and offer to make another appointment. Communicate politely to everyone how busy you are, because if the prospect feels you aren't busy, he will feel you aren't selling much to anybody else and begin to wonder why he should buy from you if no one else is. Also, don't be afraid to leave an appointment when you have been kept waiting too long. (We think more than 15 minutes is too long.) Make another appointment to come back, but leave. Remember, you are a very busy, successful professional with lots of prospects to see and clients or customers to whom you sell a lot of products and services, and you can't sit on your duff for a half-hour wasting time. You've just got too many other people to tend to.

Perhaps it is also valuable at this point to offer a few words on deportment while you are in a reception area waiting (remember, for no more than 15 minutes, plus a few minutes of early arrival time). Be friendly and avoid telling your favorite joke, but otherwise, be busy. Checking over the accuracy of your last order is *always* a positive thing to do. Don't read magazines (or comic books) and expect to be treated as a serious salesperson— and *never* say anything to yourself or the receptionist you wouldn't say to your prospect's face. (Remember, many reception areas have electronic and visual security systems that may record any and everything you say.)

Don't Be Lazy or Lethargic

Selling takes energy. You have to work to sell, and don't ever forget it. Do what your prospect requires (assuming it is reasonable). Product and services don't sell themselves, otherwise you'd be unnecessary. Be sure to return phone calls, follow up on leads, study call reports, analyze trends, and so on.

Listen—Pay Attention

You know this. You've heard this before. Many sales are lost because salespeople just don't listen. There are legendary stories of sales lost because the salesperson never knew what the prospect wanted to buy. You have to listen to your prospects, their ideas, their wants and desires, and so on. Studies show that the typical salesperson who thinks he or she talks "half the time" is probably talking 75 percent to 90 percent of the time. A good salesperson really only talks a small percentage of the time (under half) in most sales situations. There are many good books, audio CDs, and DVDs on the subject of being a good listener. Get them! Listening truly is an essential skill for any salesperson, and we highly recommend investigating the subject further.

SALES TECHNIQUES TO USE WITH A PRICE-BUYER

You're going to have some prospects who think they're price-buyers, whether they are or not. We don't think there are that many pure price-buyers out there, but there are certainly many people who think they are. What are some of the things you can do to get their orders, even though your prices are higher than your competitors?

Know Your Buyer's Needs

If you really want to sell to a hard-core price-buyer, you've got to do your homework. You've got to know what he or she wants and needs—and it isn't just the lowest price. In brief, price-buyers need good supply and delivery; they need reliable, predictable help in getting what they need; they need good services and no excuses. Selling to a price-buyer also requires knowing, from an esoteric standpoint, what it is they need and want. Again, you have to do your homework—precall planning and effective questioning will help you learn these things. If you do, you will often be able to face down the prospect who says, "I can get the same stuff down the street," because you know full well that while he can get a similar thing or perhaps even the identical stuff from that competitor, he really isn't going to have his needs satisfied unless he buys from you.

Never Argue with a Prospect or Customer

When a prospect or customer says anything wrong or bad about you, your organization, or your product or service, don't argue. You are not going to win those kinds of arguments. Instead, learn to agree with anything that is said if it is correct, and try to take control over the situation from that point on. Many prospects who really study how to be tough as a customer are told to complain, because complaining makes salespeople nervous. That is why a lot of them will criticize your company, your product, your service, the last order, and on and on. That is why we've said again and again that when they are saying things about you, your company, or your product, it's often just to scare you into thinking you are about to lose the account. Remember, their objective is to instill enough fear in you that you will cut your price as low as you can, as quickly as you can.

As we've suggested, the best way to handle this is to use a technique called *fogging*—being essentially noncommittal and not resisting or arguing. But when your prospect says, "Of course, you guys did do okay on this," or, "Well, one thing about it, at least you got it here on time," that's the time to try to take over and say, "Yes, as a matter of fact, I wanted to point out to you that one of the things that we have done for you is to always have on-time, reliable delivery. And let me point out another thing. . . ." At this point, you are back in control of the conversation.

Explain to Your Prospect Why Customers Buy from You at That Price

When a prospect says, "Hey, your price is too high," you might come back with, "Of course we're 20 percent higher than those guys. And I'm real proud of it. In fact, let me tell you why I'm so proud of being 20 percent higher. . . ." You may want to take that a step further, for example, by coming back with, "We're higher—you bet. But you know, we sell a lot of this, and we sell it to a lot of people. Why, we sell to this customer and that customer, and we sell to these guys, too." (As previously pointed out, it doesn't hurt to do a little name-dropping here and let them know who your other customers are. It's the equivalent of using references and is a *very* effective technique. If, in fact, you can tell them that you're selling to one of their competitors, it might just prove to be the most valuable reference that you can give them.)

When you use this strategy, it is good to embellish on why those other customers actually do buy from you. For example, you can say, "Well, you know, we sell to this company and we sell to that company. They buy from us because they have found that our delivery is so reliable, or that our service is indispensable to them, or that our inventory of spare parts has saved them countless times in emergencies," or whatever it is that you feel is your real competitive advantage. In short, it's a good idea to tell your prospect why your current customers buy from you. This is effective because the honest truth is what will probably keep them buying from you in the future as well.

Emphasize How Your Product or Service Will Help the User of the Product

If you know enough about your product or service and how it's used by the people who actually work with it (who are likely not the people you're talking to), you should be able to explain to them (very carefully, knowledgeably, comfortably, and credibly) why it is that the people who use whatever you sell actually prefer your product or service. You should be able to say something like, "Your people out there in the field will really prefer using our configuration. Let me tell you why. They have found that our design *is* better for . . . [whatever reason]."

Always, always, always remember that if you've got prospects who are telling you that "your price is too high" and that they "can get it cheaper from someone else," you must ask yourself this question: Why is he talking to me? (Does this sound familiar? Have you read this before in this book?) If any significant amount of time is spent explaining to you that they can get it cheaper elsewhere and why they would prefer to get it cheaper from your competitor, after a while you'd think they would run you off because you are just wasting their time. But, if they don't run you off, they're clearly *signaling* to you that they really prefer to buy it from you, maybe *have* to buy it from you, or can't *really* get it (on time) from your competitor. In other words, they are simply trying to figure out some way to get you to crack—knuckle under and cut your price a little more before they give you the order. Do you see why we've revisited this concept over and over?

Explain the Economics of Price

Often, there are economies to be realized with large orders versus small orders. If a prospect really does need a lower price, maybe he or she is going to have to buy two years' quantity from you at one time. Explain to them,

"We can give you a larger quantity price, but frankly you'd have to commit to (so many) units in order to do that." A few words of caution if you use this technique: (1) Remember the quantities needed to offset a price cut (see Chapter 8); (2) Be certain you'll get paid; and (3) Write a noncancelable, nonpostponable order (i.e., make sure you will get paid).

Ask Yourself Why You (and Your Employer) Have Ever Switched Vendors

Why do individuals switch vendors? Why do companies switch vendors? Remember, the most common reason (over 70 percent of the time) is a lack of acceptable delivery. And delivery relates not only to hard, durable goods. Delivery can relate to *any* type of service as well. Very few companies actually drop vendors because their prices are too high. Thus, if you have a prospect or customer who is spending a good deal of professional time talking to you, it's probably because his current vendor is not meeting his needs in some way (even though he may indicate that he is "very happy" with the current vendor). If a prospect is willing to spend time talking to you, it is probably a signal that there is a delivery, quality, or service problem with his current vendor. Try to ascertain what that problem is, and then sell your ability to eliminate that problem for your prospect. This point is *especially critical* if your prospect is experiencing any form of delivery problem. If that is the case, it's imperative that he find another source. The prospect (and his company) may find that by trying your solution, he'll have no reason to go back to the old vendor even though he's paying your company more money.

Don't Invite Price Comparison

Many salespeople make the mistake of saying, "We're the best bargain, even though we're higher priced." Such a statement invites a comparison, and you become the matador out there waving a red flag at the bull. If you communicate that you think your price is a bargain, you trigger the mentality of, "Oh, yeah! Well, I'm going to go out there and find somebody that's got a better one." Sometimes it's how you say things and the words you use, rather than exactly what you say. Saying, "I think we're the best value," is far different than saying, "We've really got the best price if you figure it out." If you tell somebody you've got the best value (in contrast to *price*), you convey a value judgment, which is harder to go out and prove. But if you say you have the best price, a lot of people are hard-headed enough to want to prove you wrong if they get the chance, and you may cause your customer to shop around.

LEARN TO USE STOPPERS

We've mentioned *stoppers* before. Those are the things you might say or do that stop customers from thinking they can get yet a better price. Research shows that many prospects or customers will keep beating you up on price until they sense that you're really no longer willing to negotiate. Thus, the earlier in the game you can convince them that there isn't any more to gain by trying to get you to cut your price, the sooner they will quit hassling you, and you may very well get the order at a higher price because of it. Following are some examples of stoppers.

I Can't Do Any Better than This (Be Ready to Walk Out)

One thing you can say is, "I can't do any better than this. I've already given you my best price." But you've got to be convincing and say it with finality. Using the past tense is helpful in achieving this, particularly if you're in a negotiable deal. A second thing you might do is to give the clear appearance that you're ready to walk out. If you're a good actor, you can say, "You know, I've already given you the best price I can. I suppose I may as well put everything back in my briefcase and . . ." prepare to leave. Presumably, they get the idea that they've got you just as low as you're going to go.

Do You Know What You'll Be Losing?

Another stopper is a really firm statement (or question) to the effect of: "You know what you're going to be losing if you don't buy from us? Do you realize you're not going to get our . . . (backup of spare parts, trained people, repair facilities, overnight delivery, experienced underwriters, highly rated components, etc.)?" Make them start thinking that if they don't sign that agreement, they are in trouble and are going to lose something far more important than price.

We Are Better

An additional stopper is just a firm, self-assured statement to the customer, "Yes, I know we're 10 percent higher than those guys, but we're far more than 10 percent better. And I've already explained to you why we are. But let me just review this with you one more time . . ."

Use the *Nonquote*

The nonquote is yet another tactic you can use as a stopper. The nonquote is a false breaking-off point, if you will, but it gives you the opportunity to keep your foot in the door and to test your price. You say, "I don't know how well we could really do, but you're obviously still negotiating with other people. Rather than trying to finalize this now, maybe I ought to come again next week to see where things stand at that time." Then walk out without giving your "best quote." This technique ensures that you will get a last look, especially with price-buyers, who will always work to be sure they know everybody's "best price." And remember, if they spend some time seeing you next week, they are signaling that they are still very interested in buying from you. You must have the quality, service, and delivery they need—you are only negotiating price.

Use of the False Breaking-Off Point

You can also take the false breaking-off point a step further. Again, this is a "pack your tent and get ready to go" strategy, but you say something to the effect of, "I really don't think this is getting anywhere, and maybe we ought to break off discussions for now. You might need to think this through some more, and I need to, also. Maybe your situation will change; maybe ours will. Let's just break off our discussion for now, and I'll plan on giving you a call next week." Again, that's a form of the nonquote, but it even suggests the possibility that you've given up, and might not even call back next week. This tactic is, therefore, a stronger tactic than the nonquote, but has the same advantages.

I've Got to Get to Another Customer

Another stopper is the strategy of stopping discussing things now, because you've got "another (hot) customer." This technique is a little bit like the slam-dunk. You say to the customer, "This is taking more time than I realized, and I really do have another appointment that I've got to get to. We're not making any headway here; maybe it would be better if I came back some other time." Again, this is another way to put some pressure on the prospect, particularly if he's running out of time to get what he needs—the quality product or service that he needs to have there by a *certain time*. This also effectively communicates that you do sell a lot of whatever you sell to others at this price.

We Are Pushing Capacity Now

A very strong stopper to use is the line, "We're starting to push capacity this year, and one of the things we really are quite proud of is that when we promise a delivery date, we make that delivery date. Once we get our capacity maximized (personnel, bandwidth, trainers, etc.), we won't be able to offer anything to you at any price. Plus, we absolutely refuse to sell anything we can't deliver on time or service correctly, and we are getting close to filling up our capacity for both." Using this line depends on what you're selling and the nature of your business, but the emphasis is on the fact that you are not going to take any more pressure for a lower price because you are worried that you might not be able to deliver a high quality product or service on time.

Our Quality Requirements Limit What We Can Do

One more stopper (similar to the previous one) is to use your quality requirements as a reason you might not be interested in writing an order, especially at a lower price. It works the same way, only with a slight deviation. The line is essentially this, "We pride ourselves on our quality control. In fact, our strict quality requirements this year are really going to limit our growth. In the past years, we really tried to service everybody, and we found it was very difficult. We're going to put a limit on our production capacity this year, because we want to be absolutely sure that everything that goes out our door is going to be top quality."

Naturally, you're more apt to use this quality issue technique with somebody who is very concerned about quality requirements, and whether or not they're going to get that right quality stuff in their hands at the right time. Again, it's the, "We might not be able to fit you in as a customer this year at any price, let alone the price you say you want, given the requirements that we're leveling on ourselves to have absolutely perfect quality going out the door" strategy. You can do that either from a quality standpoint or from the standpoint of your production capacity, or both.

In using stoppers, you must remember you are trying to convince the prospect or prospects that you are no longer willing to negotiate. You put the pressure on them—fish or cut bait. But you must be willing to lose the sale. Remember: Think like a premium seller—not a low-price beggar!

Make Sure That Your Customer Knows That Other Things Aren't Equal

Your prospect is always going to tell you, "Other things are equal, and I can get the same thing somewhere else, only cheaper," or, "Those guys are just as good as you are—they have the same quality, service, and delivery." But you should know by now that many times it's not the same product or service, it's just similar. Second, even if it is the same, they are not getting it from the same source. It's not the same policies, it's not the same procedures, and it's just not going to be the same. So again, always know why other things aren't equal, even though your prospects will say they are. Point out to them why your product or service *is* different and why buying from you absolutely makes it different. Say to them that, "You may think that we are just like XYZ, but we're really not. And these are some of the things that I think you should know about us." Then you start enumerating those reasons why you're a better option, even if you're selling the same stuff. And remember, too, if they are willing to waste very much of their time telling you they can get it cheaper, they probably can't get it cheaper . . . or if they can, they don't want to or had better not!

Point Out to Your Prospect, "This Is What Your People Want"

A good sales strategy to use on a price-buyer is to say, "This is what the people that use this stuff want. I've been talking to your salespeople (or manufacturers, technical, engineers, distributors, etc.) and they say that they've really got to have these things. I realize that our price is higher, but I'm sure you realize that you pretty much get what you pay for. And I'm here to tell you that the reason our price is higher is because we're better. And, let me tell you why we're better." Then you talk about why your product or service is better, whether it's because of quality, service, or some other advantage. But emphasize it.

CHAPTER 18

GENERAL GUIDELINES ON HOW TO PRICE

The mechanics of running a business are really not very complicated when you get down to essentials. You have to make some stuff and sell it to somebody for more than it costs you. That's about all there is to it, except for a few million details.

—John L. McCaffrey

We'll grant you that it is exceedingly difficult to price any product or service properly. It's also true that most businesspeople are terrified of overpricing. Consequently, when most people have any doubt about their price, they tend to err on the low side. It's not unlike someone approaching the edge of a cliff, so terrified of going "off the deep end" that they will inevitably tend to be ultraconservative in their approach.

It is not easy to try to determine if your prices are too high or too low. Earlier chapters have presented some of the indicators of overpricing and underpricing on products and services. However, now let's take a look at some philosophical guidelines behind pricing. For example, there is always the most basic, yet essential question: Should we compete as a higher priced competitor, or should we go to market as a lower priced competitor?

Anyone who has read this book to this point will know that our recommendation to any business or salesperson is to lean toward being a higher priced source for your product or service. However, there are some serious reasons why you might wish to consider being a lower priced provider. The strategy behind being a lower priced competitor, or at least being on the low side of the competitive arena, generally occurs when the following conditions and circumstances prevail.

211

WHAT YOU SELL (OR YOUR BUSINESS) IS IN A WELL-ESTABLISHED MARKET THAT HAS NOT SEEN MANY CHANGES

Some products or services and some markets simply become well established, and frankly, not much innovation occurs in them. It is often very difficult to be a higher priced alternative in such a stable environment. The primary reason for this is that everybody and his dog has the same product or can do a comparable job or provide an identical service. When this happens, you are competing in a "me, too" market, and you'll generally have to get down there with the rest of the crowd in order to sell anything.

THERE ARE TOO MANY SIMILAR OR IDENTICAL PRODUCTS IN YOUR MARKET

When you cannot differentiate your product or your service from your competitors' products or services in any meaningful way, it is difficult to establish and maintain higher prices than your competition. However, it certainly can be accomplished and is done on a regular basis. In Chapter 3, when we talked about gaining a competitive advantage, we made it clear that even if you are selling a commodity, you can sell at a higher price. But to do so, you must be very good at selling your service and/or have a unique capacity to deliver the product or service into the customer's hands at precisely the right place and time.

Many businesspeople, however, don't wish to be competing in terms of service and/or they can't think of any way to be any better than their competitors relative to the service that they do provide their customer. When someone has this mindset, almost out of necessity they have to be a lower priced competitor.

YOU OWN THE MARKET

If you "own" the market, or have an exceptionally large share of the market, you may wish to price low. The usual reason for this strategy is a simple one: To keep your competitors out.

However, this tactic could prove to be rather foolhardy for one very important reason: Some people will enter virtually any market no matter how dominant a given major player is in that field. The bottom line is that no one should ever allow a large market share to fool them into believing their presence will always keep competitors out.

Another essential point that should be made is that intentionally pricing low to maintain market share almost always results in having such a low profit margin that you cannot earn an adequate return on investment. That will ultimately doom you, even if you have a 100 percent market share. There are several circumstances at work in this scenario. One is your inability to replace capital equipment because of the inevitable inflationary pressures in every business. A second is the possibility of technological change requiring investment that you simply can't afford. And a third is that something critical could go wrong that precludes you from continuing to survive. For example, the evolution of a strong union that extracts totally unreasonable wages can even put a dominant player out of business.

If you need an example of how some businesses can have a dominant market share, but still end up going out of business, look at the small package delivery business in the United States. Back in the 1950s, the dominant player was Railway Express Agency. But they don't exist today, and they haven't for a long time. Since then, we have seen the emergence of United Parcel Service (UPS), Federal Express (FedEx), Emery Air Freight, DHL, and scores of others. And today, UPS is gravitating toward supply chain management and leaving the small package business to the others.

IT DOESN'T COST MUCH TO SELL YOUR PRODUCT OR SERVICE

Some products and services can be sold without a major expense in advertising and promoting the product. Obviously, if you're selling something that can simply be put on the street, and sales are virtually guaranteed, you'll probably have to be a low priced competitor, because you can bet you'll have a lot of competition that also easily can put the same product on the street.

The contrasting side to this occurs when selling your product requires major expenditures on advertising and promotion. One of the better examples of an industry where you had better be high priced because the cost of promoting the products is so high is the cosmetics industry.

YOU GET A LOT OF HELP WITH THE ADVERTISING AND PROMOTION OF YOUR PRODUCTS OR SERVICES

Some products and services are expensive to sell, but the people who sell them get a lot of help from the people who supply those products (or components of the products) to them. It is not unusual for manufacturers to provide advertising and promotion help to resellers of their product. It is also not unusual for major component manufacturers to share the promotional costs for the sale of a manufacturer's product when that component supplier's product is a brand that is easily identifiable as being part of the final product.

For example, let's say a company is selling agricultural irrigation equipment, and part of its offering is an engine that powers pumps to raise water out of the ground and push the water through the irrigation system. The manufacturer of that engine may very well find that its brand name is obvious and ever-present on the engine installation, and it may find that it is very much to its advantage to help the manufacturer sell the system (which includes their engine). This is also true with component parts of hardware or with software included with a computer hardware purchase.

The bottom line is the net impact on the expenses of selling your product. If it is not expensive to sell your product, you can price low. Or, even though it is expensive to sell what you sell, if you get help with your expenses and exposure in selling it, you can still price low.

THERE APPEARS TO BE A BASIC DEMAND FOR YOUR PRODUCT THAT IS PROBABLY GOING TO SUSTAIN ITSELF INTO THE VERY DISTANT FUTURE

Some products and services, by their very nature, seem to be in perennial demand. For example, there will probably always be a need for hair salons of one form or another. While it is true that hairstyles do change and the frequency with which people receive haircuts waxes and wanes, there will probably always be people with hair and people who will want their hair cut or styled on a regular basis.

When you are in a competitive environment and are selling a product or service that is in ongoing demand, there is probably some argument to be "competitive" with your price. But do keep this one thing in mind: Being competitive tends to make you a loser rather than a winner, and in every product or service, there is almost always room for improvement in some area; that is, a competitive advantage.

YOU CAN SPIN OUT ADDITIONAL BUSINESS OPPORTUNITIES BY SELLING ONE PRODUCT AT A LOW PRICE

A classic example of selling something at a low price in order to make money from the business opportunities spun out of the sale is the razor.

For all intents and purposes, companies give your customers the razor and then heal financially by selling the customer the blades.

This tactic is sometimes known as *buy-in/heal-up*. Not only has it been done successfully in the razor blade industry, it has also proven to be viable in many, many others as well. For example, sell your copy machine at a relatively low price and then "heal up" on the sale of paper, toner, or other products that can be sold as add-ons or spin-outs from the sale of the basic product. Today, the requirement for toner cartridges with printers is in the same vein, as is the cell phone market.

The trouble with this, of course, is that sometimes your customers get a bit unhappy about the deal. They realize that you're "gouging them" with your "heal up" products or service. Consequently, it is not unusual to find your customers doing whatever they can—including legal action—to preclude you from "healing up" on them. One of the more famous cases of this was the old IBM card-sorters. The tactic at that time was to give the customer a relatively good deal on a card-sorter, but then require the customer to buy all the cards that had to be used in the card-sorter from the manufacturer (IBM).

Your Customers Know What It Costs You to Provide Your Product or Service

If your customers have a pretty good idea of what it costs to provide your product or service, they'll tend to be resentful if you are making what they consider to be an excess amount of money on them. Therefore, it may be politically astute to be "competitive" in such a market condition. But when you follow that guideline, you need to remember that a certain percentage of your customers really don't want you to make *any* money on them. Consequently, no matter how generously priced you are relative to your competitors, if you're making any kind of a profit, your prospects may very well think that you're making too much. And keep one other thought in mind: Appreciation is not a major character trait of pure price-buyers. They believe that if your product or service were worth any more, you'd be charging more for it anyway. Therefore, whatever (low) price you're charging, they will probably feel that's the best you can get for it or you would not be willing to sell to them at that (low) price.

Perhaps these guidelines have provided you some food for thought on when it is reasonable to consider pricing lower than your competitors. However, the reverse conditions could also help you to determine when you would be better advised to be a *higher priced* competitor.

You should be a higher priced competitor when:

1. You're in a very dynamic, changing marketplace.
2. There's nobody like you or your product or service in the marketplace.
3. You're fighting for a very small market share but can identify a niche for your product or service.
4. It is very expensive to advertise or promote your product.
5. You can't get any financial help in advertising and promoting your product.
6. You're selling something for which there is probably going to be a very short-term demand.
7. There's no way you can spin out any additional business by selling your product.
8. Your customers have no idea what it costs you to produce or provide your product or service to them.

WHEN TO PRICE HIGH AND WHEN TO PRICE LOW

As we've pointed out, it is not easy to decide when to price high and/or when to price low. Obviously, you must be aware of competition. But as we have repeatedly asserted in this book, it is totally foolhardy to base your price strictly on any competitor's price. A competitor may be going broke, not know what he's doing, or have so much money to lose that there's no way that you can remain viable and be "competitive" with that competitor's price.

Although it is difficult to determine if you should be a low price or a high price competitor, the nature of market conditions can be a fairly good indicator of when one or the other strategy makes more sense. The following observations are offered merely as a set of guidelines to decision making from a competitive standpoint. Studying these various points should give you an idea of when your pricing strategy should be high versus when it should be low.

Mature Market versus New or Declining Market

You will probably want to price low if you are in a *mature* market. The reason for that is that mature markets seem to be full of people with "me, too" products. You can be assured that when you have a very mature market, with many competitors in the arena, everyone is going to know what the going price "ought to be" anyway. You'll probably have to be in there with the rest of them in order to remain viable and have any decent volume of business. Hopefully, you're as effective as everybody else in keeping the costs of delivering your products or services low, thereby ensuring your own margins.

If you are either in a *new or declining* market, you should price high. The reason to price high in a new market is that if you are one of only a few players in that business, you can probably get a higher price. And if you're the only game in town, there should be no problem with pricing high. Short of not buying, prospects and customers will have to buy from you. When you only have a few competitors, you still should be able to maintain profitable sales volume at relatively high margins.

In a declining market, of course, you're going to have to price high because you're not going to be selling very much. Therefore, every sale that you get will have to be profitable in and of itself.

INTENSIVE MARKET COVERAGE VERSUS SELECTIVE MARKET COVERAGE

You'll probably want to price low if you have intensive market coverage. If you're "everywhere," you'll probably find it strategically advantageous to pursue market share, and in an effort to maintain that market share, you will probably want a lower competitive price. However, you'll need to be sure that you maintain adequate gross margins to maintain profitability on your sales. So, be careful.

You'll want to price high if you have selective market coverage. If you only sell to left-handed plumbers on the fifth Tuesday of the month, you better be making a profit on every single item that you sell. There just aren't that many left-handed plumbers—and even fewer who will either need what you sell or only buy it on the fifth Tuesday!

LARGE MARKET SHARE VERSUS SMALL MARKET SHARE

You'll want to be a lower priced competitor if you have a large market share. Part of this strategy is to keep competition out. The problem with this is that sometimes your competition's so dumb they keep coming in anyway.

The flip-flop is true, too. If you have a small market share, your need to make money will require that you be a higher priced competitor.

LOW PROMOTIONAL COSTS VERSUS HIGH PROMOTIONAL COSTS

If your promotional costs are small, you'll probably want to be a low price competitor because you can afford to be a low price competitor. In contrast, if you've got to spend a fortune promoting your product or service (something we see in situations such as the cosmetics industry), you'll want to be higher priced, because you'll need higher prices to cover your margin requirements.

Sometimes you'll find that your own vendors and suppliers will provide help to you with your promotional costs. If you get a lot of such help, it could be that you could still maintain a lower priced posture. If you receive little or no promotional help, you'll have to price higher.

COMMODITY PRODUCTS VERSUS ESOTERIC/EXOTIC PRODUCTS

If you compete in a commodity situation, you'll likely have to be competitive in price. When everybody has one, they're all the same, and everybody knows what the price "ought to be," you must be competitive or you're not going to sell very much unless there is a way (and you really are willing) to sell service and delivery. However, if you have a very unusual, esoteric, or exotic product, you'll want to be a higher priced competitor. Why is that? Because people are willing to pay more for unusual, esoteric, and exotic products. Also, if you have a proprietary product—no one can make one quite like yours because of patent protection, brand identification, or anything else that differentiates and insulates yours from someone else's—you can get away with a higher priced strategy relative to your competition.

MASS-PRODUCED PRODUCTS VERSUS CUSTOM-MADE PRODUCTS

If you're manufacturing a mass-produced product, you'll probably need to be a low priced competitor. Long production runs and economies of scale can work to your advantage. However, if you're producing a custom-made product, each one is a little different, and there are no efficiencies or economies to be had from producing large quantities of your product, you'll want to be a higher priced competitor.

CAPITAL-INTENSIVE PRODUCTS VERSUS LABOR-INTENSIVE PRODUCTS

Another criterion to consider in your pricing strategy is whether or not you are a capital-intensive producer or a labor-intensive producer. If you're fully automated, mass-produced, and very capital intensive, you can probably figure on large, efficient production runs and be more price-competitive. However, if you're making one-of-a-kind items or delivering expensive personal services that are very labor-intensive, and it is very difficult to achieve any economies of scale or efficiencies from personnel, machinery, and equipment, you'll want to be a higher priced competitor.

SINGLE-USE PRODUCT VERSUS MULTIPLE-USE PRODUCT

The versatility of your product is another consideration in pricing. If your product can only be used for one thing and you've got competition, you need to be competitive with that competition. Conversely, if your product is quite versatile and can be used for a multiplicity of purposes, you can probably get away with a higher price. An example of a single-use product might be a paintbrush. You can apply paint and other liquids with a paintbrush. Period. However, a multiple-use product might be an air compressor. You can certainly apply paint and other liquids with an air compressor, but you can also run power tools, operate lots of equipment, and inflate things.

SHORT PRODUCT LIFE VERSUS LONG PRODUCT LIFE

You should also consider the useful life of the product. If what you are selling has a short product life, being price-competitive is probably necessary because your customer will be using a lot of your product and will quickly see disadvantages if your price is much higher than your competitior's. However, if your product has a long, useful product life, you can probably get away with being higher priced, because your customer will not be able to make quick comparisons as to the value of your product versus your competitor's product.

SLOW PRODUCT OBSOLESCENCE VERSUS FAST PRODUCT OBSOLESCENCE

Product obsolescence must also be considered. You can price lower if your product will not be obsolete quickly. This is because you can spread development costs over a longer product life. However, if there's a high degree of probability that the product will soon be obsolete, you need to get back all that you can during the short product life.

LOW SERVICE NEEDS VERSUS HIGH SERVICE NEEDS

If you have to provide few or no ancillary services with your product, you can probably be a lower priced competitor. On the other hand, if you have to offer all kinds of service with your product—customer service, warranty work, training, and instruction on how to use your product (particularly if you can't or won't charge for such services)—you should charge a very high price to cover all of the additional expenses incurred after the sale.

SLOW TECHNOLOGICAL CHANGE VERSUS RAPID TECHNOLOGICAL CHANGE

If your product is seeing slow technological change or advancement, you can probably price low. This is driven by the same reasoning as the earlier point on product obsolescence. However, if your product or service is undergoing rapid technological change and advancement, you'll have to price high.

SHORT DISTRIBUTION CHANNELS VERSUS LONG DISTRIBUTION CHANNELS

The cost of distribution must also be considered. If you have short channels of distribution that are very inexpensive, you can be a lower priced competitor. However, if you have very long channels of distribution, and particularly if you have to go through several levels of distribution, you had better charge a higher price.

FAST INVENTORY TURNOVER VERSUS SLOW INVENTORY TURNOVER

"Give me margin or give me turn." Many people feel that they can make their money on the turnover of the product. If you have fast inventory turnover, you can possibly generate sufficient revenue by selling a high volume at a low price. However, if you have very slow inventory turnover, charge a higher price. But again, pay attention to Chapter 8, where we dealt with the volume requirements for price cuts. Remember: *Turn* does rhyme with *churn,* and it is possible to churn and make absolutely no money while still working very hard. Profitability still comes to those who realize margins; it may or may not come to those who have high turnover.

PROSPECTS FOR LONG-TERM PROFITABILITY VERSUS SHORT-TERM PROFITABILITY

Your long-term perspective relative to profits may enter into whether you want to be a low- or a high-priced competitor. If you have a long-term profit perspective and don't feel any real obligation to earn near-term profits, you can probably be a low-priced competitor. But if you need (or simply require because of your own standards) short-term profitability, you'll probably want to be a higher priced competitor and not worry about the long run. Of course, as one eminent scholar once said, "In the long run, we'll all be dead," so you should probably question the wisdom of seeking long-term profitability at the expense of short-term profits.

LIKELIHOOD OF SPIN-OUT BUSINESS VERSUS ONE-TIME SALE

If you're likely to create additional business from the sale of your product or service, you might want to be a lower priced competitor. That is, if you feel that you can "heal up" on the profitability from the additional spin-out sales on product B that you realize by selling product A at a low price, this strategy may pay off. However, if it's unlikely that you'll receive any additional business by selling product A, you'll probably want to be a higher priced competitor, because you're not going to generate any additional money from any other sales.

LARGE MARKET POTENTIAL VERSUS SMALL MARKET POTENTIAL

The size of your potential market is also a consideration. If you have a very large market potential, you might think in terms of selling a high volume and being a lower priced competitor. Certainly, if there is a very small market potential for your product, you'll want to be a higher priced competitor. Again, don't forget the economies of pricing explained in Chapters 1 and 8.

INSIGNIFICANT CUSTOMER BENEFITS VERSUS SIGNIFICANT CUSTOMER BENEFITS

If your product or service offering provides insignificant benefits to your customer, you'll probably have to be a lower priced competitor. People who don't receive significant benefits from buying a product aren't very likely to pay a premium price for it. However, if your customer is likely to realize a significant gain by buying your product or service, you'll want to be a higher priced competitor. If what you sell changes somebody's total outlook on life or quality of life, you can bet he or she will be willing to pay a high price for it.

BUSINESS-TO-BUSINESS MARKET VERSUS HOUSEHOLD CONSUMER MARKET

Business-to-business buyers tend to be tougher in the marketplace than household consumers. If you're selling to trained, capable business prospects, you'll probably have to be more competitive than if you're selling to a person who has little or no training in purchasing, acquisition, or procurement skills. But always remember, business-to-business buyers really are less likely to be as price-conscious as household consumers.

LIKELIHOOD OF FUTURE TIE-IN SALES VERSUS NO TIE-IN SALES

Sometimes you can lock a customer into future purchases. If you can do that, you can get away with a lower price. However, it may not always be possible to tie them into future purchases. In those cases, you can't "heal up" on future sales. There are legal ramifications for tie-in sales, and you should be aware of these before attempting to pursue this strategy.

NEED FOR LARGE PARTS INVENTORY VERSUS NO PARTS NEEDED

If your customers will be committed to a large parts inventory to keep your product functioning or operating, you might be able to get away with being a low priced competitor by "healing up" on the sale of parts for your customer's inventory. However, if your customer will not be committed to a large parts inventory, you're not going to have anything to "heal up" on, so you had better charge a high price for your basic product.

HIGH LEVEL OF TRAINING VERSUS MINIMAL TRAINING REQUIRED FOR PRODUCT USE

If prospects buy your product, and as a result, have to retrain employees to use your product (or service)—and particularly if such retraining takes significant time—you will probably want to be a low priced competitor. The converse is likewise true: If, as a result of buying your product, your prospect will not have to retrain employees to use it, you can probably get away with a higher price. The basic point here revolves around the reality that it is very expensive to train people. If a lot of training or retraining is required to use your product, you have to give new customers a real reason to try your product. But you can rely on the premise that if they do switch to your product and have spent the time to retrain employees, they will probably not switch again for a long period of time. Therefore, your lower price at getting your customer to use your product or service will, perhaps, enable you to "heal up" with future sales because of the unlikelihood that your customer will switch to a competitor's product once they have started using yours.

GENERIC PARTS REQUIREMENTS VERSUS SPECIALIZED PARTS REQUIREMENTS

If your product requires parts that anybody can supply, you'd better charge a lower price, because somebody will try to heal up on *your* parts business. On the other hand, if your product requires parts that only you can supply (because of patent or production capabilities or whatever), you can get away with a higher price.

EASE OF NEW PRODUCT ENTRENCHMENT VERSUS EASE OF PRODUCT DUPLICATION IN THE MARKETPLACE

If you can get your new product entrenched in the market before it is copied by "me too-ers," it's probably a worthwhile strategy to come in at a low price. However, if there's no way you can get entrenched before competition enters, you'd better come in at a higher price that will enable you to realize your margins. By the way, the time between your new, unique product introduction and the ability of the "me too-ers" to enter the market is shrinking daily.

RAPID QUALITY ASSESSMENT VERSUS LENGTHY DETERMINATION OF QUALITY

If the quality of your product is quickly tested (e.g., food), you will probably have to charge a lower price. If somebody can simply test the quality of your product by tasting, smelling, or feeling it, you can bet they'll switch quickly to somebody else's lower priced competitive product. However, if it takes a long time to test the quality of your product—months, years, or even decades—you can probably get a higher price. For example, a product that takes a long time to test is house paint. Even a poor paint ought to last at least three or four years, and a good paint will last maybe 10 or 15. If it's going to take your customer a minimum of three or four years to decide whether or not your product is any good, in the near-term you ought to be able to get a higher price.

LOW PRODUCT LIABILITY RISK VERSUS HIGH PRODUCT LIABILITY RISK

Product liability must also be considered. If you have a very low product liability risk, you can probably get away with a lower price because of the low probability of expensive litigation and other margin-eroding activity concerning your business and your product. However, if there's a very strong probability of product liability risk, lawsuit, or litigation, you better charge a high price. One serious judgment against you could wipe out several years, or perhaps a lifetime, of work.

CONCLUSION

All of these considerations are nothing more than a guide to help you in decision making. Any single factor will likely not determine whether or not you should pursue a low-priced or a high-priced competitive stance. However, if in reviewing the previous issues, you determine that the bulk of the indicators of when you should price low do apply to your product or service, you would certainly be well advised to be a lower priced competitor. Conversely, if the bulk of them indicate that your product is in the higher priced competitive bracket, you would probably be better advised to pursue a high-price competitive stance, and rely on the other factors to help you sell your product and maintain the margins and profitability that you should realize.

CHAPTER 19

FINAL THOUGHTS ON SELLING AT PRICES HIGHER THAN YOUR COMPETITORS

Even if you're on the right track, you'll get run over if you just sit there.

—Will Rogers

There are many ways to sell at prices higher than your competitors do. However, there are certain things you absolutely should never do if you expect to get business from your prospects or customers at a premium price. Most of these "can't do" items are things that lower priced sellers do that antagonize or inconvenience their prospects and customers. Let's take a look at some of them.

LATE DELIVERIES

You *cannot* have late deliveries. End of story! No one will pay big bucks for excuses, and your customer is not going to put up with late deliveries for very long. If your customer orders it, he probably needs it or wants to have it. If you have late delivery of a tangible product or intangible service, it reveals a series of weaknesses on your part. Your planning is bad, your scheduling is poor, or maybe your vendor relations are terrible or you have cash-flow problems. But the bottom line is that if your customer can't count on you to get the product or service to him on time it will mean grief and aggravation for him and big losses for you.

PARTIAL DELIVERIES

Partial deliveries highlight the same problems as late deliveries. Your customer thinks, "Well, these guys are limping through so far, but one of these days they'll probably completely fail me and I'll be left high and dry without anything." Nobody likes to take partial deliveries, certainly not as a regular diet. It fouls up receiving records and creates more paperwork for the customer. Why should they put up with your miscues, disorganization, and confusion, and still pay you a premium price? They shouldn't. And you shouldn't expect them to, should you?

DESTRUCTIVE PRICING

Destructive pricing is when you quote someone a price (you "cut" a deal) and then you change the price, terms, or conditions of the agreement. For example, you "lose" a large order and then claim you didn't write it at that price, or you tell your customer you "couldn't possibly have sold it at that price." Your customer will get the idea that all you are trying to do is sucker him into giving you an order, and then raising the price after the order is placed (when it is too late for him to order from someone else).

CANCELING OR DELAYING ORDERS

If you tell your customer, "We can't honor these orders on time," you will totally destroy your credibility and concurrently put your customer in a bind. Delaying or canceling an order is a surefire way for you to lose future sales; you will become identified as an unreliable source.

REQUIRING "ADD-ONS" OR RENEGOTIATING ORDERS

Some salespeople get into the (bad) habit of requiring extra orders; that is, they ask for "add-ons" in an effort to renegotiate previously placed orders. Trust us, your customers know what you're doing. You're trying to get them to commit to a low-ball quote and then trying to spool it up into bigger dollars. They, too, will clearly see that you are misleading them and are creating a lot of extra paperwork for them at the same time.

SUPPLYING DEFECTIVE PRODUCTS OR PARTS OR UNQUALIFIED PEOPLE

Any parts, materials, supplies, or even people that you put into place that aren't exactly as promised will cost you sales. Customers don't want to put up with shoddy materials, service, or results. This not only costs them money directly by requiring them to redo things or to inspect every item before they use it, it also makes them worry about your ability to control quality and service in the future. Why should they buy from you at any price if that is their outlook toward you?

ASSERTING QUICK PAYMENT SCHEDULES

There's nothing wrong with giving a customer terms that will encourage quick payment. It's not unusual, for example, to give terms to your customer that expedite payment like "2/10, net 30." Those terms are fine and are clearly understood. But when you try to push payment schedules or ask for too much money in advance, it will send a signal that you have cash-flow problems. That can cause your customers to wonder about whether or not you are really keeping up with your quality requirements and how things are going in your plant, operation, or business. They will begin to wonder if you will be able to continue to give them the wonderful service you keep telling them that they should expect from you.

SUBSTITUTING MATERIALS, PARTS, SUPPLIES, OR PEOPLE

When you start making substitutions of materials, parts, supplies, or even human capital, your customer needs to know about it. Those things could be critical to your customer, even though you may think it is unimportant. If you substitute any kind of material, ingredient, or anything else that goes into the making of your product or delivering your service, you may very well create problems for your customer. Again, the usual reaction to that is that it shows you're not really reputable to do business with—not to mention the very expensive legal, moral, or ethical problems it can cause for them in dealing with *their* customers.

HIGH PERSONNEL TURNOVER

You may not think that your customers should care if you have high turnover. Maybe they don't. But you should know that turnover could have a definite, negative impact on your customer or client relationships. Often, your customers only know the salesperson—you. However, there are other times when they do have contact with customer service, accounting, and other support staff as well. There is nothing more maddening than for a customer to have a good working relationship with a person in one of those departments, only to call and find out, "Ms. So-and-so has quit, and I don't know anything about it. She didn't tell me anything, so you've got to pay right now or we will cancel your order," or "I don't know anything about the repair order."

The same thing can occur in your customers' relationships with your production, warehouse, shipping, or other personnel. When those things happen, you are provoking and aggravating your customers. That gives them reasons to start looking for other sources, even though you may be more than competitive in price. This does not mean that your organization should never replace an employee, but a consistently high level of visible turnover can have a detrimental effect.

LABOR RELATIONS PROBLEMS

When any organization has union or other labor problems, people start worrying about on-time delivery of correct quality products and services. Some may even worry about sabotage, and they certainly will worry about the predictability and reliability of your performance on their contracts.

A POOR REPUTATION RELATIVE TO ETHICS AND INTEGRITY

Most people believe that, "Where there's smoke, there's fire." If you have a poor reputation when it comes to ethics and integrity, it's going to be very difficult for you to support a higher price structure. Just as your customers simply will not pay you big bucks for "me, too" quality, service, and delivery, they absolutely will not pay you big bucks for an inferior, difficult, or untrustworthy business relationship.

Hopefully, neither of these issues exists in your world. You need to be aware, however, of how a lack of integrity and poor reputation can harm the sale of your products and services at premium prices. If any negative aspects relative to your reputation do exist, you and/or your employer must take steps to eliminate them if you expect to sell at premium prices. They are often the very reasons why customers are willing to leave a lower priced supplier and pay more to get a product or service from someone else with greater integrity, a better reputation, and a cleaner track record.

IN CONCLUSION: SOME BASIC GUIDELINES

No doubt about it, once in a while you're going to be faced by a price-cutting fool no matter what we write in this book. What are you to do when you are up against a competitor who is really hammering on your price? Keep these ideas in mind:

- *Never let the dumbest (or the fattest) guy in town set your price.* Remember how much more volume you're going to need just to make the same profit dollars if you cut your price (Chapter 8).
- *Determine how much, if any, your customer will really benefit from any price reduction.* There may be a problem of image if you cut the price of your product or service. If you are associated with "cheap," you may rue the day you cut your price, because you can hurt sales by pricing too low.
- *Learn to resist the temptation to take action just for the sake of doing something.* Cutting price may only get your competition to cut their prices even further. And the real truth is that it seldom gets you a lot more volume anyway. This is especially true in a recessional period. Cutting price only means that you get even less money for what you sell.
- *Be prepared to sustain some loss, but not all loss.* Distress selling seldom earns any decent margin. All you usually move out of inventory are your better products. Then all you have left is your Chapter 11 inventory.
- *Don't believe that your competition have cut their prices unless you can substantiate it as fact.* Never rely on a customer's word that "so-and-so" has a lower price. Get accurate information before offering any kind of a discount. Is their product or service really being offered at the lower price, and is your competitor actually shipping (filling orders) at that price? Furthermore, find out if your competitor is restocking to sell more at that price. And, even if all this is true, is his lower price affecting your volume? There are several steps that you must go through before you consider cutting price. Before you get stampeded into cutting price, *find out what's going on!*
- *Don't ever feel that price is either the cause of, or the solution for, a sales decline.* A sales decline is usually caused by something other than price—like poor delivery, poor quality, inept marketing, or bad service.
- *Concentrate on the price of your total line of products and services rather than individual offerings.* Quite often, someone who requires a lower price may not need merchandise that is as good as your standard product.
- *Consider whether you even have the capacity to produce more quality product if you do lower price and get an increase in demand.* If you do get an increase in demand, you may not be able to provide quality product or fulfill service requirements on time (remember those potentially big volume swings associated with a price cut). The facts are that if you do cut your price and you do get the orders, if you can't

ship quality product or provide superior service on time, you will only antagonize your customer, and if you do that, what will you have gained? Don't ever overlook the volume requirements for both product and service that occur as a consequence of cutting price.

SUMMARY

Never forget that *business is a game of margin*. It is not a game of volume. And all business success is driven by sales and marketing success. Any fool can cut price, get volume, and go broke. And salespeople who sell at low prices aren't going to make any money. If your employer is not making money, you aren't going to make any money, either. We know that price is virtually always more significant in the mind of the seller than in the mind of the buyer, and if your price is going to be cut, it is going to be cut by you. Your competition does not cut your price, you do. Furthermore, it is easy to make money when you sell on some basis other than price; such as quality, service, delivery, advertising, promotion, or salesmanship. Very few customers buy anything on price. Virtually always there are other primary and secondary reasons for buying from anybody. Your job is to make sure that the reasons to buy from you are presented in a meaningful, useful sense to your customer.

There are two philosophical thoughts you must always retain in the back of your mind: (1) If price were the only reason anybody bought anything, only one source would sell all that is sold of it, and (2) if price were the only reason that anybody bought anything, we wouldn't need salespeople.

Remember that prospects will always *tell* you they buy on price, even if it is not the case, because they are trying to get you to cut your price. That is part of negotiation.

Also recall that there is a certain amount of gamesmanship to selling. A favorite story of ours, which makes this point, is one that Allan Hurst often told. It seems there was a salesperson who called on a prospect, and during his negotiation with the customer, he noticed a price quote from his major competitor on the customer's desk, sitting right on top of a pile of papers. The only problem was that a soft drink can was sitting right on the quote. This drove him literally insane for about 10 minutes—until the prospect's phone rang. It was the prospect's boss, who wanted to see the prospect in his office "right now." "Yes, sir," said the prospect. "I'll be right there." He excused himself from the salesperson, saying, "This will only take a minute or two—seems we have a little problem—just make yourself comfortable," and shot out of the room.

The salesperson, of course, couldn't help but seize this opportunity to lift the can to see the dollars on the quotation—and hundreds of BBs bounced all over the room from out of the bottom of the can, where they had been hidden.

There are two morals to this story. First, *never* pick anything up off your prospect's or customer's desk—always just slide it sideways to see what is underneath (we're only kidding). Second, remember that you are the one who cuts your price, and your prospect has every right to try to get you to do so. But, again, it is you who will actually do the price-cutting, not your competitor. *It's always a self-inflicted wound, isn't it?*

Appendix

The Premium Price Seller's Ready Reference Guide

A Companion to the How to Sell at Margins Higher Than Your Competitors System

Introduction

What if a group of experienced sales representatives met and wrote down the 33 toughest strategies that their customers have used to successfully negotiate better prices as well as the responses they have used to best avert or curtail those maneuvers? The purpose of this reference guide is to outline those 33 strategies and give you the responses that will keep you on track with your sales presentation and assist you in sticking to your premium prices.

Prospect Strategy	*Your Strategy and Response*

Stiff-arming you.

"I can't pay any more" or "I can only pay X amount."

To identify the decision maker.

"Why not?"

Making you believe competitor is as good or better.

"I can get the same stuff down the street from your competitor, and cheaper."

To level the field.

"If you want everything about my product, you'll just have to pay my price. If you want my competitor's price then you'll get everything that goes with it including his lack of inventory, investment, parts, experience, his inability to deliver, his lack of warranty or guarantee, etc."

Leading you to believe you can get your foot in the door with a lower price.

"Let's write it up at a lower price this time. We'll see if we can pay more later when we know how well you can perform."

Stick to your price because customers talk to one another.

"I'm sorry. We've given you our best price and told you all that goes with it. And those benefits are the same now as they would be with later purchases. We are consistent.

Making you believe that price is everything.

"We don't care about quality, service, or delivery. It doesn't make any difference; price is all that's important."

Most customers say they buy on price but they do not.

"Okay! We'll ship it to you in four years."

To change the quality, service, delivery once you have struck the deal.

"We will have to have a better quality, more service and faster delivery (even a lower price)."

If your customer ever wants a "superlative anything," you must raise the price.

"If that's the case, we do have to revisit the price that we have agreed on since the standards of performance have changed."

Intimidating you by having the big boss stop by.

"Are you still buying from these guys?"

If you're there, they want to buy from you. This is planned intimidation.

"Yes. And I'm glad you are!"

Playing both ends against the middle.

"I just received a telephone call from (your competitor) and he says that his price on those products like yours is only . . ."

This trick is psychological; don't fall for it.

"I can understand why he'd say that. However, does his include . . . ?" "Is it the same thing?"

Prospect Strategy	*Your Strategy and Response*
Mandating that you have to meet certain requirements to win the sale. "My boss said that we have to do this for less than ($15) per unit. Now I don't care how you get to that price, but that's what it's got to be."	**This trick is just another variation of the stiff-arm:** • Never itemize any cost breakdown or how you build your price. • You will inevitably identify where your slack is to your customer. • If you talk in terms of a package deal, then only have a package price. Bottom line—Don't be cherry picked!
Criticizing your quality, service, and delivery to win a better price. "You guys are terrible. You guys are always messing up. We didn't get one completely satisfactory shipment from you last year. Etc., etc., etc. . . ."	**Never argue with them; never disagree with them (particularly if they said something that was true).** "Yeah, that's right (if it's true). We did. But you know what? It's now been over five years, and we've not failed you since, and we aren't going to fail you for another 50 years."
Misrepresenting their purchasing volume to get you to lower your price. "We're going to buy 100,000 of these widgets."	**You know something is up if the order is exceedingly high based on past orders.** Ask them to put the order in writing and/or protect your company by getting payment up front and giving them a credit for orders in the future.
Allowing you to use their name and reference. "Use our name as a reference."	**You can use the name anyway and it's not a reason to reduce price.**
Stalling and looking for concessions.	**Time pressure is virtually always greater on the salesperson than on the customer.** Don't rush to close the sale. Ultimately, they will have to order from somebody; and when they feel that pressure, they won't be so demanding.

(continued)

Prospect Strategy	*Your Strategy and Response*
Making the claim that people in the field do not see any difference in your product or service as opposed to others they could buy.	**Sell to decision makers and people who influence decision makers, not people who handle paperwork with no decision-making authority.** "You mean the people out in the field don't see why we are superior? I can't believe that. Would you mind if I go talk to them?"
Citing problems your organization is supposedly having. "We know about the problems your company is having."	**They are on a fishing expedition and are trying to get you to rat on yourself.** If they are specific about your problems, they know; but if they only refer to "problems" in general, they are fishing.
Appearing to be busy and forcing you to state your price. "Hey, look, I don't have time to listen to all this garbage about quality, service, and delivery. Just give me your price."	**If they won't make an appointment, they aren't going to buy from you anyway—at least not at a profitable price.** Test this statement by offering to come back when they do have time.
Using the "rock bottom price" ploy. "Look, I don't have time to make an appointment. I'm leaving here in 10 minutes. Give me your best price, and you better give it to me right now because this whole decision is based on price."	**Go for the sale. They must be ready to sign when they get your price.** "Great! Tell you what! Get your pen out. Get ready to sign your purchase order because I'm going to give you my best price. This price that I'm going to give you is only going to be good for two minutes. I want you to know that before I give you this price." (If that is too tough for you to do, just say, "Hey, great, that means you can commit to the order right now if my price is the best price. Right?") Put the same pressure on them that they've put on you. If the answer is "yes," write up the order. If the answer is "no," leave. "When can you commit?" is a good question to ask in any selling situation, particularly when they try to stampede you into giving your very best price, "RIGHT NOW."

Prospect Strategy	*Your Strategy and Response*
"Using the "If Come" strategy by saying: "I can't commit now because our order with you is contingent on winning the contract we are bidding on."	**Get the customer to commit in writing. Ask for a contingency contract that states, "If you (the customer) get that contract, we (seller) have the order at that (two-minute) price."** "When can you commit?" is a good question to ask in any selling situation, particularly when they try to stampede you into giving your very best price, "RIGHT NOW."
Acting unreasonably and doing crazy acts, like throwing things—such as a stack of paper up in the air, etc. "You know what I like to do? I keep an old stack of papers on my desk, and when salespeople like you give me their price, I say, 'What? You crazy!' and throw the paper up in the air. You'd be amazed at what a bunch of paper floating around in the air will do to terrify people like you!"	**The more bizarre their behavior, the higher the probability is that they have to buy from you.** "Hey, that's great! I'm glad you did that; it looks like fun; but you know, I'm here to get your order. Why don't you sign this order and then I'll help you pick up that paper."
Offering terms that are only to their advantage and advancing false breaking-off points. "Look, that's it! There's no point in talking about it. If you can't come in at $16, you're out in the cold."	**Break away from the table (but leave the door open) with a statement like:** "Well, we can't really do that, so I suppose I shouldn't waste any more of my time—or yours for that matter. Why don't we both think it over and see how it goes for you with those other guys. I'll make it a point to call again in a few days (weeks, months) and see how things are going." You have to learn to lose a few sales if you want to sell at top dollar. You can't make every sale. And really don't want to, either!
Asking for throw-ins or nibbling. "I'll buy! Where do I sign?" "Now this software will come with 120 days of help desk assistance, won't it?"	**Say, "No." If you find that impossible, say, "Yes, but only if you can sign the contract right now."** Translation: "Yeah, you get the help desk service, but don't even think about on-site assistance. You try for the on-site service and you are going to lose the 120-day help desk."

(continued)

Prospect Strategy	*Your Strategy and Response*
Playing the "if " game. "We could buy at any price if only . . ." or, "my boss said we could pay anything if you could only get it here by Thursday.	**Ask for the order. Never make a concession without asking for something (like the order).** "Let's suppose we could get it by Thursday, could you sign the contract right now?" Or better yet, say, "Let's suppose we could get it by Thursday, what are you willing to pay?" "Let's suppose we can. What are you willing to pay?" or "That will cost you X dollars." That clearly puts forward the fact that you are negotiating the value of delivery on Thursday to them (which is what they're really trying to buy and may be the real reason they know they will [must] buy from you).
Walking out on a deal occasionally—just to "teach you." "Look, I told you—you'll have to do better than that and I'll prove it."	**Return to the subject of your superior quality, service, and delivery.** "Hey, do you know what you'll be losing?"
Negotiating trivia. "Listen, will you include the downloadable manual?" Get tougher at the end of negotiations.	**This is another variation of nibbling.** "If I could do that, could you commit to the order right now?" When customers start to take tough stands, you should quit making concessions and use up some of their valuable time. When they've clearly decided to buy, and then they start getting tough, they have probably wasted all their slack time. Time pressure is beginning to be greater on them than on you.
Whipsawing "We need to reduce everything to only two vendors. If you want to be one of them, you will have to cut your price."	**Whipsaw them back.** "Could you commit if I give you my best price right now—or do you have to go shopping? I'll give you my best price, but it's only good for two minutes."

Prospect Strategy	*Your Strategy and Response*
Playing the long-term vendor game. "I need a reason to cut off this long-term vendor. For me to do so, you must be below their price."	**Ask them to buy right now, and tell them your price is only going to be good for two minutes.** You must put the same heat on them that they are putting on you.
Playing the bright light game. Put the salesperson in a position in which the sun or other bright light is in his/her face.	**Acknowledgment: "That light's really blinding me."** "You don't mind if I pull these drapes, do you?"
Insisting that they need a prototype.	**You must charge for it.** "Yes, we'll be glad to build your prototype (or submit a proposal or give you our drawings), but we must warn you, we do charge X dollars for this developmental activity unless, of course, it is not going out for bid. In that case, of course, we copy-right and register our drawings (designs, etc.) to be sure they are not expropriated." "We're going to charge you for it; but if you buy from us, it's applied to the pur-chase price." "This is an expensive undertaking. We're going to have to charge you for it." If your prospect says, "The others don't charge," always reply that this doesn't sur-prise you because you have often won-dered how professional and/or competent organizations that don't that really are.
Playing the power game: • How the furniture is organized • Where to sit • What chair	**Acknowledge and encroach.** "My, my, this chair is uncomfortable. You don't mind if I stand, do you?" "Look at that! Somebody shortened the legs on this chair. You don't mind if I stand, do you?"
Playing the power lunch game.	**Enjoy your lunch and never feel guilty or obligated to cut them a deal.**

(continued)

Prospect Strategy	*Your Strategy and Response*
Competitor's literature on customer's desk during appointment.	**Acknowledge and encroach.** "Ah. I see you're talking to our competition. I'm so glad you've talked to them because now you know how different we are in quality, service, and delivery.
Splitting your team—dividing and conquering. "Hey, your compatriot said we can get that for $18."	**Record on tape any conversations when your partner isn't there so he or she can review the salient points of what was said.** "You'll have to talk to my partner about that because I'm not authorized to say that."
Playing the "we're great customers" game.	**You don't have to cut your price. If they are a great customer, they will only be doing what they said they were going to do.**

NOTES

Chapter 1   Employers Can Fail or Go Broke—And Yours Can, Too

1. Thomas. J. Watson, *A Business and Its Beliefs: The Ideas That Helped Build IBM,* New York: McGraw-Hill, 1963.
2. Nathan Paul, *How to Make Money in the Printing Business,* New York: The Lotus Press, 1900, p. 114.
3. *Inc.,* May 1988, p. 21, column 2.
4. Advertising piece, Columbia Executive Programs, Columbia University Graduate School of Business, New York, NY 10027, November 1988.
5. Kimes, Beverly Rae, and Clark, Henry Austin Jr., *Standard Catalog of American Cars, 1805–1942,* 2nd ed., Iola, WI: Krause Publications, Inc., 1989.

Chapter 2   But Competition Keeps Cutting My Price

1. The complete breakdown was as follows: 70.2 percent dropped a vendor because of delivery problems, 9.4% because of quality problems, 8.1 percent because of price, 6.2 percent because of service (mostly poor), and 6.1 percent because the vendor went out of business—another form of delivery problem.
2. *BusinessWeek,* October 6, 1986, p. 62.

Chapter 3   Determining Your Competitive Advantage

1. *Small Business Report,* January 1987.

Chapter 8   Your Competitors' Delivery Problems Will Get You Profitable Sales

1. For more information, see Robert Morris Associates, *Annual Statement Studies,* Philadelphia, PA.
2. For example, if you're a manufacturer, it costs you 65¢ to make it to sell; if you're a wholesaler, distributor, or retailer, it costs you 65¢ to buy it to have it to resell. You must always subtract that 65¢ (what it costs you to have it to sell) from your $1.00 of sales.

Chapter 9   Yeah, But I'll Make More Money If I Cut My Price—And I Don't Care If My Employer Does Go Broke

1. *Inc.,* April 1967, p. 23.
2. Mussolini used to sit on an elevated throne to intimidate people; that's also why judges sit on benches. It's a military tactic; take the high ground.

About the Authors

Lawrence L. Steinmetz, PhD, is an internationally acclaimed author and speaker who practices what he preaches. Larry has founded 11 highly successful small businesses, two of which he still operates today as CEO.

All of Larry's degrees are in business. His BS and Master's Degree are from the University of Missouri, and his PhD is from the University of Michigan. As professor and head of the Management Department at the Graduate School of Business at the University of Colorado, Larry developed a keen understanding of what it takes to operate businesses profitably.

Having honed his knowledge of business in both the academic and practical world, Larry then authored the pioneering book on *How to Sell at Prices Higher Than Your Competitors* (1992), which contains the underpinnings on which this book is based.

Larry has authored 12 other books on sales and business management, including *Nice Guys Finish Last*. In addition to managing his businesses, Larry maintains a highly active speaking schedule. He can be contacted through his offices in Boulder, Colorado, at:

High Yield Management, Inc.
Suite 201
3333 Iris Ave.
Boulder, Colorado, 80301
(800) 323-2835, (303) 442-8115, or (fax) (303) 442-2803
pricexpert@aol.com
www.pricingexpert.com.

William T. Brooks is considered America's foremost sales strategist. The author or coauthor of 14 previous books, he is CEO and founder of The Brooks Group, a sales and sales management screening, development, and retention firm based in Greensboro, NC.

An honors graduate of Gettysburg College, he also holds a master's degree from Syracuse University. One of the country's busiest and most in-demand sales and business speakers, he is a Certified Speaking Professional, Certified Management Consultant, and a member of the Speaking Hall of Fame.

Mr. Brooks numbers among his clients the world's best-known and prestigious organizations from more than 400 different industries. A former college football coach, he has been president of a national sales organization with more than 3,500 salespeople. He is also a military veteran with 23 months duty in Southeast Asia.

He and his wife, Nancy Greever Brooks, are the parents of two sons, Will and Jeb.

The Brooks Group
3810 N. Elm Street, Suite 202
Greensboro, NC 27455
(336) 282-6303
(336) 282-5707 (fax)
bill@thebrooksgroup.com
www.thebrooksgroup.com
www.billbrooks.com

INDEX